CW00950101

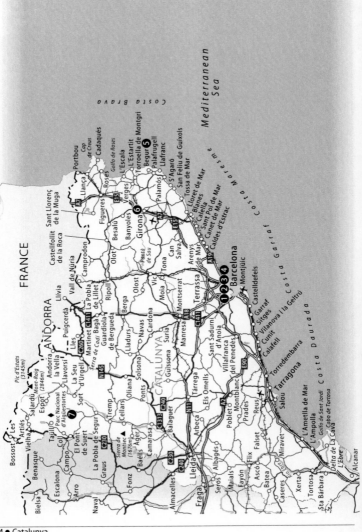

Catalunya

Mary-Ann Gallagher

Credits

Footprint credits

Editorial: Felicity Laughton
Maps: Kevin Feeney
Cover: Pepi Bluck

Publisher: Patrick Dawson
Advertising: Elizabeth Taylor
Sales and marketing: Kirsty Holmes

Photography credits
Front cover: r.nagy/Shutterstock
Back cover: stocker1970/Shutterstock

MIX
Paper from
responsible sources
FSC® C013604
www.fsc.org

Printed in Great Britain by CPI Antony Rowe,
Chippenham, Wiltshire

Every effort has been made to ensure that
the facts in this guidebook are accurate.
However, travellers should still obtain advice
from consulates, airlines etc about travel
and visa requirements before travelling.
The authors and publishers cannot accept
responsibility for any loss, injury or
inconvenience however caused.

Publishing information

Footprint *Focus Catalunya*
1st edition
© Footprint Handbooks Ltd
February 2013

ISBN: 978 1 909268 00 5
CIP DATA: A catalogue record for this book
is available from the British Library

® Footprint Handbooks and the Footprint
mark are a registered trademark of Footprint
Handbooks Ltd

Published by Footprint
6 Riverside Court,
Lower Bristol Road, Bath BA2 3DZ, UK
T +44 (0)1225 469141
F +44 (0)1225 469461
www.footprinttravelguides.com

All rights reserved. No part of this publication
may be reproduced, stored in a retrieval
system, or transmitted, in any form or by
any means, electronic, mechanical,
photocopying, recording, or otherwise
without the prior permission of Footprint
Handbooks Ltd.

The content of Footprint *Focus Catalunya* has
been taken directly from Footprint's *Spain
Handbook*, which was researched and written
by Mary-Ann Gallagher and Andy Symington
and with the invaluable help of Tom Hill.

Catalunya packs a lot into a small space. Bounded by the Pyrenees to the north and the Mediterranean coast to the east, the Catalan interior veers dramatically from endless wetlands to sudden volcanic eruptions, or waterfall-studded cliffs.

Barcelona, Catalunya's proud, flamboyant capital, really has got it all. Just for starters, there's the location: the city dips its toes in the Mediterranean, leans back against the Pyrenees, and basks in year-round sunshine. Then there is the skyline: this is Gaudí's city after all, and his buildings seem to have erupted magically between Gothic spires and glassy 21st-century design. Add to that a fantastic and varied nightlife, a discerning cuisine, and a nose for the latest and best in fashion and design, and it's hardly surprising that Barcelona has become the most popular city in Europe.

The rest of the region boasts a dazzling array of attractions too. The Belle of the Catalan coast is Sitges, a fun-loving town which goes wild during Carnaval. The southern tip of Catalunya is swallowed up by the haunting flat wetlands of the Delta de l'Ebre.

To the north of Barcelona is the the wild, remote Cap de Creus which Dalí made his home. Girona, Catalunya's second city, has a beautiful medieval core barely touched by time, and a lively nightlife. The Pyrenees are wilder, craggier and altogether less civilized. Trek across the hauntingly beautiful Parc Nacional Aigüestortes or snowboard at one of a dozen resorts. West of Barcelona are the eerie jagged peaks of Montserrat, Catalunya's holy mountain, with great hiking and climbing. More medieval monasteries dream silently in the quiet villages of Poblet and Santa Creus, and in Villafranca de Penedès, you can taste the local fizz, *cava*.

The tiny Principality of Andorra, wedged between Spain and France and deep in the Pyrenees, is best known for its duty-free shopping and winter sports. Avoid the brash capital and head into the hills.

Planning your trip

Best time to visit Catalunya

Catalunya, at least the coast, can get crammed in July and August; late spring and early autumn are the best times to visit if you want to avoid the crowds. If you are interested in winter sports, Andorra and the lesser-known ski resorts of Catalunya are best in January and February when the snow can be counted on. The Pyrenees are perfect for walkers and climbers in summer, with plenty of adventure sports on offer from rafting to canyoning.

The region has a packed calendar of festivals, see page 20, which take place throughout the year, and there is almost always something going on in even the smallest village. Some of the biggest include La Mercè in Barcelona and Carnival in Sitges.

Getting to Catalunya

Air

Spain is one of Europe's most popular holiday destinations, and there are hundreds of flights run by dozens of operators. This usually means a good deal for visitors, but you have to be prepared to shop around. Fares depend on the season, and the kind of ticket you buy. Ticket prices are highest from June to September, and around Christmas and Easter, but it's usually possible to find a reasonably priced ticket at all times of the year thanks to the tight competition. One of the best ways of finding the cheapest offers is to look on the internet: some of the most useful websites are www.expedia.co.uk, www.cheapflights.co.uk, wwwlastminute.com, e-bookers.com, www.flynow.com, www.dialaflight.co.uk, www.kelcoo.co.uk and www.opodo.com (a useful website set up by many of the larger European carriers, including British Airways and Iberia). Most airlines offer a discount when tickets are booked online.

Charter flights can be incredibly cheap, and many also depart from local airports. In the UK, which has the biggest selection of charter flight operators, companies such as Thomson can offer return flights from as little £60.

Airport information → *All taxes are now paid with the relevant plane ticket.*
Barcelona's international airport is in El Prat de Llobregat, 12 km to the south of the city. Each airline is allocated to one of the two main terminals – 1 and 2 – for its arrivals and departures. There are tourist information offices in both terminals, as well as car hire agencies, ATMs, bureaux de change open 0700-2300, left-luggage offices, cafés and small shops. There are trains to Passeig de Gracia and Sants station every 30 minutes in the day. The Aerobús ① *daily, every 5-20 min; take A1 for Terminal 1, A2 for Terminal 2, aerobusbcn.com, T902 100 104, single €5.75, return €9.95*, departs from terminals 1 and 2, for the Plaça de Catalunya, via Sants and Plaça d'Espanya.
There are taxi ranks outside both terminals; it costs about €20-25 to get to the centre of town. Use the taxi ranks outside the terminals rather than the touts who will approach you in the arrival halls. There are several airport hotels in the area, plus one – **Air Rooms** (T973 758 600) – in Terminal 1.

Don't miss...

Rail

Travelling from the UK to Northern Spain by train is unlikely to save either time or money; the only two advantages lie in the pleasure of the journey itself, and the chance to stop along the way. You can take the Eurostar (www.eurostar.com, T08432 186186) to Paris, the main rail gateway from the rest of Europe to Spain, which has overnight high-speed services to Barcelona. The new high-speed rail link between Paris and Barcelona is due for completion in 2014; for now there are fast trains from Paris to Figueres-Vilafant (5½ hours), which connect to regional services. There are cheaper, slower trains from Paris to Portbou, which connect to Spanish rail services. For more information, contact www.sncf.fr (also in English), www.raileurope.co.uk or www.seat61.com. Fares vary considerably, but you can get a flexible return from London to Madrid for about £300 if you book early enough. The overnight train to Barcelona costs from €120 (return), but you'll have to book well in advance.

Road

Car The main route into Catalunya is the E7, which crosses the eastern Pyrenees to Barcelona. Although heavily tolled it is worthwhile compared to the slow, traffic-plagued *rutas nacionales* on these sectors. Several more scenic but much slower routes cross the Pyrenees at various points. Motorways charge expensive tolls in France and Spain and ferry fares can be extremely expensive in high season. Petrol is considerably more expensive than in North America but roughly the same price in France, Spain and the UK. For information on driving through France, check www.autoroute.fr.

Coach Eurolines, 52 Grosvenor Gardens, London SW1, T020-7730 8235, www.gobycoach. com, run several buses from major European cities to a variety of destinations in Spain, including Barcelona, Valencia, Madrid, Bilbao, Murcia, Granada, and Seville. Fares to Madrid from London start at around £90 one-way, and £75-150 return. Peak-season fares are slightly higher, but there are good discounts for students, under-26s, senior citizens and children under 12. Journey times to Madrid are between 26 and 36 hours – considerably longer to cities in the south, and, unless you hate flying, air tickets will often work out cheaper.

Sea

P&O runs a ferry service from Portsmouth to Bilbao but in reality it's more of a cruise than a transport connection. It's a two-night trip, and cabin accommodation is mandatory. There are crossings twice-weekly except for a three-week break in January.

Peak season runs from mid-July to mid-August when the return fare for an average-length car and four adults is around £1100, including accommodation in a four-berth cabin. In winter, the price drops to around £700. Foot passengers pay around £350 return in high-season, and about half that in winter; prices include accommodation in a two-berth cabin. Children between four and 15 years travel for just over half-price and under-4s go free. Look out for special offers. Book online at www.poports mouth.com (although it's frequently off sick) or on T0870-242 4999; Bilbao office at Cosmé Echevarría 1, 48009 Bilbao, T944 234 477. The ferry port is at Santurtzi, 13 km from the city centre.

A cheaper and faster option is the **Brittany Ferries** service from Plymouth to Santander, 100 km west of Bilbao. These leave the UK twice-weekly, three times during high season, taking a shade under 24 hours. Book online at www.brittanyferries.co.uk, or by phone T08705-360360; in Santander there's an office at the Estación Marítima, T942 214 500. Prices are variable but can usually be had for about £70-90 each way in a reclining seat. A car adds about £140 each way, and cabins start from about £80 a twin. The service doesn't run in winter. Cheaper offers can sometimes be found at www.ferrysavers.com, T0870-442 4223.

Transport in Catalunya

Public transport is generally good in Catalunya. The train network is very good (except, inexplicably, along the Costa Brava where it is non-existent), and is supplemented by an excellent network of local buses, which include express services between the larger towns and cities. Barcelona and, to a lesser degree, the provincial capitals of Girona, Tarragona and Lleia, are the main transport hubs.

Rail
The Spanish national rail network, RENFE, offers a bewildering variety of services. The website, www.renfe.com, has online timetables and ticketing. As a general guide, there are roughly three categories of train in Catalunya. The local trains (*rodalies* in Catalan, *cercanías* in Spanish) are the cheapest and operate for relatively short distances around the main cities. The medium-distance and regional trains may have a few more frills (mainly bathrooms and possibly, although rarely, a trolley service for drinks and snacks). The most luxurious trains are the high-speed services (such as **Euromed** and **Talgo** trains) which will have restaurant cars, films and other perks, but are considerably more expensive and not always much faster over comparatively short distances. For example, for a journey between Barcelona and Girona, a medium-distance train, takes 1¼ hours and costs €9.90; a regional train takes 1½ hours and costs €7.40; and a high-speed **Talgo** train takes one hour and costs €20.40.

Road
Bus Buses are the staple of Spanish public transport. Services between major cities are fast, frequent, reliable, and fairly cheap. The bus from Barcelona to Girona takes 90 minutes and costs €6.85. *Express* buses run on some routes; these are more expensive but luxurious and significantly faster.

While some cities have several departure points for buses, most have a single terminal, the *estació de autobuses*, which is where all short- and long-haul services leave from. Buy your tickets at the relevant window; if there isn't one, buy it from the driver. Many companies don't allow any baggage at all in the cabin of the bus, but security is pretty good. Most tickets will have a seat number (*asiento*) on them; ask when buying the ticket if you prefer a window (*fenestre/ventana*) or aisle (*passadís/pasillo*) seat. If you're travelling at busy times (particularly a *festa* or national holiday) always book the bus ticket ahead. If the bus station is out of town, there are usually travel agents in the centre who can do this for you for no extra charge.

Rural bus services are slower, less frequent, and more difficult to co-ordinate. They typically run early in the morning and late in the evening; they're designed for villagers who visit the 'big smoke' once a month or so to shop. If you're trying to catch a bus from a small stop, you'll often need to almost jump out under the wheels to get the driver to pull up. The same goes when trying to get off a bus; even if you've asked the driver to let you know when your stop comes up, keep an eye out as they tend to forget. There are hundreds of different bus companies, but most bus stations have an information window and a general inquiry line to help you out. Unfortunately, English is rarely spoken, even in the larger towns. The tourist information offices usually have timetables for bus services to tourist destinations and are a good first port-of-call before you brave the ranks of ticket windows.

All bus services are reduced on Sundays, and many on Saturdays too; some services don't run at all on weekends.

While most large villages will have at least some bus service to their provincial capital, the same doesn't apply for many touristed spots; it's assumed that all tourists have cars.

Most Catalan cities have their sights closely packed into the centre, so you won't find local buses particularly necessary. There's a fairly comprehensive network in most towns, though; the travel text throughout the book indicates where they come in handy.

Car The roads in Catalunya are good, excellent in many parts. While driving isn't as sedate as in parts of northern Europe, it's generally pretty good, and you'll have few problems. To drive in Spain, you'll need a full driving licence from your home country. This applies to virtually all foreign nationals, but, in practice, if you're from an 'unusual' country, consider an International Driving Licence or official translation of your licence into Spanish. Drivers are required by law to wear seatbelts, and to carry warning triangles, spares (tyres, bulbs, fanbelt) and the tools to fit them. You may also need to fit special prisms to your headlights for driving on the right if you are bringing your car from the UK or Ireland (so that they dip to the right). Front and rear seatbelts are compulsory, and children under 10 years are not permitted to ride in the front seat. Traffic circulates on the right.

There are two types of motorway in Spain, *autovías* and *autopistas*; the main difference is that the latter have tolls. Tolls are expensive but the quality of the roads is generally excellent. The speed limit on motorways is 120 kmph.

Carreteras/Rutas Nacionales form the backbone of Spain's road network. Centrally administered, they vary wildly in quality. Typically, they are choked with traffic backed up behind trucks, and there are few stretches of dual carriageway. Driving at siesta time is a good idea if you're going to be on a busy stretch. They are marked with a red 'N'. The speed limit is 100 kmph outside built-up areas, as it is for secondary roads, which are marked with a prefix 'C'.

In urban areas, the **speed limit** is 50 kmph. Many towns and villages have sensors that will turn traffic lights red if you're over the limit on approach. City driving can be confusing, with signposting generally poor and traffic heavy. While not overly concerned about rural speed limits, police enforce the urban limits quite thoroughly; foreign drivers are liable to a large on-the-spot fine. Drivers can also be punished for not carrying two red warning triangles to place on the road in case of breakdown.

Parking is a problem, particularly in Barcelona and the bigger cities. Red or yellow lines on the side of the street mean no parking. Blue or white lines mean that some restrictions are in place; a sign will indicate what these are (typically it means that the parking is metered). Parking meters can usually only be dosed up for a maximum of two hours, but they take a siesta at lunchtime too. Print the ticket off and display it in the car. Underground parking stations are common, but fairly pricey; €10-15 a day is normal.

Liability **insurance** is required for every car driven in Spain and you must carry proof of it. If bringing your own car, check carefully with your insurers that you're covered, and get a certificate (green card). If your insurer doesn't cover you for breakdowns, consider joining the RACE, www.race.es, T902 404 545, Spain's automobile association, that provides breakdown cover.

Car hire in Spain is easy but not especially cheap. The major multinationals have offices at all large towns and airports; cheaper organizations include **ATESA**, www.atesa.es, which has offices at most of the larger train stations, and **Holiday Autos**, www.holidayautos.com. All major international car hire firms including **Avis**, www.avis.com; **National**, www.nationalcar.com (who often share offices with **ATESA**); **Hertz**, www.hertz.com are all represented in most cities. It's also worth checking with your airline when you book your flight if they offer any special deals on car rental. Prices start at around €250 per week for a small car with unlimited mileage. You'll need a credit card and your passport, and most agencies will either not accept under-25s or demand a surcharge.

Cycling Cycling presents a curious contrast; Spaniards are mad for the competitive sport, but comparatively uninterested in cycling as a means of transport. Thus there are plenty of cycling shops (although beware; it can be time-consuming to find replacement parts for non-standard cycles) but very few bike lanes. By far the best places to cycle are parts of the coast and the mountains, especially the Pyrenees.

Motorcycling Motorcycling is a good way to enjoy Catalunya, and there are few difficulties to trouble the biker; bike shops and mechanics are relatively common. Hiring a motorbike, however, can be difficult; most outlets are in the major cities. **Federació Catalana de de Motociclisme** ① *www.fcm.cat*. can help with links and advice.

Taxis Taxis are a convenient and reasonable option; flagfall in Barcelona is €2 (it increases slightly at night) and it gets you a good distance. A taxi is available if its green light is lit; hail one on the street or ask for the nearest rank (*parada de taxis*).

Maps
The Michelin series of road maps are by far the most accurate for general navigation, although if you're getting off the beaten track you'll often find a local map handy. Tourist offices provide these, which vary in quality from province to province. The *Everest* series of maps cover provinces and their main towns; they're not bad, although tend to be a bit out of date. The Instituto Geográfico Nacional publishes provincial maps, available at bookshops. Good bookshops include the **Llibrería Quera** ① *C/Petritxol 2, Barcelona, T933*

180 743, www.llibreriaquera.com, or **Altaïr** ① *Gran Vía 616, T933 427 171, www.altair.es*, a large travel bookshop which also has an online shop. Pick up maps in advance from Stanford's at 12 Long Acre, London, WC2, T020-7836 1321, www.stanfords.co.uk.

Where to stay in Catalunya → *See box, page 13, for price code information.*

The standard of accommodation in Spain is reasonably high: even the most modest of *pensions* are usually very clean and respectable. However, a great number of Spanish hotels are well equipped but characterless places on the ugly edges of town. This guide has expressly minimized these in the listings, preferring to concentrate on more atmospheric options. If booking accommodation using this guide, always be sure to check the location if that's important to you – it's easy to find yourself a 15-minute cab ride from the town you want to be in.

All registered accommodations charge a 10%t value-added tax; this is often included at cheaper places and may be waived if you pay cash. If you have any problems, a last resort is to ask for the *llibre de reclamaciones* (complaints book), an official document that, like stepping on cracks in the pavement, means uncertain but definitely horrible consequences for the hotel if anything is written in it.

Hoteles, hostales and pensions

Places to stay (*allotjamients*) are divided into three main categories; the distinctions between them are in an arcane series of regulations devised by the government. *Hoteles* (marked H or HR) are graded from one to five stars and usually occupy their own building, which distinguishes them from *hostales* (Hs or HsR), which go from one to three stars. *Pensiones* (P) are the standard budget option, and are usually family-run flats in an apartment block. Although it's worth looking at a room before taking it, the majority are very acceptable. The Spanish traditions of hospitality are alive and well; even the simplest of *pensions* will generally provide a towel and soap, and check-out time is almost uniformly a very civilized midday.

Paradors

Spain's famous chain of state-owned hotels, the paradors, are often set in castles, convents and other historic buildings, although there are plenty of modern ones too. Most are very luxurious, with pools, bars, fine restaurants and other fancy trimmings but standards can vary considerably. They are usually expensive, but they offer all kinds of special deals, including a youth package, which can make them surprisingly affordable. Contact one of their representatives in your own country or check out the website: www.parador.es. There are seven paradors in Catalunya; those in Tortosa and Cardona occupy historic castles, but the others are all modern.

Rural homes

An excellent option, if you've got transport, are the networks of rural homes, called *cases rurales*. Although these are under a different classification system, the standard is often as high as any country hotel. The best of them are traditional farmhouses or old village cottages. Some are available to rent out whole, while others operate more or less as hotels. Rates tend to be excellent compared to hotels. While many are listed in the text, there are huge numbers, especially in the coastal and mountain areas. Each regional government publishes their own listings booklet, which is available at any tourist office in the area. A useful resource is www.toprural.co.uk.

Albergs and refugis

There are a few youth hostels (albergs/albergues) around, but the price of pensions/pensiones rarely makes it worth the trouble except for solo travellers. Spanish youth hostels frequently are populated by schoolkids, and have curfews and check-out times unsuitable for the late hours the locals keep. The exception is in mountain regions, where there are refugis/refugios; basically simple hostels for walkers and climbers along the lines of a Scottish bothy. Some official youth hostels require an international youth hostel card, available in advance from the international Youth Hostel Associations. To book a place in a refugi contact the Federació d'Entilats Excursionistes de Catalunya ① T933 720 283, www.feec.cat/refugis.

Campsites

Most campsites are set up as well-equipped holiday villages for families; many are open only in summer. While the facilities are good, they get extremely busy in peak season; the social scene is good, but sleep can be tough. In other areas, camping, unless specifically prohibited, is a matter of common sense: most locals will know of (or offer) a place where you can pitch a tent tranquilament.

Food and drink in Catalunya

Catalans eat very little for breakfast, usually just a coffee and maybe a croissant or pastry. In Madrid and central regions, they might tuck into chocolate y churros – thick, sticky hot chocolate with thin donut-like batter strips. They may have a quick bite and a drink in a café or bar before lunch, which is usually eaten between 1400-1530 or thereabouts. This is the main meal of the day and the cheapest time to eat, as most restaurants offer a cheap set menu (menu del migdia/menú del día). Lunch (and dinner) is much extended at weekends, particularly on Sundays, when it seems to go on until the football kicks off in the evening. It's common to have an evening drink or tapa in a bar after the paseo, if this is extended into a food crawl it's called a tapeo. Dinner (cena) is normally eaten from about 2200 onwards, although sitting down to dinner at midnight at weekends isn't unusual. In smaller towns and midweek you might not get fed after 2230, so beware. Most restaurants are closed Sunday nights, and usually take a day off, either Monday or Tuesday.

Food → See box, page 13, for price code information.

While the regional differences in the cuisine of Spain are important, the basics remain the same. Spanish cooking relies on meat, fish/seafood, beans and potatoes given character by the chef's holy trinity: garlic, peppers and, of course, olive oil. The influence of the colonization of the Americas is evident, and the Moors left a lasting culinary legacy, particularly in the south. The result is a hearty, filling style of meal ideally washed down with some of the nation's excellent wines.

Regional specialities are described in the travelling text, but the following is a brief overview of the most common dishes.

Price codes

Where to stay

€€€€ over €170

€€ €55-110

€€€ €110-170

€ under €55

Prices include taxes and service charge, but not meals. They are based on a double room, except in the € range, where prices are almost always per person.

Restaurants

€€€ over €20

€€ €10-20

€ under €10

Prices refer to the cost of a two-course meal, without a drink.

Fish and seafood Even in areas far from the coast, the availability of good fish and seafood can be taken for granted. *Merluza* (hake) and *bacalao* (salt cod) are the staple fish, while *gambas* (prawns) are another common and excellent choice. Calamari, squid and cuttlefish are common; if you can cope with the slightly slimy texture, *pulpo* (octopus) is particularly good, especially when simply boiled *a la gallega* (Galician style) and flavoured with paprika and olive oil. Supreme among the finny tribe are *rodaballo* (turbot, best wild or *salvaje*) and *rape* (monkfish). Fresh trout from the mountain streams of Northern Spain are hard to beat too; they are commonly cooked with bacon or ham (*trucha a la navarra*).

Meat Wherever you go, you'll find cured ham (*jamón serrano*), which is always excellent, but particularly so if it's the pricey *ibérico*, taken from acorn-eating porkers in Extremadura. Other cold meats to look out for are *cecina*, made from beef, and, of course, sausages (*embutidos*), including the versatile *chorizo*.

Pork is also popular as a cooked meat; its most common form is sliced loin (*lomo*). The Castilian plains specialize in roast sucking pig (*cochinillo* or *lechón*). *Lechazo* is the lamb equivalent, popular around Aranda de Duero in particular. Beef is common throughout; cheaper cuts predominate, but the better steaks (*solomillo, chuletón*) are usually superbly tender. Spaniards tend to eat them rare (*poco hecho*; ask for *a punto* for medium or *bien hecho* for well done). The *chuletón* is worth a mention in its own right; a massive T-bone best taken from an ox (*de buey*) and sold by weight, which often approaches a kilogram. *Pollo* (chicken) is common, but usually unremarkable; game birds such as *codorniz* (quail) and *perdiz* (partridge) are also widely eaten. The innards of animals are popular, particularly around Madrid; *callos* (tripe), *mollejas* (sweetbreads) and *morcilla* (black pudding in solid or liquid form) are all excellent, if acquired, tastes. Fans of the unusual will be keen to try *jabalí* (wild boar), *potro* (horse) and *oreja* (ear, usually from a pig or sheep).

Vegetable dishes and accompaniments Main dishes often come without any accompaniments, or chips at best. The consolation, however, is the *ensalada mixta*, whose simple name (mixed salad) can often conceal a meal in itself. The ingredients vary, but it's typically a plentiful combination of lettuce, tomato, onion, olive oil, boiled eggs, asparagus, olives and tuna. The *tortilla*, see box, page 15, is ever-present and often excellent. Another common dish is *revuelto* (scrambled eggs), usually tastily combined with prawns, asparagus or other goodies.

Most vegetable dishes are based around that American trio, the bean, the pepper, and the potato. There are numerous varieties of beans in Spain; they are normally served as some sort of hearty stew, often with bits of meat or seafood to avoid the accusation of vegetarianism. *Fabada* is the Asturian classic of this variety, while *alubias con chorizo* are a standard across the northern Spain. The Catalan version is *faves a la catalana*, broad beans cooked with ham. A *cocido* is a typical mountain dish from the centre of Spain, a massive stew of chickpeas or beans with meat and vegetables. Peppers (*pimientos*), too, come in a confusing number of forms. As well as being used to flavour dishes, they are often eaten in their own right; *pimientos rellenos* come stuffed with meat or seafood. Potatoes come as chips, *bravas* (with a garlic or spicy tomato sauce) or, more interestingly, *a la riojana*, with chorizo and paprika. Other common vegetable dishes include *menestra* (think of a good minestrone soup with the liquid drained off), which usually has some ham in it, and *ensaladilla rusa*, a tasty blend of potato, peas, peppers, carrots and mayonnaise. In the north, *setas* (wild mushrooms) are a particular delight, especially in autumn.

Desserts and cheeses Desserts focus on the sweet and milky. *Flan* (a sort of crème caramel) is ubiquitous; great when *casero* (home-made), but often out of a plastic tub. *Natillas* are a similar but more liquid version, and *arroz con leche* is a cold, sweet rice pudding typical of Northern Spain.

Cheeses tend to be bland or salty and are normally eaten as a *tapa* or entrée. There are some excellent cheeses in Spain, however; the most famous is the dry, pungent Manchego, a cured sheep's milk cheese from La Mancha, but piquant Cabrales and Basque Idiázabal also stand out.

Regional cuisine

Regional styles tend to use the same basic ingredients treated in slightly different ways, backed up by some local specialities. Food-producing regions take their responsibilities seriously, and competition is fierce. Those widely acknowledged to produce the best will often add the name of the region to the foodstuff (some foods, like wines, have denomination of origin status given by a regulatory body). Thus *pimientos de Padrón* (Padrón peppers), *cogollos de Tudela* (lettuce hearts from Tudela), *alubias de Tolosa* (Tolosa beans) and a host of others.

Most of Spain grudgingly concedes that **Basque** cuisine is the peninsula's best, the San Sebastián twilight shimmers with Michelin stars, and chummy all-male *txokos* gather in private to swap recipes and cook up feasts in members-only kitchens. But what strikes the visitor first are the *pintxos*, a stunning range of bartop snacks that in many cases seem too pretty to eat. The base of most Basque dishes is seafood, particularly *bacalao* (salt cod; occasionally stunning but often humdrum), and the region has taken full advantage of its French ties.

Navarran and Aragonese cuisine owes much to the mountains, with hearty stews and game dishes featuring alongside fresh trout. **Rioja and Castilla y León** go for filling roast meat and bean dishes more suited to the harsh winters than the baking summers. **Asturias and Cantabria** are seafood-minded on the coast but search for more warming fare in the high ground, and Galicia is seafood heaven, with more varieties of finny and shelly things than you knew there were; usually prepared with confidence in the natural flavours, whereas the rest of the area overuses garlic to eliminate any fishy taste.

A taste for tortilla

Tortilla is perhaps the classic dish of Spain. Served everywhere and eaten at virtually every time of the day, it is easy to prepare and can be eaten either hot or cold. Typically served as tapas or with a salad its key features are the layering of the potatoes and its rounded shape, enabling it to be eaten in slices.

Method (serves 6)

1 large frying pan for potatoes
1 small, fairly deep frying pan
6 fresh eggs
750 g of potatoes thinly sliced
half a medium onion (if desired)
enough good quality olive oil to cover the potatoes in a frying pan
salt
Total cooking and preparation time around 1 hour.

Wash and peel the potatoes then slice thinly so they are about ½ cm in thickness. Place them in a mixing bowl and sprinkle with salt ensuring that that each piece is coated with a little salt. Cut and slice the onion into small pieces about 2 cm long and add to the potatoes.

Place the salted potatoes and onions in a large frying pan and pour in enough olive oil nearly to cover the them. It is essential to use good quality oil – Spanish cooks would never dream of using inferior aceite for tortilla. Keep the pan at a low heat and continue to stir the potatoes regularly to ensure they do not burn. The aim is to cook the potatoes while ensuring they do not become crisp. Remove the cooked potatoes and onion from the pan and drain the oil. Total cooking time should be between 15-20 minutes depending on the thickness of the potatoes.

Mix the eggs in a mixing bowl. It is not necessary to add salt as the potatoes should have enough seasoning. Milk and pepper are rarely used in Spanish cooking but will not radically affect the taste if preferred. Prepare a new smaller pan which is deep enough to contain the egg mix and the potatoes. Place the cooked and drained potatoes in first and then add the egg mix. Fry the mixture, keeping the heat very low. When the mixture is showing signs of becoming solid remove the pan from the heat and find a plate large enough to cover the pan.

The next stage is the only tricky bit as the mixture is now to be turned over to cook the other side. Turn the solid mix on to the plate and then return it to the pan ensuring the uncooked side is facing the bottom of the pan. Continue to cook until the tortilla is solid. Total frying time should be around 10 minutes. Remove the tortilla from the pan and eat either hot or leave to cool and eat later.

The **Catalans** are almost as famous for their cuisine as the Basques. Seafood from the Mediterranean, rice and vegetables from the plains and meat and game from the mountains are combined in unusual ways; look out for *mandonguilles amb sèpia*, meatballs with cuttlefish, or *gambas con pollastre*, prawns with chicken. The local staple is *pa amb tomàquet*, country bread rubbed with fresh tomatoes, with a little olive oil and salt. **Valencia** is famous as the birthplace of *paella*, a surprisingly difficult dish that is often made badly elsewhere in Spain, much to the annoyance of Valencianos. The genuine article is made with starchy *bomba* rice grown in the Valencian plains, and real saffron (not yellow food colouring, which is common), which is simmered in a shallow pan with garlic and olive oil, and a mixture of meat and/or seafood (depending on the recipe – no one can agree on the ingredients of the definitive paella). The finishing touch is the *soccarat*, a crunchy crust formed by turning up the heat for a few minutes just before the paella is cooked.

Typical **Madrileño** cuisine reflects the city's land-locked status in the middle of a vast plain; hunks of roast meats and hearty stews, like *cocido*, a thick broth of chickpeas, vegetables and hunks of meat, which are cooked together and served in separate courses – often over several days. Spaniards in general, and Madrileños in particular, don't turn their noses up at any part of an animal, and another local speciality is *callos a la madrileño*, a tripe dish cooked in a spicy tomato sauce. It's not unusual to find *orejas* (pigs' ears), *sesos* (brains), *riñones* (kidneys) and even *criadillas* (bulls' testicles) on the menu. If you head out to Segovia, be sure to try *cochinillo*, roast suckling pig, traditionally slaughtered when they are 21 days old. Ideally, it should be tender enough to cut with a butter knife.

In **Andalucía**, the Moorish inheritance is felt most strongly. The Arabs cultivated olives, saffron and almonds, which all appear in the local cuisine. There's plenty of fresh seafood along the coast and *pescadito frito*, fried fresh fish best eaten out of a paper cone, is the specialitiy of Cádiz. Inland the emphasis is on meat and game: one of the region's best known dishes is *rabo de toro* – bull's tail slowly cooked in a rich sauce. You might already have tried *gazpacho* – a cold soup of tomatoes, onions and cucumber – but there's a delicious thicker version called *salmorejo*, usually topped with chopped ham and boiled eggs, and a white soup called *ajo blanco* in which the tomatoes have been replaced with almonds.

Extremadura is known for its *migas*, breadcrumbs fried with peppers, but it's most famous culinary export is the *jamón ibérico*. This is the king of hams – and Spain has countless varieties – and is made from the flesh of the *pata negra* (black foot) pigs which roam the Extremaduran *dehesa* and are fed on acorns. Watch out, though, if you order it in a tapas bar; it's very, very expensive.

Drink
Wine In good Catholic fashion, wine is the blood of Spain. It's the standard accompaniment to most meals, but also features prominently in bars, where a glass of cheap *tinto* or *blanco* can cost as little as €0.30, although it's normally more. A bottle of house wine in a restaurant is often no more than €2 or €3. *Tinto* is red (although if you just order *vino* it's assumed that's what you want), *blanco* is white, and rosé is either *clarete* or *rosado*.

A well-regulated system of *denominaciones de origen* (DO), similar to the French *appelation controlée*, has lifted the reputation of Spanish wines high above the party plonk status they once enjoyed. Much of Spain's wine is produced in the north, and recent years have seen regions such as the Ribera del Duero, Rueda, Navarra, Pinedes and Rías Baixas achieve worldwide recognition. But the daddy is, of course, still Rioja.

The overall standard of Riojas has improved markedly since the granting of the higher DOC status in 1991, with some fairly stringent testing in place. Red predominates; these are mostly medium-bodied bottles from the Tempranillo grape (with three other permitted red grapes often used to add depth or character). Whites from Viura and Malvasia are also produced: the majority of these are young, fresh and dry, unlike the powerful oaky Rioja whites sold in the UK. Rosés are also produced. The quality of individual Riojas varies widely according to both producer and the amount of time the wines have been aged in oak barrels and in the bottle. The words *crianza*, *reserva*, and *gran reserva* refer to the length of the aging process (see below), while the vintage date is also given. Rioja producers store their wines at the *bodega* until deemed ready for drinking, so it's common to see wines dating back a decade or more on shelves and wine lists.

A growing number of people feel, however, that Spain's best reds come from further west, in the Ribera del Duero region east of Valladolid. The king's favourite tipple, *Vega Sicilia*, has long been Spain's most prestigious wine, but other producers from the area have also gained stellar reviews. The region has been dubbed 'the Spanish Burgundy'; the description isn't wholly fanciful, as the better wines have the rich nose and dark delicacy vaguely reminiscent of the French region.

Galicia produces some excellent whites too; the coastal Albariño vineyards produce a sought-after dry wine with a very distinctive bouquet. Ribeiro is another good Galician white, and the reds from there are also tasty, having some similarity to those produced in nearby northern Portugal.

Among other regions, Navarra, long known only for rosé, is producing some quality red wines unfettered by the stricter rules governing production in neighbouring Rioja, while Bierzo, in western León province, also produces interesting wines from the red Prieto Picudo grape. Other DO wines in Northern Spain include Somontano, a red and white appelation from Aragón and Toro, whose baking climate makes for full-bodied reds.

An unusual wine worth trying is *txakolí*, with a small production on the Basque coast. The most common form is a young, refreshing, acidic white which has a green tinge and a slight sparkle, often accentuated by pouring from a height. The best examples, from around Getaria, go beautifully with seafood. The wine is made from underripe grapes of the Ondarrubi Zuria variety; there's a less common red species and some rosé.

Catalan wines are also gaining increasing recognition. Best known is *cava*, the home-grown bubbly, and a night out in Barcelona should always start with a glass or two of this crisp, sparkling white wine. The largest wine-producing region in Catalunya is Penedés, which produces a vast range of reds, whites and rosés to suit all tastes and pockets, but you'll find other local specialities including the unusual *Paxarete*, a very sweet traditional chocolatey brown wine produced around Tarragona.

One of the joys of Spain, though, is the rest of the wine. Order a *menú del día* at a cheap restaurant and you'll be unceremoniously served a cheap bottle of local red (sometimes without even asking for it). Wine snobbery can leave by the back door at this point: it may be cold, but you'll find it refreshing; it may be acidic, but once the olive-oil laden food arrives, you'll be glad of it. Wine's not a luxury item in Spain, so people add water to it if they feel like it, or lemonade, or *cola* (to make the party drink called *calimocho*).

In many bars, you can order *Ribera*, *Rueda*, or other regions by the glass. If you simply ask for *crianza* or *reserva*, you'll usually get a Rioja. A *tinto* or *blanco* will get you the house wine (although many bartenders in tourist areas assume that visitors don't want it, and will try and serve you a more expensive kind). As a general rule, only bars that serve food serve wine; most *pubs* and *discotecas* won't have it.

Beer Spanish beer is mostly lager, usually reasonably strong, fairly gassy, cold, and good. On the tapas trail, many people order *cortos,* usually about 100 ml. A *caña* is a larger draught beer, usually about 200-300 ml. Order a *cerveza* and you'll get a bottled beer. Many people order their beer *con gas*, topped up with mineral water, sometimes called a *clara*, although this normally means it's topped with lemonade. A *jarra* is a shared jug.

Cider *Sidra* is an institution in Asturias, and to a lesser extent in Euskadi, but you'll find it in Basque and Asturian restaurants in most of the larger cities. The cider is flat, sourish, and yeasty; the appley taste will be a surprise after most commercial versions of the drink. Asturias' *sidrerías* offer some of Spain's most enjoyable barlife, with excellent food, a distinctive odour, sawdust on the floor, and the cider poured from above head height by uniformed waiters to give it some bounce.

Sherry If you thought sherry was for old ladies and vicars, think again. At Seville's famous *Feria*, the standard tipple is a glass of refreshing chilled *manzanilla*, a pale, dry and delicious thirst-quencher. There are dozens of other varieties including the light *fino* which is drunk young, or sweeter *amontillados* with a caramel flavour. The very sweetest are *olorosos*, a traditional dessert accompaniment. The *bodegas* of Jerez ('sherry' is a corruption of Jerez) offer guided visits with tastings.

Spirits *Vermut* (vermouth) is a popular pre-dinner *aperitif*, usually served straight from the barrel. Many bars make their own vermouth by adding various herbs and fruits and letting it sit in barrels: this can be excellent, particularly if its from a *solera*. This is a system where liquid is drawn from the oldest of a series of barrels, which is then topped up with the next oldest, etc, resulting in some very mellow characterful drink.

After dinner people relax over a whisky or a brandy, or hit the mixed drinks: *gin tonic* is obvious, while a *cuba libre* is a rum and coke (but can refer to vodka or other spirits). Spirits are free-poured and large; don't be surprised at a 100 ml measure. Whisky is popular, and most bars have a good range. Spanish brandy is good, although it's oaky vanilla flavours don't appeal to everyone. There are numerous varieties of rum and flavoured liqueurs. When ordering a spirit, you'll be expected to choose which brand you want; the local varieties (eg *Larios* gin, *DYC* whisky) are marginally cheaper than their imported brethren. *Chupitos* are shots; restaurants will often throw in a free one at the end of a meal, or give you a bottle of *orujo* (grape spirit) to pep up your black coffee.

Non-alcoholic drinks Juice is normally bottled and expensive, although freshly squeezed orange juice is common. It's an odd thing to order after breakfast, though. *Mosto* (grape juice; really pre-fermented wine) is a cheaper and popular soft drink in bars. There's the usual range of fizzy drinks (*gaseosas*) available, but a popular and peculiarly Spanish soft drink is *Bitter-kas*, a dark red herby brew which tastes a bit like Campari. *Horchata* is a summer drink, a sort of milkshake made from tiger nuts which comes from the Valencia region but is popular throughout Spain. Water (*agua*) comes *con* (with) or *sin* (without) *gas*. The tap water is totally safe to drink, but it's not always the nicest.

Hot drinks Coffee (*café*) is usually excellent and strong. *Solo* is black, mostly served espresso style. Order *americano* if you want a long black, *cortado* if you want a dash of milk, or *con leche* for about half milk. A *carajillo* is a coffee with brandy, while *queimado* is a coffee heated with *orujo*, a Galician drink of ritual significance. *Té* (tea) is served without milk unless you ask; herbal teas (*infusiones*) can be found in many places. *Chocolate* is a reasonably popular drink at breakfast time or as a *merienda* (afternoon tea), served with *churros*, fried doughsticks that seduce about a quarter of visitors and repel the rest.

Restaurants in Catalunya

One of the great pleasures of travelling in Spain is eating out, but it's no fun sitting alone in a restaurant so try and adapt to the local hours as much as you can; it may feel strange leaving dinner until after 2200, but you'll miss out on a lot of atmosphere if you don't.

The standard distinctions of bar, café and restaurant don't apply in Spain. Many places combine all three functions, and it's not always evident; the dining room (*comedor*) is often tucked away behind the bar or upstairs. *Restaurantes* are restaurants, and will usually have a dedicated dining area with set menus and *à la carte* options. Bars and cafés will often display food on the counter, or have a list of tapas; bars tend to be known for particular dishes they do well. Many bars, cafés and restaurants don't serve food on Sunday nights, and most are closed one other night a week, most commonly Monday.

Cafés will normally have some breakfasty fare out in the mornings; croissants and sweetish pastries are the norm; fresh squeezed orange juice is also common. About 1100 they start putting out savoury fare; maybe a *tortilla*, some *ensaladilla rusa*, or little ham rolls in preparation for pre-lunch snacking.

Lunch is the biggest meal of the day for most people in Spain, and it's also the cheapest time to eat. Just about all restaurants offer a *menú del día*, which is usually a set three course meal that includes wine or soft drink. In unglamorous workers' locals this is often as little as €5 or €6; paying anything more than €9 indicates the restaurant takes itself quite seriously. There's often a choice of several starters and mains. To make the most of the meal, a handy tip is to order another starter in place of a main; most places are quite happy to do it, and the starters are usually more interesting (and sometimes larger) than the mains, which tend to be slabs of mediocre meat. Most places open for lunch at about 1300, and stop serving at 1500 or 1530, although at weekends this can extend; it's not uncommon to see people still lunching at 1800 on a Sunday. The quality of *à la carte* is usually higher than the *menú*, and quantities are large. Simpler restaurants won't offer this option except in the evenings.

Tapas has changed in meaning over the years, and now basically refers to all bar food. This range includes free snacks given with drinks (which is increasingly rare – although you'll still get a free tapa in León and Granada), *pintxos*, the Basque speciality which has taken off in bars all over Spain, and more substantial dishes, usually ordered in *raciones*. A *ración* in Northern Spain is no mean affair; it can often comfortably fill one person, so if you want to sample a range of things, you're better to ask for a half (*media*) or a *tapa* (smaller portion, when available). Prices of tapas basically depend on the ingredients; a good portion of *langostinos* (king prawns) will likely set you back €10, while more *morcilla* (black pudding) or *patatas* than you can eat might only be €3 or so.

Most restaurants open for dinner at 2030 or later; any earlier and it's likely a tourist trap. Although some places do offer a cheap set menu, you'll usually have to order *à la carte*. In quiet areas, places stop serving at 2200 on weeknights, but in cities and at weekends people tend to sit down at 2230 or later.

A cheap option at any time of day is a *plato combinado*, most commonly done in cafés. They're usually a truckstop-style combination of eggs, steak, bacon and chips or similar and are filling but rarely inspiring.

Vegetarians in Spain won't be spoiled for choice, but at least what there is tends to be good. Dedicated vegetarian restaurants are amazingly few, and most restaurants won't have a vegetarian main course on offer, although the existence of *raciones* and salads makes this less of a burden than it might be. *Ensalada mixta* nearly always has tuna in it, but it's usually made fresh, so places will happily leave it out. *Ensaladilla rusa* is normally a good option, but ask about the tuna too, just in case. Tortilla is another simple but nearly ubiquitous option. Simple potato or pepper dishes are tasty options (although beware peppers stuffed with meat), and many *revueltos* (scrambled eggs) are just mixed with asparagus. Annoyingly, most vegetable *menestras* are seeded with ham before cooking, and bean dishes usually have at least some meat or animal fat. You'll have to specify *soy vegetariano/a* (I am a vegetarian), but ask what dishes contain, as ham, fish, and even chicken are often considered suitable vegetarian fare. Vegans will have a tougher time. What doesn't have meat nearly always has cheese or egg, and waiters are unlikely to know the ingredients down to the basics.

Festivals in Catalunya

Even the smallest village in Spain has a fiesta, and some have several. Although mostly nominally religious in nature, they usually include the works; a mass and procession or two to be sure, but also live music, bullfights, competitions, fireworks and copious drinking of *calimocho*, a mix of red wine and cola (not as bad as it sounds). A feature of many are the *gigantes y cabezudos*, huge-headed papier-mâché figures based on historical personages who parade the streets. Adding to the sense of fun are peñas, boisterous social clubs which patrol the streets making music, get rowdy at the bullfights and drink wine all night and day. Most fiestas are in summer, and if you're spending much time in Spain in that period you're bound to run into one; expect some trouble finding accommodation. Details of the major town fiestas can be found in the travel text. National holidays can be difficult times to travel; it's important to reserve tickets in advance. If the holiday falls mid-week, it's usual form to take an extra day off, forming a long weekend known as a *puente* (bridge).

Major fiestas
5 January Cabalgata de Los Reyes (Three Kings). Throughout Spain. The Three Kings Parade in floats tossing out sweets to kids, who get Christmas presents the next day.

February/March Carnaval. Held in almost every town and village; although the biggest and wildest party is held in Cádiz, the parades in Sitges are also fantastic.

Easter Semana Santa. Easter celebrations are held everywhere and parades take place in every town, particularly in the south of Spain.

End May/June Feast of Corpus Christi. Held in most towns, it is celebrated with traditional dancing and parades although Toledo's processions are the grandest.

21-24 June Fiesta de San Juan, or the Midsummer's Solstice. This is celebrated across Spain, often with the strange custom of the 'Burial of the Sardine'.

September Barcelona Festes de la Mercé. Huge festival with folkloric parades, fireworks, dragons and giants.

Public holidays
1 January Año Nuevo (New Year's Day)
6 January Reyes Magos (Epiphany) when Christmas presents are given.
Easter Jueves Santo, Viernes Santo, Día de Pascua (Maundy Thursday, Good Friday, Easter Sunday).
1 May Fiesta de Trabajo (Labour Day).
15 August Asunción (Feast of the Assumption).

12 October Día de la Hispanidad (Columbus Day, Spanish National Day, Feast of the Virgin of the Pillar).

1 November Todos los Santos (All Saints' Day).

6 December El Día de la Constitución Española (Constitution Day).

8 December Inmaculada Concepción (Feast of the Immaculate Conception).

24 December Noche Buena (Christmas Eve).

25 December Navidad (Christmas Day).

Essentials A-Z

Accident and emergencies
There is now one nationwide emergency number for fire, police and ambulance: **T112**.

Electricity
The current in Spain is 220V. A round 2-pin plug is used (European standard).

Embassies and consulates
For embassies and consulates of Spain abroad, see http://embassy.goabroad.com.

Health → *See Directory, page 79, for hospitals and pharmacies in Barcelona.*
Health for travellers in Spain is rarely a problem. Medical facilities are good, and the worst most travellers experience is an upset stomach, usually merely a result of the different diet rather than any bug. The water is safe to drink, but doesn't always taste great, so many travellers (and locals) stick to bottled water. The sun can be harsh, so take precautions to avoid heat exhaustion/sunburn. Many medications that require a prescription in other countries are available over the counter at pharmacies in Spain. Pharmacists are highly trained but don't necessarily speak English. In all medium-sized towns and cities, at least one pharmacy is open 24 hrs; this is organized on a rota system; details are posted in the window of all pharmacies and listed in local newspapers.

Insurance
British and other European citizens should obtain a European Health Insurance Card (EHIC) available via www.dh.gov.uk or from post offices in the UK, before leaving home. This guarantees free medical care throughout the EU. Non-EU citizens should consider insurance to cover emergency and routine medical needs; be sure that it covers any sports/activities you may get involved in.

Insurance is a good idea anyway to cover you for theft, etc. Any theft must be reported at the local police station within 24 hrs; you'll need to obtain a written report to show your insurers.

Language
There are 3 official languages in Catalunya: Catalan, Spanish (Castellano) and Aranés (spoken in the Val d'Aran, high in the Pyrenees). Menus and road signs are generally in Catalan, although everyone (except in the most remote regions) also speaks Spanish. Any efforts to speak Catalan – even a simple '*bon día*' (hello) – are warmly welcomed by locals. Some locals may reply to a Spanish request in Catalan, a gentle reminder to visitors that Catalunya isn't Spain.

While many visitor attractions have information available in English (and sometimes French and German), many don't, or only have English tours in times of high demand. Most tourist office staff will speak at least some English, and there's a good range of translated information available in many regions. English is widely spoken in the resorts along the coast.

Money → *See www.xe.com for exchange rates.*
Currency
In 2002, Spain switched to the euro, bidding farewell to the peseta. The euro (€) is divided into 100 céntimos. Euro notes are standard across the whole zone, and come in denominations of 5, 10, 20, 50, 100, and the rarely seen 200 and 500. Coins have one standard face and one national face; all coins are, however, acceptable in all countries. The coins are slightly difficult to tell apart when you're not used to them. The coppers are 1, 2 and 5 cent pieces, the golds are 10, 20 and 50, and the silver/gold combinations are €1 and €2.

ATMs and banks

The best way to get money in Spain is by plastic. ATMs are plentiful, and just about all of them accept all the major international debit and credit cards. The Spanish bank won't charge for the transaction, though they will charge a mark-up on the exchange rate, but beware of your own bank hitting you for a hefty fee: check with them before leaving home. Even if they do, it's likely to be a better deal than exchanging cash. The website www.moneysavingexpert.com has a good rundown on the most economical ways of accessing cash while travelling.

Banks are usually open Mon-Fri 0830-1400 (and Sat in winter) and many change foreign money (sometimes only the central branch in a town will do it). Commission rates vary widely; it's usually best to change large amounts, as there's often a minimum commission of €6 or so. Nevertheless, banks nearly always give better rates than change offices (*casas de cambio*), which are fewer by the day. If you're stuck outside banking hours, some large department stores such as **El Corte Inglés** change money at knavish rates.

Traveller's cheques are accepted in many shops, although they are far less common than they were.

Tax

Nearly all goods and services in Spain are subject to a value-added tax (IVA). This is currently 10% for most things the traveller will encounter, including restaurants and hotels, but is as high as 21% on some things. IVA is normally included in the stated prices. You're technically entitled to claim it back if you're a non-EU citizen, for purchases over €90. If you're buying something pricey, make sure you get a stamped receipt clearly showing the IVA component, as well as your name and passport number; you can claim the amount back at major airports on departure. Some shops will have a form to smooth the process.

Cost of living and travelling

Prices have soared since the euro was introduced; some basics rose by 50-80% in 3 years, and hotel and restaurant prices can seem dear even by Western European standards these days. Spain's average monthly salary of €1500 is low by EU standards, and the minimum monthly salary of €800 is very low indeed.

Spain can still be a reasonably cheap place to travel if you're prepared to forgo a few luxuries. If you're travelling as a pair, staying in cheap *pensiones*, eating a set meal at lunchtime, travelling short distances by bus or train daily, and snacking on tapas in the evenings, €70 per person per day is reasonable. If you camp and grab picnic lunches from shops, you could reduce this considerably. In a cheap hotel or good hostal and using a car, €130 a day and you'll not be counting pennies; €250 per day and you'll be very comfy indeed unless you're staying in 4- or 5-star accommodation.

Accommodation is more expensive in summer than in winter, although prices drop in Barcelona in Aug when many businesses are closed and the city is stifling. The news isn't great for the solo traveller; single rooms tend not to be particularly good value, and they are in short supply. Prices range from 60-80% of the double/twin price; some places even charge the full rate. If you're going to be staying in 3- to 5-star hotels, booking them ahead on internet discount sites, such as www.booking.com or www.budgetplaces.com, can save a lot of money.

Public transport is generally cheap; intercity bus services are quick and low-priced and trains are reasonable, though the fast AVE trains cost substantially more.

Petrol is relatively cheap: standard unleaded petrol is around €1.38 per litre and diesel around €1.35. In some places, particularly in tourist areas, you may be charged up to 20% more to sit outside a restaurant. It's also worth checking if the 10% IVA (sales tax) is included in menu prices, especially in the more expensive restaurants; it should say on the menu whether this is the case.

Opening hours

Offices are usually open Mon-Fri 0800-1500. These hours might be official, but time in Spain is always fluid.

Safety

Spain is generally a safe place, with considerably less violent crime than many other European countries. However, street crime – bag-snatching and pickpocketing – in the bigger cities is on the rise. Don't invite crime by leaving luggage or cash in cars, and if you are parking in a city or a popular hiking zone, leave the glove box open so that thieves know there is nothing to steal.

There are several types of police, helpful enough in normal circumstances. The paramilitary Guardia Civil dress in green and are responsible for the roads (including speed traps and the like), borders and law enforcement away from towns. They're not a bunch to get the wrong side of but are polite to tourists and have thankfully lost the bizarre winged hats they used to sport. The Policía Nacional are responsible for most urban crimefighting. These are the ones to go to if you need to report anything stolen, etc. Policía Local/Municipal are present in large towns and cities and are responsible for some urban crime, as well as traffic control and parking. Police stations are listed in phone books under *comisarías*. See also Insurance, page 22.

Telephone → *Country code +34.*

Phone booths on the street are mostly operated by Telefónica, and all have international direct dialling (00 is the prefix for international calls). They accept coins from €0.05 upwards and pre-paid phone cards, which can be bought from newsagents, post offices and tobacconists (*estancos*) in denominations of €5, 10, 15 and 20. Calls are cheaper after 2200 during the week and all day at weekends. Phones in bars and cafés usually have more expensive rates than public payphones. Phone centres (*locutorios*) are the cheapest method for calling abroad; you'll find them in the Atocha and Chamartín train stations, and several smaller ones dotted throughout Chueca and Lavapiés.

For directory enquiries, dial T11818 for national or T11825 for international numbers. (All these numbers are operated by **Telefónica**; other operators offer the same services).

Domestic landlines have 9-digit numbers beginning with 9 (occasionally with 8). Although the first 3 digits indicate the province, you have to dial the full number from wherever you are calling, including abroad. Mobiles numbers start with 6.

Mobiles (*móviles*) are big in Spain and coverage is very good. Most foreign mobiles will work in Spain; check with your service provider about what the call costs will be like. Many mobile networks require you to call up before leaving your home country to activate overseas service ('roaming'). If you're staying a while, it may be cheaper to buy a Spanish mobile or SIM card, as there are always numerous offers and discounts. You could even purchase a 'disposable' BIC mobile phone at several outlets including **Schleker**. They cost about €20 and include €12 of calls.

Time

Spain operates on western European time, ie GMT +1, and changes its clocks in line with the rest of the EU.

'Spanish time' isn't as elastic as it used to be, but if you're told something will happen 'en seguida' ('straight away') it may take

10 mins, if you're told 'cinco minutos' (5 mins), grab a seat and a book. Transport, especially buses, leaves promptly.

Tipping

Tipping in Spain is far from compulsory, but much practised. Around 10% is considered fairly generous in a restaurant; 3-5% is more usual. It's rare for a service charge to be added to a bill. Waiters do not normally expect tips for lunchtime set meals or tapas, but here and in bars and cafés people will often leave small change, especially for table service. Taxi drivers don't expect a tip, but don't expect you to sit around waiting for twenty cents change either. In rural areas, churches will often have a local keyholder who will open it up for you; if there's no admission charge, a tip or donation is appropriate; say €1 per head; more if they've given a detailed tour.

Toilets

Public toilets are not common, although you'll find them in train stations. It's usually okay to use the ones in bars and cafés. You might have to use the bin next to the loo for your toilet paper if the system can't cope, particularly in out-of-the-way places. There are usually toilets in the big department stores, too.

Tourist information → *See individual entries for specific details of tourist offices.*

The tourist information infrastructure in Spain is organized by the regional governments and is generally excellent, with a wide range of information, often in English, German and French as well as Spanish. Offices within the region can provide maps of the area and towns, and lists of registered accommodation, usually with a booklet for hotels, *hostales*, and *pensiones*; another for campsites, and another, especially worth picking up, listing farmstay and rural accommodation, which has taken off in a big way; hundreds are added yearly. Opening hours are longer in major cities; many rural offices are only open in summer. Average opening hours are Mon-Sat 1000-1400, 1600-1900, Sun 1000-1400. Offices are often closed on Sun or Mon. Staff often speak English and other European languages

Visas and immigration

Entry requirements are subject to change, so always check with the Spanish tourist board or an embassy/consulate if you're not an EU citizen. EU citizens and those from countries within the Schengen agreement can enter Spain freely. UK/Irish citizens will need to carry a passport, while an identity card suffices for other EU/Schengen nationals. Citizens of Australia, the USA, Canada, New Zealand and Israel can enter without a visa for up to 90 days. Other citizens will require a visa, obtainable from Spanish consulates or embassies. These are usually issued very quickly and valid for all Schengen countries. The basic visa is valid for 90 days, and you'll need 2 passport photos, proof of funds covering your stay, and possibly evidence of medical cover (ie insurance). For extensions of visas, apply to an *oficina de extranjeros* in a major city.

Weights and measures

The Spanish use the metric system. Decimal places are indicated with commas, and thousands with points.

Contents

Footprint features

Barcelona

Barcelona doesn't hold back when it comes to touting its many charms. The most popular city on the Med boasts great beaches, a gorgeous climate, spectacular architecture and a stellar dining scene. It contains the largest and best-preserved medieval quarter in Europe, as well as the greatest concentration of Modernista monuments in the Quadrat d'Or, or 'Golden Square'. Gaudí's enormous temple to the Sagrada Família – now finally roofed if still incomplete – dominates the entire city, its vast spires creeping higher and higher each day. Barcelona's ongoing makeover which started with the 1992 Olympics has resulted in new parks, squares, museums and skyscrapers, many of which bear the signature of celebrity architects such as Jean Nouvel or Richard Rogers. The city's fame as a gourmet destination continues to spread, offering something for all pockets and palates, whether you're just looking for some freshly fried sardines by the beach, or an ode to molecular gastronomy by one of Barcelona's new breed of super chefs.

Arriving in Barcelona → *Populaton: around 1,625,000.*

Getting there

Barcelona's international **airport** is in El Prat de Llobregat, 12 km to the south of the city. For information on arriving by air, see page 6.

If arriving by **car**, the main access road into Barcelona is the A-7 *autopista*, which crosses the eastern Pyrenees and runs down past Girona and Figueres. The tolls are high, which means that the other main access road, the N-II, is clogged with traffic most of the time.

Barcelona's main **bus and coach station** ① *Estació d'Autobuses Barcelona-Nord, C/Ali Bei 80, metro Arc de Triomf, T902 260 606, www.barcelonanord.com,* has services for national and international destinations. Note that the bus station next to Barcelona-Sants train station is a stop on many routes, but it is the final destination for most Eurolines buses.

The main **train** station for international, regional, and local trains is Estació-Sants, metro Sants. Many trains often stop at Passeig de Gràcia station which is more convenient for the city centre. Some trains from France arrive at the Estació de Francia near the harbour. For RENFE information, see www.renfe.com.

There are regular ferries to the Balearics (Palma de Mallorca, Mahó and Ibiza) with **Acciona/Trasmediterránea**, T902 454 645, www.trasmediterranea.es. Regular ferries to Genova with **Grandi Navi Veloci**, T934 437 139, www.gnv.it.

Just the ticket

Barcelona Card This offers unlimited public transport plus more than 100 discounts at shops, restaurants and museums. It is available for two, three, four or five days and costs €29-47. Discounts include free entry to the Museu d'Història de Barcelona, MNAC, Museu Frederic Marès, among many others.

Ruta del Modernisme This ticket is available from the Centre del Modernisme in the main tourist information office, www.ruta modernisme.com. It is a self-guided tour: you buy the map and guidebook, and visit more than 100 Modernista sites around the city. A discount voucher book is included.

Art Ticket This offers free entrance to seven of Barcelona's best art museums: the Museu Picasso, Museu Nacional d'Art de Catalunya (MNAC); Fundació Joan Miró; Fundació Antoni Tàpies; Centre de Cultura Contemporània de Barcelona (CCCB); Centre Cultural Caixa Catalunya (La Pedrera); Museu d'Art Contemporani de Barcelona (MACBA). It costs €30, is valid for three months and is available from tourist offices, and participating museums.

Arqueoticket This offers free entry to four museums with archaeological collections: the Museu d'Arqueologia de Catalunya; Museu Egipci; Museu d'Història de Barcelona and the Museu Marítim.

Artcoticket Admission to six provide contemporary art collections for €15: Fundació Alorda Derksen; Fundació de les Arts y les Artistes; Fundació Foto Colectania; Fundació Francisco Godia; Fundació Suñol; and Fundació Vila Casas.

Getting around

The public transport network in Barcelona is excellent: clean, efficient, cheap, safe and easy to use. For maps and information in English, check the website, www.tmb.cat or call the TMB on T902 075 027. ▸▸ *For further details, see Transport page 77.*

Orientation

Finding your way around Barcelona isn't difficult; a glance at any map shows the **Barri Gòtic** (Gothic Quarter) squeezed into a crooked oval shape at the heart of Barcelona. It is divided from the once-sleazy, now hip and multi-cultural, **Raval** area by the famous **Rambla** promenade. On the other side of the Barri Gòtic is the fashionable **Ribera** neighbourhood. Spreading inland from the old city is the elegant grid of the **Eixample**, where the Modernistas left their fanciful mark on the bourgeois mansions. Beyond the grid lie a ring of traditional towns like **Gràcia**, which boasts the magical Park Güell. The city is ringed by the Collserola hills, of which the highest and most famous peak is **Tibidabo**, with its funfair, from where the whole city is spread out at your feet on a clear day. Hemming in the city on its western end is the hill of **Montjüic**, the city's favourite playground and site of the 1992 Olympic stadium. Along the seafront are the spanking new developments of the **Port Vell** and the **Port Olímpic**, crammed with beaches, restaurants and bars. It's an engagingly walkable city but, if you get footsore, the bus system and the metro are clean, safe and easy to negotiate, and you can swing up to Montjüic in a cable car or take a vintage tram to Tibidabo.

1 Barcelona

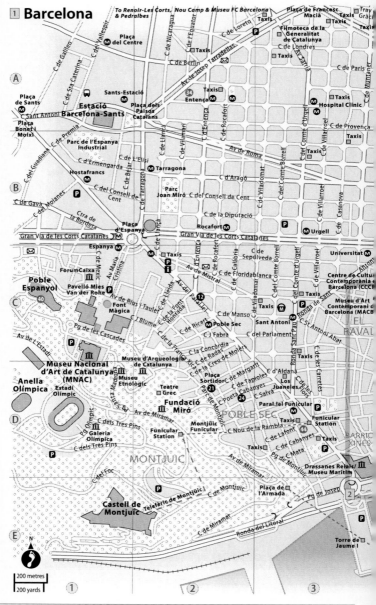

To Renoir-Les-Corts, Nou Camp & Museu FC Barcelona & Pedralbes

Plaça de Francesc Macià

Filmoteca de la Generalitat de Catalunya

Plaça del Centre

Plaça de Sants

Sants-Estació

Estació Barcelona-Sants

Plaça dels Països Catalans

Entença

Hospital Clínic

(A)

Sant Antoni

Plaça Bonet i Moixí

Parc de l'Espanya Industrial

C de Provença

Hostafrancs

Tarragona

C d'Aragó

C del Consell de Cent

Parc Joan Miró

(B)

Rocafort

Urgell

Plaça d'Espanya

Gran Via de les Corts Catalanes

Gran Via de les Corts Catalanes

Espanya

Universitat

Sepúlveda

ForumCaixa

Centre de Cultura Contemporània de Barcelona (CCCB)

Poble Espanyol

Pavelló Mies Van der Rohe

C de Floridablanca

Museu d'Art Contemporani de Barcelona (MACBA)

Font Màgica

Paral·lel

C de Manso

Poble Sec

Sant Antoni

EL RAVAL

(C)

Pg de les Cascades

C del Parlament

Av de L'Estadi

Museu Nacional d'Art de Catalunya (MNAC)

Museu d'Arqueologia de Catalunya

Plaça Sortidor

Els Juanelos

Anella Olímpica

Estadi Olímpic

Museu Etnològic

Teatre Grec

Fundació Miró

Paral·lel Funicular

Funicular Station

(D)

Galeria Olímpica

Av de Miramar

Montjuïc Funicular

Funicular Station

BARRIO CHINO

MONTJUIC

POBLE SEC

Drassanes Reials / Museu Marítim

C del Foc

Telefèric de Montjuïc

Av de Miramar

Plaça de l'Armada

Pg de Josep

Castell de Montjuïc

C de Montjuïc

(E)

C de Miramar

Ronda del Litoral

Torre de Jaume I

200 metres

200 yards

(1)   (2)   (3)

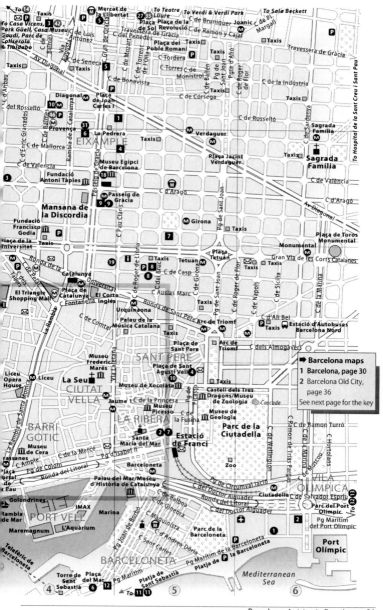

To Casa Vicens
Park Güell, Casa Museu
Gaudí, Parc de
Collserola
& Tibidabo

To Teatre Lliure
To Verdi & Verdi Park
To Sala Beckett

Mercat de la Llibertat
Plaça de la Revolució
To Bruniquer
Joanic
C de Pl Margall

To Casa Vicens

Taxis

Taxis

C de Luis Antúnez
Plaça del Poble Romaní
Travessera de Gràcia

C de Ramon y Cajal

Taxis

Travessera de Gràcia

C del Penedès
C de Mozart
C de Torrent de l'Olla
Tordera

Taxis

AV Diagonal
Via Augusta
Gran de Gràcia
C de Seneca
C de Bonavista
C Torres
C de Bailén
Pte d'Alto
Pge de Roger de Flor
C de Sant Joan
C de la Indústria

Taxis
Taxis
C de Monistrol

C de Córsega

Taxis

Diagonal
Plaça de Joan Carles I
C de Rosselló

Sagrada Família

To Hospital de la Sant Creu i Sant Pau

del Rosselló
Passeig de Gràcia
Rambla de Catalunya
La Pedrera
Verdaguer

To Sant Creu i Sant Pau

C d'Enric Granados
Provença
EIXAMPLE

Taxis

C de Mallorca
Plaça Jacint Verdaguer
Sagrada Família

Fundació Antoni Tàpies
Museu Egipci de Barcelona
C d'Aragó

Taxis

C de València
C d'Aragó
Av Diagonal

Mansana de la Discòrdia
Passeig de Gràcia
C de Pau Claris
C de Sant Joan
Girona

Fundació Francisco Godia
Plaça de la Universitat
Taxis
Plaça de Toros Monumental

Ronda de la Universitat
Taxis
Plaça Tetuan
Tetuan
C de Casp
C de Roger de Flor
Monumental
Gran Via de les Corts Catalanes

El Triangle Shopping Mall
Plaça de Catalunya
El Corte Inglés
C d'Ausiàs Marc
C de Girona
C de Sicília
C de la Marina

La Rambla
Fontanella
Ronda de Sant Pere
C de Roger de Flor
C de Nàpols
Urquinaona
Palau de la Música Catalana
Arc de Triomf
C d'Alí Bei
Estació d'Autobuses Barcelona Nord

C de Comtal
Taxis
Plaça de Sant Pere
Arc de Triomf

Museu Frederic Marès
SANT PERE
Plaça de Sant Agustí Vell
dels Almogàvers

Liceu
Opera House
Liceu
La Seu
CIUTAT VELLA
Museu de Xocolata
Taxis
Castell dels Tres Dragons/Museu de Zoologia
Museu de Geologia
Cascade

BARRI GÒTIC
Jaume I
Museu Picasso
LA RIBERA
C de la Princesa
C de la Fusina
Parc de la Ciutadella

Museu de Cera
Santa Maria del Mar
Estació de França
Zoo
C de Ramon Turró

Plaça Reial
Pg de Colom
Pg d'Isabel II
Barceloneta
Ciutadella
VILA OLÍMPICA

Golondrines
Palau del Mar/Museu d'Història de Catalunya
C de Salvador Espriu
Parc del Port Olímpic

IMAX
Marina
C de Balboa
C de Ginebra
Ronda del Litoral
C del Doctor Aiguader
Pg Marítim del Port Olímpic

Rambla de Mar
Maremagnum
L'Aquàrium
Pg de Circumval·lació
C del Doctor Aiguader

Telefèric de Barcelona
PORT VELL
BARCELONETA
Parc de la Barceloneta
Pg Marítim de la Barceloneta

Torre de Sant Sebastià
Plaça del Mar
Pg Marítim
Platja de Sant Sebastià
Platja de la Barceloneta
Port Olímpic

Mediterranean Sea

➡ **Barcelona maps**
1 Barcelona, page 30
2 Barcelona Old City, page 36
See next page for the key

Barcelona map key

Tourist information

The tourist information services in Barcelona are excellent. The **main tourist office** on the Plaça Catalunya also has a bureau de change, an accommodation-booking service, and a gift shop. You can book tours here and buy the various discount cards (see below). There is plenty of information on the excellent websites www.barcelonaturisme.com and www.bcn.cat. For telephone information, call T906 301 282 within Spain, or T+34 933 689 730 from abroad. Main office ① *Plaça Catalunya, daily 0900–2100.* Branches ① *Plaça Sant Jaume (in the corner of the Ajuntament/City Hall). Mon–Fri 1000–2000, Sat 1000–2000, Sun and hols 1000–1400; Estació Barcelona-Sants. winter Mon–Fri 0800–2000, Sat, Sun and hols 0800–1400, open daily in summer 0800–2000. Palau de Congressos (Trade Fair office), Avinguda Reina Maria Cristina, Montjüic. Open during trade fairs only. Airport (Terminals A and B), 0900–2100. Palau Robert, 107 Passeig de Gràcia, T932 384 000, www.gencat. es/probert. Open Mon–Fri 1000–1900, Sat 1000–1430.* This has information on all of Catalunya, including plenty about Barcelona. Centre d'Informació de la Virreina, ① *Palau de la Virreina, La Rambla 99, T933 017 775, Mon-Sat 1000-2000, Sun 1100-1500, ticket sales Tue-Sat 1100-2000, Sun 1100-1430.* This is the information service for the Generalitat's culture department, with details of concerts, exhibitions and festivals throughout the city.

Background

The first known settlers in the Barcelona area were the Laetani, followed by Greek and Phoenician traders from the eighth century BC onwards. Around 15BC, a fully-fledged Roman colony called Barcino was established, but it was still a backwater, outshone by Tarragona and Empúries which had better ports. Still, the next wave of invaders, the Visigoths, liked it well enough to name it a capital of one of their kingdoms in the fifth century AD. The Arabs occupied it briefly, before being expelled by the Franks from north of the Pyrenees. Wilfred the Hairy (Guifré el Pilos) united the earldoms of the area which was becoming known as Catalunya under the House of Barcelona, a dynasty which was to last 500 years.

The 12th to the 14th centuries were Barcelona's Golden Age: the city prospered as the Catalan empire began to expand, and a network of profitable trade routes was established around the Mediterranean. But, by the 15th century, with the marriage of Ferdinand of Aragón and Isabella of Castile, the balance of power shifted from Catalunya to Castile, and Barcelona was sidelined as Madrid emerged as the new political centre of Spain. Worse was to come: as Europe was ravaged by war during the 17th and 18th centuries, Barcelona always seemed to pick the losing side and was viciously punished in consequence. Revolt against the repressive Castilian regime was followed by siege and severe reprisal in 1640 and again in 1714; despite defeat, the Catalans named their national anthem after the heroic protestors of the 1640 rising, *Els Segadors* (the Reapers), and 11 September, the day the city fell to the Castilian armies in 1714, is now celebrated as Catalunya's National Day.

By the early 19th century, however, Barcelona was getting back on its feet thanks to the opening up of the trade routes with the Americas. It prospered, largely thanks to the cotton trade, and the city began to grow rapidly as factories and housing proliferated for the vast flood of workers. This was also the age of the *Renaixença*, a profound cultural revival which transformed the Catalan arts, particularly architecture: flamboyant Modernista buildings sprang up throughout the new extension (*Eixample* in Catalan) to the old city, and none were more magical than the dreamy palaces and mansions created by Antoni Gaudí. The Universal Exhibition of 1888 was held to bring Barcelona to the world's attention, and the city was transformed for the event (a harbinger of the Olympics over a century later). But the good times didn't last: ignominious defeat in the Spanish-American war of 1898 meant the loss of Spain's last remaining colonies and the trade routes. Barcelona's factory workers, crammed into slums and working in unspeakably miserable conditions, were becoming increasingly politicized. Tensions finally boiled over on the streets of Barcelona in 1909 in the *Setmana Tràgica* – a week of carnage and destruction which left 116 people dead and 80 buildings razed to the ground. In 1923 Primo de Rivera suspended the constitution and declared himself Dictator. He resigned, exhausted, seven years later and finally the country was swept up into the Spanish Civil War (1931-1936). Under Franco's repressive regime, the city suffered through the 'years of hunger', but the surge of tourism in the 1960s and 70s ushered in a new period of prosperity. Every *cava* bottle in the city was popped at the news of Franco's death in 1975, and, in 1980, the Catalan government (*Generalitat*) was finally reinstated under Jordí Pujol. The city was utterly transformed for the 1992 Olympic Games which really put it on the international map, and other high-profile events, such as the Universal Forum of Cultures in 2004, continued to remake the city's skyline. 'Starchitects' from Jean Nouvel to Richard Rogers created spectacular new buildings (such as Nouvel's Torre Agbar) and cleverly renovated old ones for new uses (such as Rogers' conversion of a Modernista bullring into a recreational complex) until the world financial crisis hit in 2008, causing most new projects to be put on hold or shelved indefinitely.

One project which hasn't been shelved is the extension of the high-speed railway, which already connects Barcelona with Madrid in about 2½ hours and which will soon link the Catalan capital with Paris in about 5½ hours.

La Rambla and down to the sea

Almost inevitably, everyone's first glimpse of Barcelona will be the Rambla, the city's most famous promenade, a mile-long ribbon shaded with plane trees which meanders down to the sea. Caught somewhere between banality and beauty, it's a strange and oddly appealing mixture of the picturesque and the tacky: almost lost among the fleets of 'human statues' are pretty turn-of-the-century kiosks overflowing with flowers, fast-food outlets are squeezed between crumbling theatres and mansions, and banks pop up in whimsical Modernista houses. It's at its best early in the morning and especially on Sunday lunchtimes, when families stroll among the flower kiosks and couples amble towards the seaside.

Plaça Catalunya

The mouth of the Rambla, and the inevitable starting point for a stroll, is the Plaça Catalunya, a huge square which links the old city with the new, dotted with fountains and benches. It's the main transport hub of the city, where buses and trains converge, disgorging endless crowds on to the Rambla. The Rambla looks like one street, but in fact it is five, all placed end-to-end in a seamless progress down to the harbour and referred to as La Rambla or Les Ramblas with equal ease by locals.

Les Ramblas

Each section has its own name and its own characteristics. The first stretch of the five adjoining Ramblas is the **Rambla de las Canaletes**, named for the **Font de las Canaletes**, a florid 19th-century fountain which is where fans of FC Barça come to celebrate victories. Drink from this fountain, a legend says, and you'll return to Barcelona.

Next up is **La Rambla de les Ocells**, the Rambla of the Birds, full, until recently, of kiosks selling cages full of parrots, canaries and other birds.

Rambla de las Flores is the prettiest and most sweet-smelling section of the street, with dozens of kiosks spilling over with brightly coloured bouquets. Set back on the right is the elegant **Palau de la Virreina**, which houses the city's cultural information offices and an exhibition space called the **Centre de la Imatge**, which focuses on photography exhibitions.

Further down on the right is the colourful Mercat de Sant Josep, affectionately and more usually known as **La Boquería**, capped with a lacy wrought-iron roof and a Modernista sign in bright jewel colours in 1914. Inside are piles of gleaming produce and there's a liberal sprinkling of tiny bars for a coffee or some oysters. Dive straight to the back of the market to avoid tourist prices and to enjoy better its unique atmosphere.

Back on the Rambla, there's a large colourful pavement mosaic by Miró, overlooked by the delightful **Casa Bruno Quadros**, formerly a Modernista umbrella shop, with a Chinese dragon supporting an umbrella. Stop off for cakes in the Modernista **Antigua Casa Figueres**, now an outpost of the famous **Escribà** patisserie (see page 65).

Rambla de les Caputxins is named after a Capuchin monastery which was destroyed in 1835. A new opera house, the **Liceu** ① *La Rambla 51-59, T934 859 900, www.liceubarcelona.cat; open for visits daily 1000-1300, guided visits at 1000, express non-guided tours at 1130, 1200, 1230 and 1300; Metro Liceu. Bus 14, 38, 51, 59*, was built in its place and has become one of Barcelona's best-loved institutions (making tickets very hard to come by). It's had its share of disasters since it first opened in 1847, and has burned down twice (rumours of a curse persist). This latest incarnation dates from 1999 and, while faithful to the original in terms of decoration, it's now equipped with the state-of-the-art technical improvements. There are tours around its opulent interior, with marble staircases and nymphs floating across the ceilings. Look out for the contemporary fresco in the main auditorium by one of Catalunya's best known contemporary artists Perejaume, which has transformed the Liceu's trademark velvet chairs into a series of gentle mountain peaks, fading softly into the distance. Buy tickets for guided visits in the modern annexe called *L'Espai de Liceu*.

Beyond the opera house, the grandeur fizzles out into the shabby genteel kind pretty quickly. Once-grand theatres and hotels struggle gamely to keep up appearances despite their ageing façades, while life on the street below carries on cheerfully oblivious. On the left, a pair of tall arches leads into the **Plaça Reial**, a grand 19th-century square with neoclassical arcades and lofty palm trees. The fountain of the Three Graces is flanked by twin lamp posts designed by Gaudí for his first municipal commission. Until recently, the square was well known for its squatters, prostitutes and drug-sellers. Some still linger in the corners, but it's now a tourist favourite, not least for the dozens of terrace cafés. Explore the tiny passages which lead off the square to discover some of the best nightlife in the city.

The last stretch of the Rambla, called the **Rambla de Santa Mònica** after another convent, is still the shabbiest despite ongoing restoration: for a long time it got the spillover from the surrounding red-light districts, but that's almost a thing of the past now. Cafés sprawl across the pavements, and there is a daily craft market. Tucked down an alley off the Rambla is the city's waxwork museum, the **Museu de Cera** ⓘ *Passatge Banca 7, T933 172 649, www.museucerabcn.com, Oct-Jun Mon-Fri 1000-1330 and 1600-1930, weekends and holidays 1100-1930, Jul-Sep daily 1000-2200, €15, children €9; guided night visits by the city executioner daily Jun 2000, Jul-Sep 2100 (over 8s only) €19; Metro Liceu, Bus 14, 36, 38, 57, 59, 64, 91.* The dummies of international criminals have been augmented by Hollywood stars, Royals and the 1992 Olympic mascot, Cobi.

It's worth taking a peek across the Rambla at the **Arts Santa Mònica** ⓘ *Rambla de Santa Mònica 7, T933 162 810, Mon-Fri 1100-2100, Sat 1100-1400, 1600-2000, free, Metro Liceu Bus 14, 36, 38, 59, 64, 91,* a gleaming modern building which incorporates the ruins of the old convent and which features very interesting temporary exhibitions.

Almost at the harbour, the Rambla opens out into the **Plaça Portal de la Pau** (Gate of Peace), where the **Monument a Colom** ⓘ *Plaça Portal de la Pau (closed temporarily); Metro Drassanes, bus 14, 36, 38, 59, 64, 91,* the world's largest statue of Christopher Columbus, enjoys a bird's eye view of the city. The statue was erected in 1888 and was immediately popular thanks to the unusual addition of an interior lift which still swoops visitors up to a viewing platform.

Barri Gòtic

The Rambla marks the southern boundary of the Barri Gòtic (The Gothic Quarter); the heart of the city for more than 2000 years. It is one of the best preserved Gothic quarters in Europe, a dizzy maze of palaces, squares and churches piled on top of the remnants of the

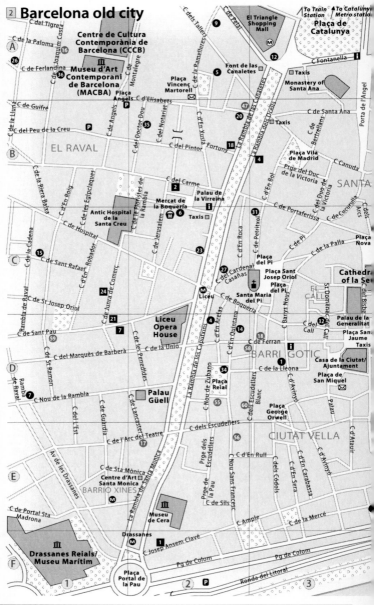

Barcelona old city

C del Tigre
C de la Paloma
C de Ferlandina
EL RAVAL
C de Guifre
C del Peu de la Creu
C de la Riera Baixa
C d'En Roig
C de les Esplanques
C de Hospital
C de la Cadena
C de Sant Rafael
C d'En Robador
C de St Josep Oriol
C de Sant Pau
C de St Ramon
C de Junta de Comerç
C del Marquès de Batberà
C de la Unió
C del Est
C de Guardia
C de Lancaster
C de l'Arc del Teatre
Rambla de Raval
C Nou de la Rambla
Av de les Drassanes
C de Sta Mònica
C de Portal Sta Madrona
BARRIO XINES

Centre de Cultura Contemporània de Barcelona (CCCB)
Museu d'Art Contemporani de Barcelona (MACBA)
Plaça Àngels
C de Montalegre
C d'Elisabets
C de Doctor Dou
C del Notariat
C del Pintor
C del Carme
C de les Floristes de la Rambla
Antic Hospital de la Santa Creu
C de Jerusalem
Mercat de la Boqueria
Palau de la Virreina
Plaça Vicenç Martorell
Liceu Opera House
Palau Güell
Centre d'Art Santa Mònica
Museu de Cera
Drassanes Reials/Museu Marítim
Drassanes
C Josep Ansem Clavé
Plaça Portal de la Pau

El Triangle Shopping Mall
C dels Tallers
C de Petal
Plaça de Catalunya
To Train Station
To Catalunya Metro station
Font de les Canaletes
La Rambla dels Estudis
C de la Ramelleres
La Rambla de Canaletes
Monastery of Santa Ana
C de Santa Ana
Porta de l'Angel
C de Bertrellans
Plaça Vila de Madrid
C Canuda
SANTA
Ptge del Duc de la Victoria
C d'En Bot
C Duc de la Victoria
C de Portaferissa
C de Petritxol
C de Pi
C de la Palla
Plaça Nova
Plaça del Pi
C del Cardenal Casañas
Plaça Sant Josep Oriol
Plaça del Pi
Santa Maria del Pi
C de Boqueria
C d'En Aixeles
C d'En Quintana
C de Ferran
C de la Lleona
Plaça Reial
C de Zubano
C Nou de la Rambla
C dels Escudellers Blanc
Plaça George Orwell
C d'Avinyó
Prge dels Escudellers
C d'En Rull
Nou Sant Francesc
C dels Còdols
C d'En Sera
C d'En Carabassa
C Ample
C de la Mercè
Pg de Colom
Ronda del Litoral
Cathedral of la Se
EL CALL
St Domènec del Call
Palau de la Generalitat
Plaça San Jaume
Casa de la Ciutat/Ajuntament
Plaça de San Miquel
BARRI GÒTIC
CIUTAT VELLA
La Rambla de los Caputxins

➡ **Barcelona maps**
1 Barcelona, page 30
2 Barcelona Old City, page 36

N

100 metres
100 yards

Where to stay 🛏
Bonic Barcelona 1 *F2*
Curious 2 *B2*
Denit 3 *A4*
España 7 *D1*
Itaca Hostal 16 *C4*
Le Meridien
  Barcelona 18 *B2*
Montecarlo 4 *B3*
Musik Boutique 5 *B5*
Park 20 *E5*
Peninsular 21 *D1*
Principal 24 *C1*
Room Mate Pau 6 *A4*

Restaurants 🍴
Agut 1 *D3*
Atril 2 *C5*
Bar Kasparo 5 *A2*
Bliss 8 *D4*
Bodega La Plata 3 *E3*
Café de
  l'Acadèmia 10 *D4*
Café de l'Opéra 4 *D2*
Café d'Estiu 11 *C4*
Café Zurich 12 *A3*
Cal Pep 13 *E5*
Can Culleretes 14 *D2*
Casa Leopoldo
  15 *C1*
Elisabets 20 *B2*
El Xampanyet
  22 *D5*
Escribà 23 *C2*
Euskal Etxea 24 *D5*
Imprévist 26 *A1*
Juicy Jones 27 *C2*
La Pallaresa 31 *C3*
La Vinateria
  del Call 32 *D3*
La Vinyor del
  Senyor 33 *E5*

Les Quinze Nits
  34 *D2*
Mamacafé 35 *B2*
Pla 6 *D4*
Pla dels Àngeles
  36 *A1*
Salero 37 *E5*
Senyor Parellada
  38 *D4*
Set Portes 39 *E5*
Suculent 7 *D1*
Teresa Carles 9 *A2*

Bars & clubs 🍸
Betty Ford 16 *A1*
Boadas 47 *B2*
Gimlet 53 *D5*
Jamboree 55 *D2*
La Macarena 56 *E2*
Malpaso 58 *D2*
Marsella 59 *D1*
Moog 17 *E2*
Pilé 43 60 *D2*
Pitin 61 *E5*
Ribborn 62 *E5*
Sub Rosa 18 *D3*

Cagoner

During the Feria de Santa Llúcia, artisans display their *santons* (collection of nativity scene figures) in the streets around the Cathedral of La Seu. As well as the usual figures – the crib, the Holy Family, the Three Kings, animals – the Catalans wouldn't consider a manger scene complete without the bizarre, squatting figure of the Cagoner, the Crapper, usually wearing a cheerful red Catalan cap and an entranced expression, with his little pile of poo beneath him.

original Roman settlement. But the Barri Gòtic is no picture-perfect tourist-museum – the Barcelonins have always been too pragmatic to pickle their city for posterity and the old city is a noisy, chaotic maze packed with shops, bars and clubs which cater for every possible taste, and where the streets are just as crowded at midnight as they are at midday.

Cathedral of La Seu and around

ⓘ *Pla de la Seu s/n, T933 428 260, www.catedral.bcn.org, cathedral Mon-Fri 0800-1330 and 1600-1930, Sat-Sun 0800-1330 and 1700-1930, free; lift and choir daily 1000-1330 and 1600-1800, €2 each; Museu de la Catedral, T933 102 580, 1000-1300 and 1600-1830 daily, €1 , Metro Jaume I, Bus 17, 19, 40, 45.*

It's impossible to miss the dramatic spires of the Gothic cathedral of La Seu soaring above the old city. The main entrance overlooks the wide Plaça Nova; from here you'll get the full effect of the fairytale façade which was actually stuck on in the 19th century. The main cathedral dates back to the 13th century (some sections survive of the even earlier Romanesque building), and the interior is magnificent, suitably dim and hushed, with soaring naves supported by heavily decorated Gothic cross vaults. Underneath the main altar lie the remains of the city's patron saint, Santa Eulàlia, in a 14th-century alabaster sarcophagus adorned with grisly depictions of her martyrdom. It's an operatic setting; to get the full effect, put a coin in the slot and watch the whole thing light up. Behind the altar, a lift just off the ambulatory will whip you to the roof for staggering views. The delightful cloister has a lush palm-filled garden in the centre, home to a colony of white geese. They have lived here for so long that no one can remember why. The old tradition of dancing a hollow egg (known as the *l'ou com balla*) on the delicate 15th-century fountain of St George takes place on the feast of Corpus Christi in early June. Just off the cloister, a tiny **museum** in the *Sala Capitular* (Chapter House) displays a collection of medieval paintings, including Bartolomé Bermejo's beautiful retablo of *La Pietat* (1490), one of the earliest Spanish oil paintings.

Next door to the museum is the plain Romanesque chapel of **Santa Llúcia**, dedicated to the patron saint of seamstresses who queue up here for her blessing on the saint's day, 13 December. This date also officially marks the opening of the **Fira de Santa Llúcia**, a Christmas fair which is held outside the cathedral.

Plaça Nova and around

The cathedral rises up over the dull, concrete expanse of the Plaça Nova. In the evenings it's livened up with the odd flame-thrower or tango dancer and on Sundays, from noon, you can join in with the traditional Catalan dance, the stately *sardana*. Across the square, the frieze of *sardana* dancers blazoned across the **College of Architects** was designed by Picasso, but executed by a Norwegian because Picasso refused to set foot in his homeland while it remained under a dictatorship. To the left of the main cathedral entrance is the Pia Almoina, a Gothic almshouse which has been beautifully renovated to hold the **Museu Diocesà** (Diocese Museum) ① *Av de la Catedral 4, T933 152 213, www.cultura.arqbcn. cat/museu_cat.php, Tue-Sat 1000-1400 and 1700-2000, Sun 1100-1400, Metro Jaume I, Bus 17, 19, 40, 45*, a goldmine of religious treasures from the Middle Ages onwards, including several shimmering retablos by Bernat Martorell.

Behind the Museu Diocesà is the **Museu Frederic Marés** ① *Plaça Sant Iu (off C/ des Comtes), T932 563 500, www.museumares.bcn.es, Tue-Sat 1000-1900, Sun and hols 1000-2000, €4.20, concessions €2.40, free every Sun 1500-2000 and on 1st Sun of each month 1100-2000*, devoted to the obsessive, patchwork collection of the eccentric sculptor and painter who had obviously never heard the phrase 'less is more'. On the lower floors are endless ranks of tiny Iberian ex-votos and a huge collection of sculpture spanning several centuries. The upper floors contain the Museu Sentimental, with a mind-boggling collection of 18th- and 19th-century ephemera, including 108 snuffboxes, 1,295 books of cigarette papers, and 158 pairs of opera glasses (Marés was as obsessive about itemising his finds as he was about collecting them), which eloquently convey the hothouse atmosphere of a 19th-century bourgeois home.

Plaça de St Jaume

Plaça de St Jaume would be more impressive if a street (the busy Carrer Ferran) didn't cut straight through it. Still, it's grand enough, thanks to the presence of the medieval palaces of the Generalitat (Catalan parliament) and the Ajuntament (City Council), which have been struggling for control of the city for centuries and glower at each other like two dowagers at a tea party. The square abandons its gravitas annually on 23 April – a kind of Catalan Valentine's Day, when couples exchange the traditional gifts of books and roses, and flower-sellers and book stalls fill the square in a flutter of petals.

Palau de la Generalitat ① *C del Bisbe, T934 024 600, www.gencat.cat, book in advance online or by phoning; guided visits only on second and fourth Sun of the month 1000-1400, arrive early to sign up for the English tour and bring ID*, has housed the Catalan parliament since the early 15th century, when Mark Safont designed its graceful inner courtyard and the sumptuous Chapel (1432) on the first floor. The Pati dels Tarrongers (Courtyard of Orange Trees), with its pink marble columns, was begun a century later. The Golden Room, named for its 16th-century gilded ceiling, is purely ceremonial, and the assembly prefer the modern Sala Antoni Tàpies to conduct business, blazoned with the eponymous artist's four-part series of medieval chronicles of Catalunya.

Facing the main façade of the Palau de la Generalitat is the late 14th-century Casa de la Ciutat, which contains the offices of the **Ajuntament** ① *T934 027 000, Sun 1000-1330, free*. The sumptuous Staircase of Honour leads up to the Saló de Cent, the core of the old Gothic palace. Designed by Pere Llobet, the hall was inaugurated in 1373, a masterpiece of monumental simplicity. On the other side of the Saló de Cent is the Saló de les Cróniques, awash with Josep María Sert's dramatic sepia murals depicting Catalan victories in Greece and Asia Minor during the 14th century.

The **Museu d'Idees i Invents de Barcelona (Museum of Ideas and Inventions, MIBA)** ① *www.mibamuseum.com, C/Ciutat 7, T933 327 930; Tue-Fri 1000-1400, 1600-1900, Sat*

Crazy Catalans

You won't find flamenco, paella or any of the other stock clichés about Spain in Barcelona – for the very good reason that Barcelona isn't properly part of Spain at all. It's the capital of Catalunya, a proud nation with its own language, customs and traditions and a fiercely democratic history. The Catalans are supremely proud of their *seny*, a deep-rooted natural wisdom which is treated with pious reverence. But *seny* is only half the Catalan story – the other half is *rauxa*, an outburst of uncontrollable emotion or just plain old craziness. *Rauxa* is what is going on when demons charge down narrow streets spitting flames and surrounded by leaping devils; when ice-cream houses undulate wildly to the sky without a straight line in sight; or when thousands of sweating bodies converge on the beaches for parties which might stop at dawn or maybe next week. The Catalans believe, with characteristic good sense, that a touch of madness will keep them sane.

1100-2000, Sun 1000-1400; adults e7, is a small, private museum founded by a Catalan inventor and TV personality. The displays include genuinely useful inventions, such as water purifiers, as well as enjoyably silly ones, such as the chair for inserting suppositories. There's a great gift shop.

Plaça del Rei

Plaça del Rei (King's Square) is a tiny, exquisite square just off the Plaça Sant Jaume. The rulers of Catalunya held court for centuries in the austerely beautiful **Palau Reial Major** which closes off the square, and prayed in the adjoining Royal Chapel with its dainty belltower. Incredibly, the astonishingly intact remnants of the Roman city of Barcino were unearthed beneath this square a century or so ago.

The fascinating **Museu d'Història de Barcelona (MultBa)** ① *Plaça del Rei s/n, T932 562 100, www.museuhistoria.bcn.es, Tue-Sat 1000-1900, Sun 1000-2000,* €7 (includes entry to all of MultBa's sites, including the Pedralbes Monastery, Metro Jaume I, Bus 16, 17, 19, 40, 45, reveals the history of the city layer by layer. The deepest layer contains the Roman city of Barcino, established here more than 2000 years ago. Tacked on to it are Visigothic ruins which were built during the 5th and 6th centuries and built on top of the whole lot are the palaces and churches of the middle ages which still enclose the Plaça del Rei.

A glass lift glides down a couple of millennia to the subterranean excavations of Roman Barcino. A vast swathe of the Roman city survives, an astonishing stretch of walls, watchtowers, baths, temples, homes and businesses, founded 2000 years ago and discovered by chance less than a century ago. Glass walkways lead over the ruins, where you can peer into the old wine vats or stroll along the top of a fortified wall. Still underground but heading steadily towards the site of the present cathedral, the Roman ruins become interspersed with the remnants of Visigothic churches which date back to around the 5th century. Stairs lead up to the Gothic Royal Palace and you enter the next layer of the city's history, the Golden Age of the medieval period. The echoing throne room, the Saló de Tinell, was built in 1359 and is a masterpiece of Catalan Gothic style. Seven solemn arches succeed each other in great broad arcs, creating an overwhelming

Jews in Barcelona

No one really knows when the first Jews settled in Barcelona but by 694 they had established a large enough presence for the Visigoths to find them threatening and decree that all Jews become slaves. However, the community was thriving by the 11th century, and many Jews worked for the king as advisers and translators, especially to the Arab courts. Yet, although the kings marginally improved their status, the community was taxed heavily and given no civil rights. In 1243, by decree of Jaume I, El Call became a ghetto: Jews were forced to remain within its walls (bounded by Carrer Banys Nous, Carrer el Call, and the wall of the Generalitat building) between dusk and dawn and identify themselves with capes and hats. The Jews suffered increasing persecution: bitter jealousy of their influence at court erupted in sporadic attacks on the ghetto from the end of the 13th century. Hundreds of inhabitants were massacred in a vicious pogrom in 1391; Jewish synagogues and cemeteries were suppressed throughout Catalunya a decade later; and finally, in 1424, Jews were expelled from the city, a harbinger of the expulsion of all Jews from Spain in 1492. Jews didn't return to the city until the early 20th century, and, soon after, the triumph of Franco resulted in another exodus. It wasn't until 1948 that a Jewish synagogue opened again in the city.

impression of space and grandeur. Next to the throne room is the Royal Chapel of Saint Agatha, with a single graceful nave and a dazzling polychrome ceiling supported by diaphragm arches. It was built at the beginning of the 14th century, and topped with a whimsical octagonal belltower in the form of a crown. The glittering 15th-century retablo of the *Epiphany* is by Jaume Huguet, and is considered one of the finest examples of Catalan Gothic painting.

Plaça del Pi and around

The pretty Plaça del Pi is named for a glade of pine trees which once stood here, their memory recalled now by a single pine. The hulking 15th-century Gothic church of Santa Maria del Pi is now solely remarkable for its enormous rose window, the biggest in Europe, as looters burnt the interior to a crisp during the Civil War. You can, however, visit the church treasury to see some of the few artworks which survived the fires. Plaça del Pi and the adjoining Plaça Sant Josep Oriol and miniature Plaçeta del Pi are now great spots for an evening copa out on the terrace, with plenty of wandering musicians for entertainment. On the first Friday and Saturday of the month, a market selling local cheeses, honey and *embutits* (cured meats) sets up its stalls, and on Thursdays there's a regular antiques market. Plaça Sant Josep Oriol has artists of varying quality most weekends, and an art market on the first weekend of each month.

El Call

Carrer Banys Nous, off Plaça Sant Josep Oriol, marks the boundary of the old Jewish Quarter, known as El Call from the Hebrew word *quahal*, meaning 'meeting place'. There is virtually no trace of what was once the most important Jewish population in medieval Spain – just a faded stone with a Hebrew inscription from 1314 which was erected at the corner of Carrer Arc de Sant Ramon de Call and Carrer Marlet in the 19th century and the remnants of a medieval synagogue. The **Barcelona History Museum** has an interpretation centre on the Placeta de Manuel Ribé, with exhibitions and leaflets outlining walking tours of the ancient Call. The **synagogue**, at Calle Marlet 5, is also the main seat of the privately run **Asociació del Call** (www.calldebarcelona.org), which operates tours of the area. The quarter, a shadowy maze of twisting passages and overhanging buildings, is now mainly known for its antique shops, see page 74, and is a delightful place for a wander or a good rummage.

Barri de Santa Anna

North of the Plaça Nova is the unassuming district of Santa Anna, with few eye-catching monuments or museums, but plenty of opportunities to shop. The two main shopping streets of the Barri Gòtic meet here: the **Carrer Portaferrissa**, with lots of trendy fashion stores, and the **Avinguda del Portal de l'Àngel**, with several of the major chains and a branch of El Corte Inglés. Avinguda del Portal de l'Àngel, the main artery of this neighbourhood, links the Plaça Nova with the Plaça Catalunya. The area is known as the Barri de Santa Anna after the simple, Romanesque **Monastery of Santa Anna** (just off the Carrer de Santa Anna) which was founded by the Knights Templar in the early 12th century. South of the Calle de Santa Ana is the **Plaça Vila de Madrid**, a wide square which has been mostly dug up in archaeological excavations. In a grassy corner, you can peer down into a Roman sepulchural way, a series of simple funerary monuments lined up beside one of the smaller Roman access roads into the city.

On the other side of the Avinguda del Portal de l'Àngel, the famous **Els Quatre Gats** tavern has been faithfully recreated at No 3 Carrer Montsió. Unfortunately, it is now just a pretty tourist trap. Els Quatre Gats began life here in 1897, when the painters Ramon Casas and Santiago Rusiñol, along with Miquel Utrillo and Pere Romeu, nostalgic for their old stomping ground of Montmartre, opened the tavern in order to provide a meeting place for all their friends. The tavern survived just six years, but was a roaring success among its varied clientele of artists, intellectuals, and bohemian hangers-on. It produced its own review, held concerts, poetry readings and art exhibitions and encouraged protegés, including Picasso who designed the menus and held his first exhibition here.

La Ribera

The old artisans' district of La Ribera is a funky, fashionable neighbourhood with some of the city's trendiest bars, restaurants and shopping, as well as its most popular museum (the Picasso Museum), its most beautiful church, and a string of elegant palaces along the Carrer de Montcada.

Carrer Montcada and the Museu Picasso

Carrer Montcada was the swankiest address in the city during the 12th century, when affluent merchants lined it with beautiful mansions set around elegant patios. Now it's one of the most popular streets in Barcelona, mainly thanks to the pulling power of its biggest attraction, the Museu Picasso, which draws more visitors than any other museum in the city except the FC Barça museum, see page 61 – get here early to avoid the crowds.

Picasso's Barcelona

In 1895, Picasso and his family moved from Málaga to Barcelona, where his father took up a post as professor of fine arts at the Academia Provincial de Bellas Artes.

In 1897, the famous tavern Els Quatre Gats (see page 42) was inaugurated and quickly became the heart of the city's avant garde, and Picasso designed its menus and held impromptu exhibitions. In 1899, Picasso shared a studio just off the Carrer Avinyò, a street famous for its brothels, which gave him the inspiration for his celebrated painting *Les Demoiselles d'Avignon* (it was also here that he contracted gonorrhoea). The following year, one of his paintings was chosen to be exhibited at the Universal Exhibition in Paris, and he travelled to what was then the mecca of the art world with Carlos Casegamas. Casegamas, troubled and addicted to drink and drugs, killed himself the following year, and Picasso returned to Barcelona. This time, he was able to afford a studio by himself at Carrer del Comerç 28, where he created many of the haunting works of his Blue Period, using the beggars, prostitutes and gypsies of the streets as his models.

In 1904, he moved permanently to Paris, although he regularly returned for visits. His last extended stay in the city was in 1917, when he came to oversee a production of Parade, an avant garde ballet by Serge Diaghilev and his Ballets Russes for which he had designed the costumes and sets. He was adamant that he would not set foot on Spanish soil under the dictatorship of General Franco; his only concession were the sketches he sent in 1961 for the frieze which adorns the College of Architects on the Plaça Nueva (see page 39) but which he refused to come and carry out himself.

Museu Picasso

① C/Montcada 15-23, T932 563 000, www.museupicasso.bcn.es, Tue-Sat 1000-2000, Sun 1000-1500, €9 concessions €5, Metro Jaume I, Bus 14, 17, 19, 39, 40, 45, 51, 59.

The Museu Picasso draws more visitors than any other museum in the city except the FC Barça museum, see page 61, and it is well worth getting here early to avoid shuffling along behind the crowds. The collection includes few of Picasso's most famous paintings, and focuses instead on the early works, particularly those created by the young artist in Barcelona. The early selection of works includes some of the chilly paintings of his Blue Period, like the stricken mother and child of *Desamperados* (The Despairing, 1904). Picasso was partly influenced by the grim studies of gypsies and beggars painted by Isidro Nonell, who also frequented the tavern of Els Quatre Gats (see page 42) for which the young Picasso painted the menu (you can see it here). The works of his Rose Period are well represented but there is almost nothing, just a small *Head* (1913), from the Cubist years, and a single *Harlequin* (1917), from the celebrated series. From 1917, there's another leap in time, this time to the extraordinary series of 44 paintings and drawings based on Velázquez's *Las Meninas*, which Picasso painted in a single concentrated burst over six months at the end of 1956, and in which every detail of Velázquez's masterpiece has been picked out, pored over and reinterpreted.

Disseny Hub (DHub) ① *C/Montcada 12-14, T939 254 657, www.museutextil.bcn.es, Metro Jaume*, an outpost of Barcelona's Design Hub, a group of museums dedicated to design, fashion and the decorative arts. Currently used for temporary exhibitions, its future is uncertain as all the Design Hub's collections are moving to the new purpose-built premises in late 2013.

Església de Santa Maria del Mar

① *Plaça de Santa Mara del Mar, Metro Jaume I, 0900-1330 and 1630-2000, free.*
The loveliest church in all Catalunya sits at the bottom of the Carrer Montcada: the church of Santa Maria del Mar. Construction began in 1329 and was completed in just 54 years – record speed for the era – which meant that other styles and forms couldn't creep in as successive architects took over the job. As a result, the church is considered one of the finest and purest examples of Catalan Gothic. The hulking exterior, built to withstand wind and storms, gives no hint of the spellbinding interior, a soaring central nave flanked with supporting columns of ethereal slimness. The ornate fittings accumulated over centuries were lost when the church was gutted during the Civil War; only the stained-glass windows, some dating back to the 15th century, were spared. Regular concerts are held here; the city cultural office at the Palau de la Virreina (see page 34) can provide details.

Passeig del Born and around

Passeig del Born begins at the side entrance to the church of Santa Maria del Mar. Once a theatre for medieval jousting tournaments and carnivals, nowadays the fiesta continues at the string of ultra-trendy bars and clubs which line the street. This is one of the hippest neighbourhoods in Barcelona, known simply as 'El Born', and the narrow streets which splinter off the Passeig are packed with slick tapas bars, restaurants and stylish interior design and fashion shops.

Just off the Passeig is the **Fossar de les Moreres** (Mulberry Cemetery), the burial place of the martyrs of 1714, who defended the besieged city against the Bourbon armies; they are remembered here annually on 11 September, Catalan National Day.

Just around the corner is the **Museu de Xocolata** (Chocolate Museum) ① *C/Comerç 26, T932 687 878, www.patisseria.com, Mon-Sat 1000-1900, Sun and hols 1000-1500, €4.30, Metro Jaume I, Nus 14, 16, 17, 19, 36, 39, 40, 45, 51, 59, 69*, tucked away in the old convent of San Agustí on Carrer Comerç, which describes the histories and legends behind chocolate and – best of all – does tastings.

Parc de la Ciutadella

This is one of Barcelona's most popular parks, a quiet oasis in the heart of the city with a clutch of small museums, shady walkways and fountains, and a cramped zoo. The park was originally the site of an enormous star-shaped citadel, built after Barcelona fell to the Bourbon armies in 1714. It became the most hated building in the city, and was torn down in 1869. The park was laid out in the late 19th century by a team which included the young Gaudí, and expanded again for the Universal Exhibition of 1888 – Barcelona's first taste of what an international show could do to change the face of a city.

The art of conversation

The Spanish gift of the gab is legendary and they like to boast that they have elevated their daily orations to an art form. The *tertulia*, an almost untranslatable term for discussion, was perfected a hundred years ago when writers gathered daily at celebrated cafés and expounded at length over coffee and brandies. The *tertulia* became an essential thread in the cultural revival which some compared to the Golden Age of Cervantes and Velázquez – and some of the old cafés, such as the elegant **Café Gijon** in Madrid, or Picasso's old haunt, the **Els Quatre Gats**, still survive. The fundamental criteria for a *tertulia* are that it should have no purpose save that of the sheer joy of conversation, and that the group should meet regularly and be composed of roughly the same people. They are still as much of a fixture as ever, and you'll regularly see signs in café windows advertising them – sometimes even in English. It's the perfect place for Spain's budding authors to daydream of becoming the next Javier Marías, Elvira Navarro or Manuel Vázquez Montalbán.

The **zoo** ① *Parc de la Ciutadella s/n, T932 256 780, daily Nov-Feb 1000-1700, Mar and Oct 1000-1800, Apr and Sep 1000-1900, Jun-Aug 0930-1930, €12.90/8.30 for children aged 3-12, metro Ciutadella,* takes up half of the park, but it's still not enough for the poor animals cramped into small concrete enclosures.

Domènech i Montaner's **Castell dels Tres Dragons** sits in one corner of the park, the most daring of the new buildings created for the Universal Exhibition of 1888. It's one of the earliest Modernista edifices, and is now home to the Laboratori de LA Natura (Nature Laboratory), part of the natural science museum ① *closed for remodelling, metro Arc de Triomf and Jaume I. Bus 14, 39, 40, 41, 42, 51, 141.*

Nearby is the **Museu Martorell** ① *Parc de la Ciutadella s/n, closed for remodelling; Metro Arc de Triomf and Jaume I, bus 14, 39, 40, 41, 42, 51, 141,* the oldest museum in the city, opened in 1882. Next to the museum is the charming **Hivernacle** (winter greenhouse), a glassy pavilion with a great café (see page 66). In the opposite corner of the park is the extravagant **Cascade**, a flamboyant fountain partly designed by Gaudí. It overlooks a small **boating pond**, a popular Sunday picnic spot for Barcelonin families.

Just to the north of the park is the **Passeig de Lluís Companys**, a pedestrian promenade which was designed as a spectacular entrance to the site of the Universal Exhibition (1888) in the Parc de la Ciutadella. The main gateway is the huge red-brick neo-Moorish **Arc de Triomf**, topped with a gracious figure representing Barcelona handing out gifts.

Sant Pere

Theneighbourhood of Sant Pere sits quietly across the Carrer Princessa, a wide road which divided Sant Pere from La Ribera a century ago. These two *barris* may be neighbours but they have nothing in common: fashionable La Ribera is a world away from humble Sant Pere where life continues much as it has done for decades. Nonetheless, Sant Pere does boast one important monument, the opulent Modernista Palau de la Música Catalana.

Palau de la Música Catalana

① *Carrer de Sant Francesc de Paula 2, T932 957 200, tickets T902 475 486, www.palaumusica.org, daily 1000-1530, Aug 0900-2000, visits by guided tour only, booking in advance is advisable. Tours depart every 30 mins in English, Castilian, and Catalan and last 50 mins €17, metro Urquinona. The best way to see the Palau is to come for a concert, but tickets are hard to come by.*

The Palau was built between 1905 and 1908 as a new home to the Orfeó Català, the first and biggest of the choral societies which sprang up during Catalunya's *Renaixença* (cultural renaissance) a century ago. It was designed by Domènech i Muntaner, who collaborated with many of Catalunya's most celebrated craftsmen and artists. The extraordinary sculpted façade is an elegy to music and Catalanism, and beneath it is a dense forest of floral columns, sprouting multi-coloured flowers of broken tiles. The main auditorium is spell-binding: rainbow-coloured light streams in through the vast stained glass ceiling of flowers and musical angels. Galloping winged horses bearing Valkyries seem to erupt from the stage and shimmering 3D 'spirits of music' flutter across its back wall.

The Palau won the Building of the Year award in 1908, but just two decades later it was being sneeringly referred to as the 'Palace of Catalan Junk' by architects who thought it thoroughly old-fashioned. And whatever the punters thought of the , no one argued about the appalling acoustics. The glass walls may have allowed the sunlight to flood in – but with it came all the street noise. Concerts were regularly punctuated by church bells and warbling ladies catching up on their housework. It barely escaped demolition. After decades of neglect, it was restored in the 1980s and then expanded in 2008. Its place at the forefront of the city's most prestigious venues was cemented in 1997 when it was inscribed on UNESCO's list of World Heritage Sites; it now attracts about half a million people every year.

El Raval

Part impoverished ghetto, part boho-chic *barri*, the Raval's fortunes have improved immensely over the last decades, although it remains one of the city's poorest neighbourhoods. A century or so ago, the streets nearest the port formed the most notorious red-light district on the Mediterranean, filled with whorehouses, seedy bars, and music halls. Nicknamed the Barri Xinès after San Francisco's vice-ridden Chinatown, its heyday was in the 1920s and 1930s. Like New York's Harlem, tourists flooded in to slum it at the bars and cabaret halls until Franco put an end to the party.

By the 1970s, the arrival of heroin was causing serious problems and the city hall eventually stepped in to begin the latest regeneration project: rotting tenements have been replaced with new apartment blocks, bars and bordellos have been closed down, and a new promenade, the Rambla de Raval, slices through its heart. It's still poor, but the construction of the glossy Museu d'Art Contemporani has brought in trendy new galleries, fashion shops and arty bars, and, with the arrival of immigrants particularly from north Africa and Pakistan, it's also becoming multicultural, with halal butchers and curry houses rubbing shoulders with old-fashioned haberdasheries and grocers.

The establishment of MACBA and the CCCB, see below, has drawn a glamorous crowd of art galleries, restaurants, bars and clubs – with more springing up almost daily. Many are clustered along **Carrer Carme**, **Carrer Doctor Dou**, and there's another string of great bars along **Carrer Joaquim Costa**. It's also a good place for shopping, with plenty of hip little designer boutiques and a whole street – the **Carrer de la Riera Baixa** – full of vintage fashion and music shops.

Museu d'Art Contemporani de Barcelona (MACBA)

ⓘ *Plaça dels Àngels. T934 120 810. www.macba.cat. Mon, Wed-Fri 1100-1930, Sat 1000-2000, Sun 1000-1500 (open until 2200 on Fri and Sat in summer), €8, concessions €6.60, prices vary for temporary exhibitions. Metro Universitat. Bus 9, 14, 16, 17, 22, 24, 38, 41, 55, 58, 59, 66, 91, 141.*

Richard Meiers' huge, glassy home for MACBA was built in 1995, a symbol of the city's dedication to urban renewal and a monument to its preoccupation with contemporary design. It overlooks a wide, modern square, which has become a huge favourite with skateboarders.

Although the museum's permanent collection officially begins after the Civil War, there are some earlier pieces by Alexander Calder, Paul Klee and Catalan artists like Leandre Cristòfol, Joan Ponç and Àngel Ferrant. The collection is loosely structured around four periods; the first, which roughly covers the 1940s to the 1960s, is represented by artists like Antoni Tàpies, Joan Brossa, and Antoni Saura. These artists were members of the *Dau al Set* ('seven spot die' in Catalan) group, a loose collection of writers and artists who were influenced by the surrealists, and particularly by Joan Miró, and whose works marked an end to the torpor which had settled on the cultural life of Spain after Franco's victory in the Civil War. Popular and consumer culture had more of an impact on the art of the 1960s and 1970s: there are several fun, kitsch pieces from Carlos Pazos, including the mocking *Voy a hacer de mí una estrella* (I'm going to make myself a star, 1975), a series of pouting, celebrity-style photographs. The 1980s and early 90s are marked by a return to painting and its forms of expression; among Catalan artists, Miquel Barceló's paintings and Susana Solano's stark metal sculptures reflect this return to traditional forms. Photographs from this period include works by Anselm Keifer, Jeff Wall and Suzanne Lafont. Many of the usually excellent temporary exhibitions focus on the latest digital and multi-media works. MACBA has a great bookshop and an attractive café-bar which shares a square with the CCCB (see below) around the corner.

Centre de Cultura Contemporània de Barcelona (CCCB)

ⓘ *Metro Universitat, 9 Sep-May Tue, Thu-Fri 1100-1400 and 1600-2000, Wed and Sat 1100-2000, Sun and holidays 1100-1900, Jun-8 Sep Tue-Sun 1000-2000, €5.50/4.*

The excellent Contemporary Culture Centre (CCCB) sits behind MACBA and is the second prong of the city's institution for contemporary culture. It's set in the former Casa de la Caritat, a hospice for pilgrims established in the 16th century which has undergone dramatic remodelling. The CCCB hosts wide-ranging and eclectic exhibitions on all aspects of contemporary culture not covered by MACBA, as well as running several community-based projects and dozens of other activities, including the Sonar music festival and an alternative film festival (see Festivals, page 73).

Antic Hospital de Santa Creu

① *La Capella Tue-Sat 1200-1400 and 1600-2000, Sun 1100-1400.*

An anachronistic leftover in the heart of this fashionable neighbourhood is the Antic Hospital de Santa Creu (on Carrer de Hospital), a hulking stone complex built in 1402 which comprised an orphanage, leper hospital and wards for the city's sick and dying. These vaulted Gothic wards now contain the National Library of Catalunya (entrance only to members but you can try begging for a peek), as the hospital was moved in 1926 to Domenech i Muntaner's Modernista pavilions. One of its last patients before the move was Gaudí, brought here after he fell under the wheels of a tram in 1926; he was so shabby – even his shoes were kept on his feet with elastic bands – that everyone took him for a tramp. The former chapel holds regular workshops, commissions pieces from local artists, and holds excellent shows of contemporary works from up-and-coming Barcelonin artists.

Palau Güell and around

① *C/Nou de la Rambla 3, T933 173 974, open for guided tours only Mon-Sat 1000-1330 and 1600-1830, tours fill up quickly – book in advance in summer, €2.50, Metro Liceu, bus 14, 38, 51, 59.*

Palau Güell on Carrer Nou de la Rambla was Gaudí's first major commission for the man who was to become his most important patron, Eusebi Güell. Both men were intensely Catalanist and intensely religious, and these themes are replayed throughout the tall, narrow mansion, which recently (2012) emerged from a lengthy and expensive restoration project. The small visiting room off the long glass vestibule (which Güell's horrified wife thought looked like a barber's shop) boasts a spectacularly ornate carved ceiling in which tiny spyholes were carved so that the Güells could overhear their guests' private conversations. The main salon is overwhelming, a lofty hall topped with an arched cosmic dome covered with deep blue honeycombed tiles; thin shafts of light entering through tiny windows symbolise the stars circling the moon. This is the heart of the house, with all the rooms organised around the central hall in the Mediterranean fashion, and surrounded by a series of galleries and miradors. Behind the salon is the family's dining room and private sitting room, with stained glass windows featuring historical Catalan heroes, and there's a small terrace which allows you to see the lovely tribunal which juts out at the back. Despite the sumptuousness, this was never a comfortable palace and the Güells always preferred their main residence in Pedralbes (see page 60): the dim lighting, the heavy religious solemnity and the weight of historical references combine to make it a sombre, gloomy experience (Antonioni used it as the setting for his unsettling thriller *The Passenger* in 1977). But the rooftop is its antithesis: a rippling terrace with a playful forest of swirling, *trencadi*-covered chimneys, surrounding a lofty central spire topped with a wrought iron bat, a legendary guardian of Catalan heroes.

Sant Pau del Camp and around

① *C/Sant Pau s/n. Metro Paral.lel, Wed-Mon 1120-1300 and 1800-1930, Tue 1130-1230, free.*

The Carrer de Sant Pau runs down to the tiny, delightful church of Sant Pau del Camp, the most important surviving Romanesque church in the city. The tranquil cloister has Moorish-inspired arches and simple columns carved with a menagerie of mythical creatures.The modern Rambla de Raval, nearby, is lined with terrace cafés and features one of the city's most charming pieces of art: Botero's huge, fat cat.

Museu Marítim (Drassanes Reials)

ⓘ *Av Drassanes s/n, T933 429 920, www.museumaritimbarcelona.com, closed for restoration until late 2013, Metro Drassanes.*

Almost at the harbour, in the southernmost tip of the Raval, are the magnificent Drassanes Reials, the vast medieval shipyards built at the height of the Catalan empire. Begun in 1243, the shipyards form the largest and most important civil Gothic structure in the world, and were eventually capable of accommodating 40 galley ships. Now they contain the excellent and entertaining Museu Marítim (Maritime Museum) and the star exhibit is a monstrous galley ship, a replica of the Royal Galley of John of Austria which was built to lead the Holy Alliance against the Turks in the Battle of Lepant in 1571. Down in the Port Vell, a five-minute walk away, the museum has renovated a beautiful turn-of-the-century sailing ship, the *Santa Eulàlia*, which is also part of the visit.

Barrio Xinès

The dark, narrow web of streets in this southern section of the Raval are still the poorest (and most intimidating at night), but it's also here that a glimmer of the old Barrio Xinès can still be found in a handful of old-fashioned bars – like the **Kentucky**, the **London** and **Bar Marsella**, see page 69, which haven't changed in decades. A small square is named after Jean Genet, whose novel *Journal de Voleur* (Thief's Journal) viscerally describes how he scraped a living as a rent boy and thief in these streets in the 1920s and 1930s.

Eixample

The Eixample (pronounced *Ai-sham-play*) is Barcelona's most upmarket neighbourhood, with its finest restaurants and designer boutiques, and one of the greatest concentration of Modernista monuments in Europe. Ironically, this elegant and ultra bourgeois district was created by a utopian socialist, Ildefons Cerdà, who won the commission to create a new extension (which is what 'Eixample' in Catalan) in the 19th century. Cerdà envisioned a modular city of regular blocks formed around airy central gardens in which workers and the bourgeoisie would live harmoniously side by side, but his original design was rapidly undermined by greedy speculators who filled up all the communal spaces with more houses. The poor couldn't afford to move anyway, but the rich rushed out to the new district, commissioning the greatest Modernista architects – Gaudí, Domènech i Montaner, Puig i Cadafalch and others – to create trophy mansions which would dazzle their neighbours.

Passeig de Gràcia

Passeig de Gràcia is the heart of the Eixample, a glossy boulevard of chic boutiques lined with plane trees and twirling wrought-iron lampposts. It's overlooked by an eclectic mix of spiky neo-Gothic castles, pompous neoclassic insurance offices, and fairy-tale Modernista mansions.

The most famous stretch of the Passeig de Gràcia is the block between Carrer Consell de Cent and Carrer d'Aragó, where flamboyant mansions designed by the three most famous Modernista architects – Gaudí, Domènech i Montaner, Puig i Cadafalch – are nudged up against each other. It's known as the **Mançana de la Discòrdia** (Block of Discord), the 'discord' arising from their dramatically different styles. The architects were independently invited by three of the city's most influential families to entirely remodel existing buildings. The first, at the corner of Carrer Consell de Cent, is the **Casa Lleo i Morera**, which was built in 1864, and transformed by Domènech i Montaner in 1902. Sadly, much of the beautiful façade was destroyed by the luxury leather goods shop, Loewe, who ripped out the original ground floor windows and stripped it of much of the original sculptural decoration. The surviving nymphs bearing symbols of the new age – electric light, photography, the telephone and the phonograph – flit across the façade, thickly clustered with garlands of flowers oozing like piped icing.

Casa Amatller, three doors up at No 41, was the first of the three major remodellings. Antoni Amatller's fortune was built on chocolate and Puig i Cadafalch built him a fairytale castle, with a stepped gable covered with shimmering polychrome ceramics which almost look good enough to eat. It contains a gift shop selling Amatller chocolates, and the first floor apartment is currently being restored to its original turn-of-the-20th-century glory and will be opened to the public. The Casa Amatller functions as the Centre del Modernisme where you can get information on the Ruta del Modernisme (see page 29), and which offers free guided tours of the three façades of the Mansana de la Discòrdia (the Casa Batlló was opened to visitors as part of the special activities which marked Gaudí Year 2002 but usually the interiors of all three mansions are closed to visitors).

Next door to the Casa Amatller is the fantastical **Casa Batlló** ① *Passeig de Gràcia 43, T934 880 666, www.casabatlloes, daily 0900-2000, €18.15, concessions €14.55; evening concerts are held on the terrace from end Jun to early Sep, €29* (1904-1906), unmistakably the work of Antoni Gaudí: covered with shimmering, multi-coloured *trencadís* (broken tiles) and culminating in an undulating scaly roof, it gleams like an underwater sea dragon. All kinds of theories about the symbolism of the façade have been thrown up, but the story of St George and the dragon seems to fit most neatly. The rippling waves of tiny ceramic tiles and the bone-white pillars which support the balconies evoke the curling dragon, his scaly back formed by the swaying roof ridge, and St George is represented by the bulbous cross erupting from a thick column, or lance, spearing the dragon from on high. The spiky, *trencadi*-covered, chimney is the final flick of the dragon's tail. The fibia-like columns of the lower façade gave the building its popular nickname 'the house of the bones'.

One of Gaudí's most famous buildings is a little further up the Passeig de Gracia, the **Casa Milà** ① *C/Provença 261-265, T934 845 980, T902 202 138 (to book tickets), www.caixacatalunya.es, daily Mar-Oct 0900-2000, Nov-Feb 0900-1830; €16.50, concession €14.85, free admission to temporary exhibitions, guided night visits Mar-Oct; rooftop concerts summer only; Metro Diagonal; Bus 7, 16, 17, 22, 24, 28.* Better known as **La Pedrera** ('the stone quarry'), the building rises like a creamy cliff draped with sinuous wrought iron balconies. The first occupants of the apartment building moved in around 1911, and there's a recreation of an apartment from the era on the top floor. There isn't a straight line anywhere, with the walls, ceilings, doorways and windows flowing around the interior patios. Many of the fittings in the apartment are original, including the elegant bedroom suite with its pretty polychrome floral motif which was designed by the celebrated craftsman Gaspar Homar. The attic now houses L'Espai Gaudí, a slick museum providing a systematic overview of the architect's life and works in the city with models, photos, drawings, and video installations. A spiral staircase leads up to the climax of the visit, the sinuous rooftop terrace which curls around the patios like a dreamscape studded with fantastical bulbous crosses, and plump *trencadi*-covered towers, Gaudí's magical response to the building's prosaic need for chimneys, air vents and stairwells. On summer nights, you can enjoy live music on the rooftop (see page 70).

Museums around Passeig de Gràcia

Just off the Passeig de Gràcia in Carrer Valencia is the **Museu Egipci de Barcelona** ① *C/València 284, T934 480 188, www.museuegipci.com, Mon-Sat 1000-2000, Sun 1000-1400, €11, concessions €8, Metro Passeig de Gràcia, Bus 7, 16, 17, 20, 22, 24, 28, 45, 47,* with an excellent selection of artefacts spanning more than three millennia. Among the most interesting exhibits are the sarcophagi; the earliest are made of terracotta moulded vaguely into the form of the body within, but they grow steadily more elaborate. Burial scenes are dramatically recreated, with cult chapels, mummies – including x-rays of mummified animals – and tombs. There is also a rich collection of ceramics, some dating back to 3,500BC, and jewellery – gold and silver, glittering with lapis lazuli and cornelian for the rich, painted glass paste for the poor – revealing the astonishing level of craftsmanship that the early Egyptians attained.

Another of the city's fine, privately owned museums is located nearby. The **Fundació Francisco Godia** ① *C/Diputació, T932 723 180, www.fundacionfgodia.org, Mon, Wed-Sun 1000-1900, €5.50, concessions €3.25; Metro Passeig de Gràcia; Bus 7, 16, 17, 20, 22, 24, 28, 45, 47.* Francisco Godia (1921-1990) was an odd combination: a successful racing driver for more than three decades, he also found time to acquire a dazzling collection of painting, medieval sculpture and ceramics. There's a mesmerizing gathering of polychrome, gilded statues from the 12th century onwards, and among the ceramics are lustrous 15th-century pieces from Manises. Godia also collected turn-of-the-century art, including Ramon Casas' *At the racecourse* (circa 1905) and Isidre Nonell's haunting study, *Gypsy Woman* (1905). Godia's daughters have expanded the collection by adding works from the later 20th century and some contemporary art.

On the other side of the Passeig de Gràcia, down Carrer d'Aragó, you can't miss the extraordinary red-brick building topped with what looks like a huge cloud of barbed wire, a vast sculpture entitled *Nuvol i Cadira* (*Cloud and Chair*) by recently deceased Antoni Tàpies, probably Spain's best-known contemporary artist. The building was built in 1880 by Domènech i Montaner for the family publishing house and is one of the earliest Modernista monuments. It now houses the **Fundació Antoni Tàpies** ① *C/Aragó 255, T934 870 315, www.fundaciotapies.org, Metro Passeig de Gràcia, Tue-Sun 1000-1900, €7, concessions €5.60,* which holds one of the largest collections of Tàpies' works in the world. There are interesting temporary exhibitions by contemporary artists, often featuring video and installation work, and at least one floor usually shows a selection of works by Tàpies himself. In 1948, he became part of the Dau al Set ('seven-spot die' in Catalan) group, a gathering of writers and artists whose works were the first sign of cultural revival in Spain after the grim 'hunger years' which succeeded Franco's victory. He is most celebrated for his 'material paintings', which he began after the dissolution of Dau al Set, adopting radically innovative techniques and media, particularly the use of found objects.

Never-ending story

The Sagrada Família had a gloomy start. It was commissioned by a reactionary organization known as the Josephines, who wanted an expiatory temple where the faithful could go to beg forgiveness for the depravity of the modern age. The first architect quit after a year and Gaudí, aged just 31, was given the job in 1883.

The project became an obsession and after 1914 he devoted himself solely to its construction, spending the last two years of his life living ascetically in a shack on the building site. In June 1926, he was crushed under a tram and died two days later. Some 10,000 mourners followed his coffin to its burial place in the crypt of the Sagrada Família but even so, by this time, Gaudí, his architecture and his ultra-conservative brand of Catholicism were thoroughly out of fashion. Work limped on for a few years but came to an abrupt halt with the start of the Civil War, when anarchists attacked the crypt destroying every plan, model and sketch that they could find in an attempt to ensure that it would never be completed. The temple languished for decades until finally, in 1952, a group of architects decided to continue the work by raising money through public subscription. Japanese corporations are currently the highest contributors; Gaudí-mania was big in Japan long before it really took off Europe.

In the absence of detailed plans and records, the architects are being forced to conjecture what Gaudí might have envisioned and it this which has caused such controversy: purists argue that it is simply impossible to guess Gaudí's intentions as he was infamous for his lack of reliance on plans and his buildings changed shape even as they were being constructed.

The current team is directed by Jordí Bonet, the son of one of the temple's original architects, and the sculptor Josep Subirachs. The Passion façade on the Carrer de Sardenya is now complete, but has aroused equal amounts of scorn and praise for the distinctly un-Gaudíesque sculptures which adorn it. Gaudí, in the meantime, looks set to become a saint. The Vatican announced that it would consider the case for his beatification in 2000 and the Association for the Beatification of Antoni Gaudí, founded in 1992 by architects, admirers, and artists, are getting down to the business of finding out the particulars of his miracles. They hope that he will be beatified in 2016, the 90th anniversary of his death.

Sagrada Família
① C/Mallorca 401, daily Oct-Mar 0900-1800, Apr-Sept 0900-2000, €13, concessions €11 (€15/14 with guided visit), www.sagradafamilia.cat, Metro Sagrada Família, Bus 19, 33, 34, 43, 44, 50, 51.
Gaudí's unfinished masterpiece, the Templo Expiatorio de la Sagrada Família (Expiatory Temple of the Sagrada Família), is undoubtedly the most emblematic and most controversial monument in Barcelona: Evelyn Waugh found it so depressing he refused to leave his cab to visit it, but Jean Cocteau, like most people, couldn't get his head around it: 'It's not a skyscraper, it's a mindscraper'. Love it or hate it, it's impossible to ignore: the completed towers stand at almost 100 m, and the central spire, when finished, will soar 170 m into the sky. Gaudí designed three façades: Nativity and Passion on either side of the

nave and Glory as the magnificent main entrance. Only one façade was completed by the time of his death in 1926: the craggy Nativity Façade surmounted with a green cypress tree flecked with white doves of peace. Many of the thickly clustered statues were made from life casts – including, apparently, the donkey. The Passion façade flanks the other side of the church: the antithesis of the joyful Nativity façade, this is supposed to represent death and sacrifice, but Josep Subirachs' grim sculptures are entirely devoid of any vitality. The nave was complete in 2010, and the church was consecrated in November of the same year by Pope Benedict XVI, who elevated the church to the status of basilica.

The temple is supposedly set for completion in 2026, the anniversary of Gaudí's death, but this seems increasingly unlikely in view of the technical problems surrounding the construction of the vast central tower, and delays caused by the controversial construction of a tunnel for the new high-speed rail line beneath the church.

There's a lift (with long queues) up the towers and the very brave can climb even higher into the blobby spires for an uncanny sensation of stepping out into space, and descend by the tight spirals of the vertiginous staircase. Underneath, the Crypt contains Gaudí's tomb and a museum devoted to the history of the temple, with drawings, models, and photographs.

Hospital de la Sant Creu i Sant Pau

ⓘ *C/Sant Antoni Maria Claret 167-171, T933 177 652, www.bcn.cat/visitsantpau, €10, concessions €5; guided tours in English daily at 1000, 1100, 1200, 1300; Metro Hospital Sant Pau.*

The pedestrian Avinguda Gaudí sweeps up to the other enormous Modernista project of this neighbourhood, the Hospital de la Sant Creu i Sant Pau (1926-1930), a fairytale assembly of delightful ceramic-covered pavilions ingeniously linked by underground passages and encrusted with mosaics. Visitors are guided around the grounds to admire the magical turrets and spires. No longer a working hospital, it is slowly being renovated, and one of the loveliest pavilions now contains an exhibition of the hospital's construction. The visit also includes a glimpse of the subterranean passages which linked the pavilions.

Montjuïc

The ancient promontory of Montjuïc rises up above the sea to the west of the city. A green, park-filled oasis, it's undergone a series of dramatic face lifts in the last century or so: palaces, museums and gardens were constructed for Barcelona's International Exhibition of 1929, and the upper reaches were entirely revamped to create the Olympic Ring, a string of dazzling sports complexes used during the 1992 Olympics. Despite all the development, in some ways nothing much has changed: it's still a popular weekend destination for locals, who come to wander through the parks and gaze down across the city from the hilltop castle.

Plaça d'Espanya to the (MNAC)

The circular **Plaça d'Espanya**, now a big, busy thoroughfare surrounded by whizzing traffic, was built for the International Exhibition of 1929. The Avinguda Maria Cristina, flanked by a pair of grim towers, leads to the **Font Màgica** ⓘ *shows May-Sep Thu-Sun*

2100, 2130, 2200, 22.30 and 23; Oct-Apr Fri and Sat 1900, 1930, 2000, 2030, free; Metro Espanya; Bus Nos 13, 100, 150, a magical 1920s fountain which is best appreciated during the fabulously kitsch sound and light shows in which jets of fruity-coloured water leap and dance to music.

Close by is the sleek **Pavelló Mies Van der Rohe** ① *www.miesbcn.com, Metro Espanya, Nov-Mar 1000-1830, Apr-Oct 1000-2000, €3,* a cool, glassy reconstruction of Ludwig Mies Van der Rohe's monument to rationalist architecture which was built for use as the German pavilion during the 1929 International Exhibition. Largely misunderstood at the time, it was dismantled at the close of the exhibition, but rebuilt on the same site in 1986 and is now home to the Mies Van der Rohe foundation, which hosts conferences and exhibitions.

Just across from the Mies Van der Rohe pavilion is one of Barcelona's newest museums, the **Caixa Forum** ① *Av Francesc Ferrer I Guardia, T934 768 600. www.obrasocial.lacaixa.es, Tue-Sun 1000-2000, free; Metro Espanya; Bus 13, 100, 150,* a Modernista textile mill which has been slickly redesigned to house an excellent permanent collection of contemporary art and galleries for temporary exhibitions (this is the main venue for major international touring exhibitions). Pick up a brochure for details of seasonal events, which include concerts, dance performances and other cultural events.

The huge Palau Nacional which looms from the hilltop houses the **Museu Nacional d'Art de Catalunya** ① *Palau Nacional, T936 220 360, www.mnac.es, Tue-Sat 1000-1900, Sun and hols 1000-1430, €10, concessions €7, metro Espanya, bus 9, 13, 30, 50, 55,* which contains a vast collection spanning over 1000 year, and includes everything from Romanesque murals to Modernista furnishings, along with coins, graphics and photography. The utterly spellbinding array of Romanesque murals gathered from the tiny churches of the Catalan hinterlands, is hauntingly lit and displayed on reconstructed church interiors. The stars of the exhibition are the murals from the Boí Valley, which was designated a World Heritage Site for the richness of its Romanesque heritage. The most important comes from the Church of Sant Climent in Taüll: a resplendent Pantocrater with a serene, hypnotic gaze. The paintings from the parish Church of Santa Maria (also in Taüll) are the most complete set in the museum, a blazing, richly coloured series which reaches its apotheosis in the splendid depiction of Mary as the Seat of Wisdom in the apse. The Gothic collection is less magical than the Romanesque, but equally magnificent. The 13th to the 15th centuries were Catalunya's glory years, when her ships ruled the seas and the arts flourished. Several galleries are devoted to one of the most brilliant periods in Catalan art and the three outstanding painters of the time: Bernat Martorell, Lluís Dalmau and Jaume Huguet. The museum also includes about 100 paintings, including masterpieces by Fra Angelico, Titian and Tiepolo, from the Thyssen-Bornemisza Collection, as well as more outstanding works from the likes of Fragonard, Cranach and Goya. Some of Gaudí's furnishings for the Casa Batlló have been preserved in the Modern Art collections, and there is also an excellent selection of photography and coins. Note that you don't have to see it all at once: entrance tickets are valid for visits on any two days during one month from the date of purchase.

Poble Espanyol

① *Av Francesc Ferrer i Guàrdia s/n, T935 086 300. Mon 0900-2000, Tue-Thu 0900-0200, Friand Sat 0900-0500. Sun 0900-2300; shops close earlier (1800-2000); €7, concessions €3.90; guided visits in Catalan, Castillian, English and French every hour, €2. Metro Espanya; Bus Nos 13, 100, 150 (take a bus up the hill if you don't want to face a long walk from the metro).*

After all the high art at MNAC, there's the pure kitsch of the Poble Espanyol to look forward to. The 'Spanish Village' was also built for the 1929 Exhibition, a gloriously tacky collection of traditional architectural styles from around the country. The entrance way is marked by a couple of fake medieval-style copies of the towers in the Castilian town of Avila, which were turned into the most over-the-top designer bar in Barcelona by Alfredo Arribas and Javier Mariscal in the 1980s. Inside, there's an arcaded Plaça Mayor, a pretty little Barrio Andaluz, a Catalan village, and streets copied from villages all over Spain, from Extremadura to the Basque lands, all lined with scores of souvenir and craft shops, cafés, galleries and restaurants.

Anella Olímpica (Olympic Ring)

ⓘ *Metro Espanya, then bus No 55, 150.*

The stadia and other buildings erected for the 1992 Olympics are strung along the Avinguda de l'Estadi, half-way up the hill. The main stadium (*estadi*) was originally built in 1929 (the Catalans beat Bolton Wanderers in the inaugural football match), but only the external structure of the stadium was retained during the radical alterations necessitated by the 1992 Olympics. Next door is the **Museu Olímpic I de l'Esport** ⓘ *T932 925 379, Tue-Sat 1000-1800, Sun 1000-1430; in summer Tue-Sat 1000-2000, Sun 1000-1430*, a museum devoted to the Games, where you can relive the highlights through videos, photos and displays.

Fundació Miró

ⓘ *Parc de Montjüic s/n, T934 439 470, www.fundaciomiro-bcn.org, Oct-Jun Tue-Wed and Fri-Sat 1000-1900, Thu 1000-2130, Sun and holidays 1000-1430, Jul-Sep Tue-Wed and Fri-Sat 1000-2000, Thu 1000-2130, Sun and holidays 1000-1430, €10, concessions €7 for permanent and temporary exhibitions; €7, concessions €5 for temporary exhibitions only.*

Further down the Avinguda de l'Estadi is the fabulous Fundació Miró, set in a white, light-drenched building designed by Josep Lluís Sert. The Foundation was established in 1971 and contains the most important and comprehensive gathering of Miró's works in the world. The opening rooms hold some of Miró's huge tapestries, including one created specially for the Foundation (*Tapestry of the Foundation*, 1979), with a huge figure of a woman dancing ecstatically beneath a star and moon.

During the war years, a growing colony of exiled artists brought new stimuli to local painters, including Miró, who began to experiment; *Carrer de Pedralbes* (1917), a skewed, glowing street, shows him dabbling with Cubism, and *Chapel of Sant Joan d'Horta* (1917), with its rich colouring and broad brushstrokes, is Fauvist in inspiration. Increasingly, objects float weightlessly in space – as in *The White Glove* (1925) and *The Music-hall Usher* (1925) – as Miró stripped away the unnecessary in pursuit of the essence.

He never forgot his earthy Catalanism; *Man and Woman in front of a pile of excrement* (1935), has two figures, enormous feet planted firmly on Catalan soil, gesturing lewdly with their bulging genitalia in front of a turd raised up as though looking on with interest. He was completely fascinated by hair, which sprouts on snakes, in stars, on genitalia throughout his works. In 1937, war broke out in Spain and Miró was devastated. He took his family to Normandy, where his work began to reflect his 'profound desire to escape...night, music and the stars began to play an increasing role'. The poetic series of *Constellations*, of which the Foundation holds one, *Morning Star* (1940) date from this period. Delicate lines trace between the floating symbols, suggesting an interconnectedness between the earth and the sky, flooded with wheeling stars.

The constant themes of the post-war years were woman, birds and stars – as in *Woman dreaming of escape* (1945), and *Woman and birds at daybreak* (1946). His sign language was being constantly refined and stripped and his paintings became increasingly gestural and impulsive – like the *Woman in a pretty hat* (1960), in which there are just two isolated spots of colour, and the *Figure in front of the sun* (1968). This Zen-like urge to strip things to their essence is beautifully illustrated in the series of paintings he made after a visit to Japan, including the spare, luminous *The Day* (1974). There are some spectacular sculptures from this later period, including the soaring white *Solarbird* (1968), blazing against a brilliant blue background, and more in a sculpture terrace on the roof.

Castell de Montjüic
① *T932 564 445, free admission, daily 0900-1900 (until 2100 in summer).*
Just beyond the Fundació Miró is the funicular station which trundles down to the Paral.lel, and which is also the starting point for the cable car ride up to the castle at the top of Montjüic. At the brow of the hill is the Castell de Montjüic, formerly a prison and torture centre, which is now being converted into a peace and reconciliation centre. You can still visit the castle's interior courtyard (with a café) and walk around the ramparts enjoying the spectacular views.

Other musems and the Ciutat del Teatre
At the bottom of Montjüic is a cluster of less visited museums in a crop of fanciful pavilions left over from the 1929 Exhibition. The best is the **Museu d'Arqueologia de Catalunya** ① *Passeig Santa Madrona 39-41, www.mac.cat; Metro Espanya; Bus 55, Tue-Sat 0930-1900, Sun and holidays 1000-1430, €3, concessions €2.10*, which opens with copies of early cave paintings, dramatic hunting and battle scenes, discovered in the Pyrenenean regions. There's a whole gallery devoted to the findings from the Greek colony of Empúries on the Costa Brava, an extensive collection of Roman artefacts, and a reconstruction of a magnificent palace room in Pompeii.

Just across the road is another revamped pavilion from the 1929 Exhibition, now home to the prestigious **Teatre Lliure**. Behind it is the **Mercat de las Flors**, a former flower market now transformed into a performance space, largely devoted to contemporary dance (see page 71).

Close by is the **Museu Etnològic** ① *Passeig Santa Madrona s/n, T934 246 807, www.museuetnologic.bcn.es, closed for renovation; due to reopen spring 2013; Metro Espanya*, with extensive holdings from Africa, Oceania, Asia, South America and Spain. They are shown on a rotating basis – there is simply too much to show at one time – but the short, temporary exhibitions are usually the most interesting. Below the museum, steps lead down to the **Teatre Grec**, an amphitheatre inspired by a model of Epidaurus and built over an old quarry for the 1929 Exhibition. It's the main venue for the Grec Festival, the city's main performing arts festival, which is held in June and July (see page 73).

Gràcia and Parc Güell

Gràcia was an independent town until 1897 when it was dragged, under protest, into the burgeoning city of Barcelona. The 'Liberation for Gràcia' movement hasn't quite died out, with the occasional T-shirt and graffited scrawl demanding freedom from big, bad Barcelona, and most *Graciencs* are still fiercely protective of their distinct identity. In the 19th century, Gràcia was a hotbed of radicalism, but now it has largely settled down to its role as a mildly bohemian, traditional neighbourhood of narrow streets and charming squares far from the flashiness and pace of the Diagonal which divides it from the Eixample. Gràcia's unique identity is best expressed in the Festa Major (held in August) which turns the streets into a riot of streamers, stars and balloons, as everyone vies for the prize of best-decorated street. On the edge of Gràcia is Gaudí's magical Park Güell, a dreamy wonderland which looks over the whole city and out to sea.

Squares, markets and Modernista mansions

The centre of Gràcia has no really big sights or monuments; its distinctive charm is best appreciated with a stroll, especially in the evening, when the names of streets and squares – the **Mercat de la Libertat**, the **Plaça de la Revolució** – evoke its fiercely liberal past. **Plaça de Sol** is the hub of the area's nightlife, with dozens of bars and cafés. A couple of blocks away is the **Plaça de la Virreina**, a quiet attractive square lined with a row of simple cottages and a pretty church. The oldest section of Gràcia is squeezed between the broad avenues of the Carrer Gran de Gràcia and the Via Augusta; at the heart of the district stands the neighbourhood's oldest market, the pretty Modernista **Mercat de Lliertat**. Two streets to the north is the delightful **Rambla de Prat**, with a cluster of Modernista buildings showing off their swirling façades. Dedicated Gaudí fans should make a pilgrimage to the Carrer de Carolines, the site of Gaudí's first major architectural project in Barcelona, the neo-Mudéjar **Casa Vicens** (1883-1888), designed for the ceramics manufacturer Manuel Vicens, whose business was advertised by the eye-popping proliferation of sea-green and white tiles.

Parc Güell

ⓘ *C/Olot 7, T934 132 400, Nov-Feb 1000-1800, Mar and Oct 1000-1900, Apr and Sep 1000-2000, May to Aug 1000-2100, free, Metro Lesseps, then a 10-min walk, or bus 24 to the gate; Casa Museu Gaudí Oct-Mar 1000-1800, Apr-Sep 1000-1900, €3.*

The whimsical turrets, fabulous *trencadí*-covered creatures, floating balconies and sloping parklands of the Parc Güell are perhaps the most delightful and varied of Gaudí's visionary creations. It wasn't originally designed as a park: it was meant to be an aristocratic housing estate. Gaudí's benefactor and friend, Eusebi Güell, had visions of an exclusive garden city, modelled on the English fashion, but it never took off and the empty grounds passed to the city for use as a public park in 1922.

Two fairy-tale **pavilions**, with their swirling roofs and shimmering coats of *trencadís* guard the entrance to the park. A flight of steps guarded by a multi-coloured **salamander**, which has become one of Barcelona's best-known symbols, culminate in the **Hall of a Hundred Columns**, name after for the forest of thick, Doric columns which support its undulating roof. Gaudí's talented collaborator, the architect and mosaicist Josep Maria Jujol, was given free reign to colour the vaulted ceiling with elaborate whimsy; look carefully and you'll see the designs are made of smashed china, ceramic dolls heads, wine glasses, and old bottles.

More steps lead up from the Hall to the **main square** which offers beautiful views of the city below. The endless bench which snakes around the square is thickly encrusted with trencadís, which shimmer and change colour in the sunlight. This, too, is the product of Gaudí's collaboration with Jujol, a dazzling collage of bizarre symbols, fragments of text, stars, butterflies, moons and flowers which presaged Cubism and Surrealism.

Surrounding the square are **porticoes and viaducts**, which hug the slopes and stretch for more than 3 km. The arches and columns are made from unworked stone quarried in situ, which seem to erupt organically, swooping overhead like cresting waves.

Just off the main esplanade is the modest, pink Torre Rosa, Gaudí's home for the last 20 years of his life. It's now the **Casa Museu Gaudí**, a delightful little cottage covered in creamy swirls and topped with a trencadí-covered spire surmounted with a cross. Inside, the modest rooms are filled with plans and drawings, examples of Gaudí's furniture designs for the grand mansions of the Eixample, and a sparse collection of his few personal possessions. His bedroom, which has been conserved much as he left it, contains a narrow bed, a copy of his prayer book and his death mask.

The **Gaudí Experiència** ① C/Larrard 41, T932 854 440, www.gaudiexperiencia.com, daily 1000-1800 (until 2000 in July and Aug), €9, concessions €7.50, is a new hih-tech museum which provides an overview of the great architect's life and work with a 4D 'experience', which includes a 4D film, audio-visuals, touch-screen information panels, models and more.

Port Vell, Barceloneta and Vila Olímpica

The seafront in Barcelona was the main focus for the frenzy of construction and redevelopment which heralded the 1992 Olympic Games. The brash, glistening development of the Port Olímpic was erected in all its towering, neon-lit splendour, and the old port was utterly transformed: now, yachts and gin palaces bob in the harbour, and smart restaurants have spread their awnings on to broad boulevards. Behind all the tourist gimmicks and laminated menus of the Port Vell sprawls the old fishermen's neighbourhood of Barceloneta, a shabby, old-fashioned district of narrow streets and traditional bars serving fresh seafood tapas. Beyond Barceloneta stretch the city's beaches, not especially lovely, but buzzy and always packed in summer. They edge past the glitzy Port Olímpic and culminate at the seafront of another quiet old workers' district, Poble Nou, now being swallowed up amid the hotels and skyscrapers and shopping centres of the modern Diagonal Mar district.

Port Vell

Port Vell ('old port'), once a grimy working port, was transformed beyond recognition for the 1992 Olympics. The port's activity was shunted down the coast and the docks and warehouses were demolished or restored to house elegant restaurants, shops and a marina. Designed with tourists in mind, it's pretty rare to find any Barcelonins here.

Now the crowds sweep down from the Rambla and across the undulating **Rambla de Mar**, a floating wooden walkway which leads to the Maremagnum shopping centre, the IMAX cinema, and the aquarium. The glassy **Maremagnum** building is stuffed full of shops, bars and restaurants, many with terraces overlooking the yacht-filled harbour. **IMAX** ① Moll d'Espanya-Port Vell, T932 251 111, open daily (see website for show times); Metro Barceloneta, Bus 14, 17, 19, 36, 40, 45, 57, 59, 64 and 157, offers everything from dinosaurs to dolphins in 3D and surround sound. Next door at **L'Aquàrium** ① *T932 217 474, Jul and Aug 0930-2300, rest of the year 0930-2100 (2130 at weekends), €11, children €7.70*, the highlight is still the enormous central tank, which you can coast through gently on a conveyor belt to a schmaltzy sound-track as sharks and glinting shoals of silvery fish wheel overhead.

The engaging **Museu d'Història de Catalunya** ① *Plaça Pau Vila 3, T932 254 758, www.mac.es, Metro Barceloneta, Tue-Sat 0930-1900, Sun and holidays 1000-1430, €3*, in a renovated warehouse overlooking the marina, is devoted to the story of Catalunya's fortunes from prehistory to the present with plenty of interactive toys and gimmicks. The rooftop café has fantastic harbour views.

Passeig Joan de Borbó culminates in the scruffy little Plaça del Mar, overlooked by the Torre de Sant Sebastià, where cable cars begin their terrifying journey over the harbour, see page 77, and up to Montjüic. The tower now holds a very slinky designer restaurant, see page 68, with more fabulous views.

Barceloneta

While tourists sit under canvas umbrellas and sip their cocktails in between visits to the beach, the shabby little neighbourhood of Barceloneta just behind it goes about its business undisturbed. The pre-Olympic reforms only touched the fringes of the old neighbourhood, leaving its unassuming, down-to-earth heart largely intact. The best time to appreciate it is during the **Festa Major de Barceloneta**, see page 73, at the end of September. There are no sights or monuments, but it's a great place for an evening wander when you'll discover scruffy little bars serving up wine from the barrel and freshly fried sardines. There's also a great market with a striking contemporary shell, good for picking up picnic supplies.

The **beaches** which extend for several kilometres from the Platja Sant Sebastià at the end of Passeig Joan de Borbó in Barceloneta all the way to the Platja Nova Mar Bella near the Besos River, are not the most beautiful nor the cleanest on the Mediterranean, but they are fun, easy to get to, and conveniently lined with cafés and snack bars. You can rent a sun-lounger for about €3 if you want to work on your tan for a while, but if you'd prefer something more active, stroll along to Mar Bella beach where you can get sailing and wind-surfing lessons, or hire snorkelling equipment, see page 76. The crowds thin out slightly the further you walk.

Vila Olímpica and the Port Olímpic

The Vila Olímpica (Olympic Village)was designed by the city's finest architects for the 1992 Olympic Games,although the result is a sterile mini-city of boxy, uninspired buildings. Do as everyone else does and head straight for the beach by the **Port Olímpic**. This neon-lit development is the undisputed success of the Olympic Village and encompasses a marina, sailing school and leisure complex stuffed with cafés, restaurants and shops. Above it flaps Frank Gehry's enormous shimmering copper fish and a pair of glassy towers, one of which contains the luxurious **Hotel Arts Barcelona** (see page 64).

Poble Nou and Diagonal Mar

The renovation of Barcelona's seaside neighbourhoods, which began with the 1992 Olympics, is ongoing. Diagonal Mar is the name of a new district which has developed at the point where the Avinguda Diagonal (one of the city's main arteries) meets the beach, and has a forest of glassy new towers containing plush hotels, offices and businesses, as well as a huge shopping centre. This area has been the focus of the city's efforts to promote Poble Nou as an innovative business district, known as **22@Barcelona** ① www.22barcelona.com. However, some delightfully old-fashioned pockets of traditional Poble Nou survive, including the **Ramble del Prim**, a semi-pedestrianized avenue with cafés, the perfect spot to refuel after the beach.

Tibidabo and the outlying districts

There are plenty of things to do around the edge of the city centre in Barcelona. Few attractions – besides the giddy peak of Tibidabo with its funfair and the huge Camp Nou stadium in Les Corts – are on the tourist trail but some lesser known sights, like the quiet monastery of Pedralbes and the surprisingly big and wild Parc de Collserola.

Camp Nou and the Camp Nou Experience

① *Museu FC Barcelona, C/Aristides Maillol 7-9, T934 963 608, www.fcbarcelona.es, Mon-Sat 1000-1830, Sun and hols 1000-1400, €5, €9 with guided tour of stadium. Metro Collblanc. Bus 15, 52, 54, 56, 57, 75.*

The Nou Camp stadium is one of the largest in Europe, built to accommodate 120,000 fans, and yet getting tickets for a match – particularly with arch-rivals Real Madrid – can be unbelievably tough. If you can't get into a game, a visit to the **Camp Nou Experience**, FC Barça's glossy museum, which includes a tour of the legendary stadium, is well worthwhile. The museum displays include the impressive line-up of silverware, including the record six cups earned during a single season in 2009. In the multimedia zone you can relive some of the club's finest moments on touch-screen panels and huge screens. But the highlight for most fans is the visit to the ground itself; you can go into the changing rooms and walk through the tunnel out onto the fabled pitch itself. ▸▸ *For information on getting tickets, see page 76.*

Pedralbes

North of the western end of the Avinguda Diagonal is the affluent suburb of Pedralbes, spilling down the once-wooded slopes of Collserola. Just off the Diagonal is the stately mid-19th-century **Palau Reial de Pedralbes**, originally built for the Güell family, Gaudí's benefactors. There's a small gallery with works by Picasso, Miró and the Catalan sculptor Josep Llorens Artigas, who gave Miró his first ceramics lessons.

At the top of Avinguda Pedralbes is the lovely 14th-century **Monestir de Santa Maria de Pedralbes**. The convent still houses a small community of Poor Clares, but a section of it is open to the public as the **Museu Monestir Pedralbes** ① *T932 039 282, www.bcn.es/museus, Tue-Sun 1000-1400, €3.50, free first Sun of the month.* The unusual three-tiered Gothic cloister, one of the best preserved in Europe, is a still, contemplative arcade of slender columns, surrounding groves of cypress trees, rose gardens and a small pond.

Temptation of Christ

According to legend, this is where the Devil is supposed to have shown Christ the world's treasures spread out at his feet, and tempted him with the words *'haec omnia tibi dabo si cadens adoraberis me'* (All this will I give you if you will fall down and worship me). Not even this vision of the city curled around the sea in one direction, and the Collserolas undulating gently inland towards Montserrat and the Pyrenees were enough to tempt Christ, but the name stuck, and the views are usually tremendous – at least when a salty blast of sea air lifts the smoggy pall.

Tibidabo

Tibidibo, the highest peak of the Collserola hills which surround Barcelona, is the city's mountain of fun. At the summit, reached by a rickety tram and a funicular railway, is a bizarre (but dull) church and a great old-fashioned funfair, the **Parc d'Atraccions** ① *www.tibidabo.cat, open daily in summer, weekends only in winter (check website for opening hours which change monthly), admission €28.20 for unlimited rides, children under 1.2 m €10*. The ferris wheel, dodgems and other rides are great for little kids, and there is a handful of attractions, including a couple of terrifying rollercoasters, to keep adrenalin kunkies happy. The views across the city can be breathtaking on a clear day.

From up here (or pretty much anywhere, for that matter) you can't miss the needle-like **Torre de Collserola** ① *Ctra Vallvidrera-Tibidabo, T932 117 942, www.torredecollserola.com, daily in Jul and Aug, weekends only the rest of the year (see website for opening hours)*, which spikes the horizon. A glass lift will whoosh you up to the mirador, with panoramic views stretching for miles in all directions. A free 'mini-train' plies between the funfair and the tower in summer; otherwise you can walk, or take the T2 or 211 bus from outside the main entrance to the funfair.

At the bottom of Tibidabo is the **Cosmo Caixa** ① *T932 126 050, www.obrasocial.lacaixa.es, Tue-Sun and holidays 1000-2000, €3, concessions €2, free for children under 6, free first Sun of the month, bus 17, 22, 58, 60, 73*. This is a big touchy-feely museum and planetarium set in an old Modernista asylum. Most of the descriptions are in Catalan orCastilian, but there are enough gadgets to keep kids occupied for hours; best is a wonderful exhibit called *Toca, toca!* (touch touch) which shows kids how to pick up all kinds of peculiar Mediterranean creatures, from sea anemones to starfish.

Parc de Collserola

The most unexpected delight in Barcelona is this beautiful natural park, which stretches for more than 6500 ha across the undulating Serra de Collserola, the ring of hills which contain the sprawling city. Despite being hemmed in by towns on all sides, it's still possible to forget completely the existence of the bustling city, and stroll, ride or mountain bike through wooded paths, between old farmhouses (*masies*), ancient chapels and half-forgotten springs. For maps and information on the various activities, visit the helpful park information office ① *T932 803 552, www.parccollserola.amb.es, 0930-1500*.

Barcelona listings

For Where to stay and Restaurant price codes and other relevant information, see pages 11-20.

🛏 Where to stay

Barcelona is a hugely popular destination year-round, so book accommodation well in advance. Surprisingly, you'll get the best deals in Aug (when most businesses are on holiday). The city has a great range of accommodation, from plush 5-star options with all the trimmings to budget hostels offering bunks at a bargain price. Short-term apartment lets have become increasingly popular in recent years, and are a particularly good option for families.

Most of the cheaper places can be found in the old neighbourhoods in the centre of the city (the Barri Gòtic, La Ribera, and the Raval) which are also the noisiest places to stay. The smartest (and quietest) places are generally concentrated in the Eixample. There are relatively few places near the seaside, although Diagonal Mar has a growing number and you might want to think about staying in Gràcia to get a feel for Barcelona without the tourists. There are no campsites close to the city centre – the nearest is 7 km away.

La Rambla *p34, map p36*

€€€€ Le Meridien Barcelona, La Rambla 111, T933 186 200, www.lemeridien.com/ barcelona. A swanky hotel with plush, newly revamped suites, a spa and all the luxury trimmings. Great location on La Rambla.

€€ Montecarlo, La Rambla 124, T934 120 404, www.montecarlobcn.com. With a fantastic location right on the Rambla, this has a lavish turn-of-the-20th-century lobby, and offers modern, comfortable rooms at a bargain price.

Barri Gòtic *p35, map p36*

€€ Bonic Barcelona, C/Josep Anselm Clavé 9, T62-605 3434, www.bonic-barcelona.com. There are just a few rooms (with shared bathrooms) at this little charmer in the Gothic Quarter, each individually decorated and filled with thoughtful extras, such as magazines and flowers.

€€ Hotel Denit, C/Estruc 24-26, T935 454 000, www.hoteldenit.com. A great-value option in a strategic location at the heart of the Gothic Quarter, just a couple of mins from the Plaça de Catalunya, this has pristine, contemporary rooms and helpful staff.

€ Itaca Hostel, C/Ripoll 21, T933 019 751, www.itacahostel.com. A bright, friendly *hostal* with colourful murals and laid-back owners. Dormitory accommodation in large rooms all with balconies, plus one twin room with en suite bathroom. Facilities include a lively café-bar shared kitchen and free Wi-Fi.

La Ribera and Sant Pere
p42, maps p30 and p36

€€€ Hotel Park, 11 Av Marquès de l'Argentera 11, T933 196 000, www.parkhotel barcelona.com. Built in the early 1950s by the celebrated architect Antoni de Moragas, the **Hotel Park** was renovated in 1990 by Moragas' son using the original plans. It's a narrow, slim hotel with good-sized balconies looking out towards Barceloneta, an exquisite interior wraparound staircase and comfortable, well-equipped rooms. It's also got a fantastic tapas bar – **10's** – with star chef Jordi Cruz at the helm.

€€ Musik Boutique Hotel, C/Sant Pere mes Baix 62, T932 225 544, www.musikboutique hotel.com. Handily situated near the Palau de la Música, this elegant small hotel offers stylish rooms with extras like iPod docks. Great service and a surprisingly reasonable price make this perfect for a weekend break.

El Raval p46, maps p30 and p36

€€€ **Hotel España**, C/Sant Pau 9-11, T935 500 000, www.hotelespanya.com. A swirling Modernista dining room and bar designed by Domènech i Montaner greets patrons at this smart hotel, which also boasts a fabulous roof terrace.

€€ **Curious**, C/Carme 25, T933 014 484, www.hotelcurious.com. Simple and affordable, this is a stylish option for those on a budget. It's just a few mins' walk from the MACBA museum and the Rambla.

€€ **Peninsular**, C/ de Sant Pau 34-36, T933 023 138, F934 123 699. **Peninsular** is a good moderately priced choice set in an old convent almost opposite the **Hotel España**. There's a charming interior patio filled with plants and greenery and the rooms are comfortable and good value.

€€ **Principal**, 8 C/ Junta de Comerç, T933 188 970, www.hotelprincipal.es. The nicest of several cheaper *hostales* along this street, the Principal is possibly the most eccentric, with florid rooms decorated with a mixture of antiques, and nick-nacks. The friendly owners also run the **Joventut** (up the street at No 12 with the same email and website).

€€ **Room Mate Pau**, C/Fontanella 7, T933 146 300, www.pau.room-matehotels.com. Small but perfectly formed, this design hotel offers compact rooms with fabulous, futuristic design at an affordable price.

Eixample p49, map p30

€€€€ **The Alma**, C/Mallorca 271, T932 164 490, www.almabarcelona.com. Modern and minimalistic yet warm and inviting, this is a chic urban hideaway with a charming secret courtyard. There's a great restaurant, and it offers excellent service.

€€€€ **Hotel Casa Fuster**, Passeig de Gràcia 132, T932 553 000, www.barcelonacasafuster hotel.com. If it's fin-de-siècle opulence you're looking for, this sumptuous Modernista hotel, designed by Domènech i Montaner who created the Palau de la Música, fits the bill perfectly.

€€€€ **Mandarin Oriental Hotel**, Passeig de Gràcia 38-40, T931 518 888, www.mandarin oriental.com/barcelona. A sumptuous addition to the city's luxury hotel scene, the **Mandarin Oriental** offers spectacular white and gold interiors, a Michelin-starred restaurant, a fabulous spa and all the luxurious extras you'd expect from this brand.

€€€€ **Palace**, 668 Gran Vía des les Corts Catalanes, T933 185 200, www.hotelpalace barcelona.com. Classic luxury, with all the Belle Epoque trimmings. The **Palace**, formerly the **Ritz** opened in 1919 and has hosted everyone from Ava Gardner to Salvador Dalí (who holed up in room 110). Come for pure old-fashioned luxury, superb service and lavish interiors.

€€€ **Constanza**, C/Bruc 33, T932 701 910, www.hotelconstanza.com. Chic and stylish, with very elegant rooms, a great tapas bar, and wonderful views from the roof terrace. The location is ideal too, just a few mins on foot from the Plaça Catalunya, the Gothic Quarter and the Passeig de Gràcia.

€€ **Circa 1905**, C/Provença 286, T935 056 960, www.circa1905.com. A sweet little boutique guesthouse, with just a handful of cosy, antique-filled rooms, and charming staff.

€€ **Close to Passeig de Gràcia B&B**, C/Diputació 327, T696 531 439, www.bedand break.es. An elegantly restored Modernista mansion contains this delightful B&B, which boasts just 4 rooms, including 2 very spacio us suites. One even has its own fireplace and a pretty gallery. There's a small kitchen for the use of guests.

€€ **Room Mate Emma**, C/Rosselló 205, T932 385 606, http://emma.room-mate hotels.com. The ideal option if you're looking for style on a budget, this has white-on-white futuristic design and a great central location.

€€-€ **Actual**, C/Rossello 238, T935 520 550, www.hotelactual.com. Trendy hotel, fashion-ably decorated in the slickest minimalist style, with plenty of white marble and dark wood. Fantastically located and surprisingly affordable.

Port Vell, Barceloneta and Vila Olímpica
p58, maps p30 and p36

€€€€ Arts Barcelona, C/ Marina 19-21, T932 211 000, www.hotelartsbarcelona.com. Easily the most glamorous hotel in the city, set in one of the enormous glassy towers at the entrance to the Port Olímpic. Inaugurated in 1992, it offers 33 floors of unbridled luxury, including a stunning spa (by **Six Senses Spas**), several excellent eating and drinking options, and the best service in the city.

€€€€ W Barcelona, Plaça de la Rosa dels Vents 1, T932 952 800, www.w-barcelona.com. This huge, sail-shaped hotel overlooking the beach has rapidly become an iconic landmark. Floor-to-ceiling windows in the bedrooms give you the sense of being at sea, and the hotel boasts all the luxurious extras you'd expect from the chain, including a gym, pool, spa and fabulous bar on the 26th floor.

€ Sea Point Hostel, www.seapoint hostel.com. Right next to the San Sebastian beach in Barceloneta, this offers all kind of amenities including internet access and bike hire. Breakfast is included in the price. Dorms for 4, 6 or 8, all with heating and a/c.

Tibidabo and the outlying districts *p60*

€€€€ ABaC, Av Tibidabo 1, T933 196 600, www.abacbarcelona.com. The gorgeous rooms and spa aren't the biggest draw at this elegant boutique hotel: it's attached to the city's finest restaurant.

⊘ Restaurants

The Catalans are renowned for their cuisine. The dishes are often simple, and rely on the freshness of the local ingredients. The Catalan staple, for example, is *pa amb tomàquet*, bread rubbed with fresh tomatoes, drizzled with olive oil and a sprinkling of salt. With extra toppings (like ham or cheese) it becomes a *torrada*.

Meat and fish are often served simply grilled, or cooked slowly in the oven (*al forn*) in a tomato-based sauce. There are some delicious vegetable dishes – such as the refreshing *escalivada*, a salad of roasted aubergine, peppers and onions, or *espinacs a la catalana*, spinach cooked with pine nuts and raisins.

Rice dishes are also popular, with variations on the famous Valencian dish *paella* like *arròs negre*, rice cooked slowly with squid ink and shellfish, or *fideuà*, which is made with tiny noodles cooked in with meat and fish. The most popular Catalan dessert is *crema catalana*, a local version of crème brûlée, or you could finish up with local curd cheese drizzled with honey, *mel i mató*.

There are plenty of old-fashioned bars near the harbour which offer fresh seafood tapas – like *sardines* (grilled sardines) – but the most common Catalan tapas are *truita*, thick omelettes (*tortilla*) or platters of cheeses or *embutits* (charcuterie). Don't forget to wash them all down in style with Catalan wine, or the local *Estrella* beer.

La Rambla *p34, map p36*

€ Les Quinze Nits, Plaça Reial 6, T933 173 075. Daily 1300-1545 and 2030-2330. Metro Liceu. Those long queues snaking across the Plaça Reial are for this good-value restaurant, which serves up simple, fresh Catalan dishes in coolly modern surroundings. No bookings, so be prepared to wait.

Tapas bars and cafés

Bar Pinotxo, Mercat de la Boquería 66-67, T933 171 731, www.pintxobar.com. Mon-Sat 0630-1600. Metro Liceu. The best-known and most well-loved counter bar in the market, serving excellent, freshly prepared food – don't miss the tortilla with artichokes.

Café Zurich, Plaça Catalunya, T933 179 153. Mon-Fri 0800-2300, Sat and Sun 0900-2300. Metro Catalunya. When the new **El Triangle** shopping mall was built, the infamous old **Café Zurich** was swept away. This new version doesn't have the same charm, but it's got a fine location at the top of the Rambla.

El Café de l'Opéra, La Rambla 74, T933 177 585. Daily 0830-0230. Metro Liceu. Sitting right on the Rambla opposite the Liceu Opera house, this is the perfect café for people-watching. Original Modernista-style fittings and an Old World ambience add to its charm.
Escribà, La Rambla de les Flors 83, T933 016 027. Open 0830-2100. A delightful outpost of the mouth-watering patisserie set in a gilded Modernista shop.

Barri Gòtic *p35, map p36*
€€ Agut, C/Gignàs 16, T933 151 709. Established in 1924, this local favourite remains a wonderful option for traditional Catalan cuisine. The menu includes a wide range of delicious roast meats, fresh fish and classic Mediterranean rice dishes.
€€ Café de l'Acadèmia, C/Lledó 1, T933 198 253. Mon-Fri 0900-1200 and 1330-1600 and 2045-1130. Metro Jaume I. An elegant and romantic restaurant just off the lovely Plaça Sant Just, with torch-lit tables out on the square in summer. Classic Catalan cuisine prepared with a modern twist. There's a great-value set lunch for around €14.
€€ Can Culleretes, C/d'en Quintana 5, T933 173 022. Tue-Sat 1330-1600 and 2100-2300, Sun 1330-1600. Metro Liceu. This is the city's oldest restaurant, founded in 1786, with a series of interconnected, wooden panelled and beamed rooms papered with pictures of celebrity visitors. Great desserts.
€€ Pla, C/Bellafila 5, T934 126 552, www.elpla.cat. A stylish restaurant tucked down a narrow street in the Gothic Quarter, this serves up delicious and creative dishes, such as roast lamb with licorice and honey, or monkfish with artichoke stew.

Tapas bars and cafés
Bliss, Plaça Sants Just i Pastor, T932 681 022. Mon-Sat 1330-1530, 2030-2315, closed Aug. metro Jaume I. A small, cosy café, with a couple of leopard-print sofas to sink into. Delicious home-made quiches, salads and

cakes. There are tables out on a pretty little square by the church in summer.
Bodega la Plata, C/Mercé 28, T933 151 009. This minuscule, prettily tiled *bodega* serves wine straight from the barrel, and some of the best, freshly fried sardines in town.
Café d'Estiu, Plaça Sant Iu 5, T933 103 014. Easter to Sep Tue-Sun 1000-2200. Metro Jaume I. This is prettily set among the orange trees in the courtyard outside the Museu Frederic Marés (see page 39). Simple snacks, pastries and cakes are on offer.
Juicy Jones, C/Cardenal Casañas 7, T933 024 330. Daily 1300-2400. Metro Liceu. A brightly lit juice counter with a small vegetarian restaurant downstairs, painted with big bold flowers. Good-value set menu (including vegetarian thali) and organic beers and wines, as well as the delicious, freshly made juices and smoothies.
La Pallaresa, C/ Petritxol 11, T933 022 036, www.lapallaresa.com. Mon-Sat 0900-1300, 1600-2100, Sun 0900-1300, 1700-2100. Metro Liceu. This is where to get your *xocolata amb xurros* (hot chocolate and fried dough sticks) in the morning – locals swear it's the best *xocolatería* in the city. It's still got the lino, formica tables and waiters in dicky bows.
La Vinateria del Call, C/de Sant Domènec del Call 9, T933 026 092. Open 1900-0100. Metro Liceu. Down a tiny side street, this is a dark, wooden-panelled bar with very friendly and knowledgeable staff. Excellent, very fresh tapas (choose from the menu) – platters of cheese or cured meats, *pa amb tomaquet*, and a fine wine list featuring local wines. It's so popular that it has 2 sittings at weekends (2100-2300 and 2300-0100).
Milk, C/Gignas 21, T932 680 922, www.milkbarcelona.com. Popular for Sun brunch, this is one of the few places in Barcelona where you can enjoy eggs Benedict or pancakes with maple syrup.

La Ribera and Sant Pere
p42, maps p30 and p36

€€€ Comerç 24, C/Comerç 24, T933 192 102, www.comerc24.com. Carles Abellán's award-winning cuisine offers a master class in molecular gastronomy, and encompasses everything from the signature 'Kinder Egg Surprise' (an apparently simple egg with an earthy, truffled centre) to razor clam *yakisoba* with tangerine.

€€€ Senyor Parellada, C/de l'Argenteria 37, T933 105 094, www.senyorparellada.com. Mon-Sat 1300-1530 and 2100-2330. Metro Jaume I. Set in a handsome 19th-century building, this is a stylish, buzzy restaurant. The menu concentrates on modern Catalan dishes using the freshest market produce; try the *papillotte* of French beans with mushrooms or the delicious sole cooked with almonds and pine nuts.

€€ Big Fish, Comerç 9, T932 681 728, www.bigfish.cat. A fashionable address, this combines retro-chic decor, including worn Chesterfield sofas and an enormous mother-of-pearl chandelier, with fabulously fresh fish, plus an excellent sushi counter.

€€ La Paradeta, C/Comercial 7, T932 681 939, www.laparadeta.com. Cheap and cheerful, it's no wonder that there are always huge queues here. Pick out your fish from the freshly landed selection and then wait for it to be fried up and served. No reservations.

€€ Salero, C/del Rec 60, T933 198 022, www.restaurantesalero.com. Mon-Thu 0845-1730 and 2000-0100, Fri 0845-1730 and 2000-0300, Sat 2000-0300. Metro Jaume I. An ultra-stylish cool white New York style restaurant in the heart of the Born district, serving creative fusion cuisine and a good-value set lunch.

€ Atril, C/Carders 23. T933 101 220, www.atril barcelona.com. There's a great 3-course lunch deal here for about €10, or you could just come for some of the generous portions of tapas. The Sun brunch is a local institution.

Tapas bars and cafés

Cal Pep, Plaça Olles 8, T933 107 961, www.calpep.com. Mon-Fri 1930-2330, Tue-Fri 1300-1545, Sat 1300-1545. Metro Barceloneta. A classic: there's a smart, brick-lined restaurant at the back, but it's more entertaining to stand at the bar as charismatic Pep grills fish and steaks and holds court at the same time. Refreshing house *cava*.

El Xampanyet, C/ Montcada 22, T933 197 003. Tue-Sat 1200-1530 and 1830-2330, Sun 1200-1530. Metro Jaume I. A classic little bar with old barrels and colourful tiles, serving simple tapas like salt cod and anchovies and tortilla washed down with a delicious house *xampanyet* – poor man's *cava*.

Euskal Etxea, Plaçeta Montcada, T933 435 410, www.euskaletxea.com. Bar Tue-Sat 0900-2330, Sun 1245-1530, restaurant Tue-Sat 1330-1530 and 2100-2330. Metro Jaume I. Where better to tuck into Basque *pintxos* than the Basque cultural centre. Get a plate from the bar staff, help yourself and then count up the cocktail sticks at the end.

La Vinya del Senyor, Plaça Santa Maria 5, T933 103 379. Mon-Thu1200-0100, Fri and Sat 1200-0200, Sun 1200-2400. Metro Jaume I. This features a fine selection of wines, *cavas* and sherries accompanied by excellent tapas (in minuscule portions). A summer terrace faces the beautiful church of Santa María del Mar.

Mosquito, Carrer Carders 46, T932 687 569. This friendly neigbourhoood bar serves great pan-Asian tapas, including delicious dim sum, and a wide range of international beers, to a relaxed, trendy crowd.

El Raval *p46, maps p30 and p36*

€€€ Casa Leopoldo, C/ Sant Rafael 24, T934 413 014. Mon-Sat 1330-1600 and Tue-Sat 2130-2300. Metro Liceu. This classic, family-run restaurant has been going since 1939 and not much has changed since – you'll still find solid wooden tables and chairs, dark beams and tile-covered walls. Hearty Catalan dishes using the freshest market produce are on offer, like an excellent *sopa de pesca* (fish soup) and perfectly grilled seafood and meat. The set lunch at €24 is a great option.

€€ Imprévist, C/Ferlandina 34, T933 425 859. Daily 1330-1600, 2000-2330. Metro Universitat. This cool café-bar, with funky industrial-style decor, is relaxed and arty. It serves good light dishes – salads, pasta and noodle dishes, falafel platters – and there are sometimes poetry readings, or performances.

€€ Mamacafé, C/Doctor Dou 10, T933 012 940. Open 1300-0100, until 1700 on Sun and Mon. Food served 1300-1730, and 2100-2330. Closed Aug. Metro Catalunya. Bright colours, bold design and great music have made the **Mamacafé** a stylish hang out in El Raval: the menu offers a selection of dishes from around the world including several vegetarian options.

€€ Silenus, C/dels Àngels 8, T933 022 680, www.restaurantsilenus.com. Mon 1300-1600, Tue-Sat 1300-1600 and 2100-2345. Metro Catalunya. A coolly arty restaurant serving top-notch international and Catalan dishes. It's a long narrow space with pale walls lined with comfy sofas and dotted with changing art and projections. Good set lunch for around €14.

€ Elisabets, C/Elisabets 2-4, T933 175 826. Mon-Thu and Sat 1300-1600, Fri 1300-1600 and 2100-2330. Metro Catalunya. Classic neighbourhood restaurant catering to locals and serving up tasty Catalan dishes at very low prices. The *menú del día* usually offers several choices and is very good value.

€ Pla dels Àngels, C/Ferlandina 23 (opposite MACBA), T933 294 047. Daily 1300-1500, 2030-0030. Metro Universitat. Bright, modern decor, dark blue walls, this is a large, popular restaurant which serves well priced dishes (salads, meats, pastas) and a bargain set lunch. Great terrace opposite MACBA.

€ Teresa Carles, C/Jovellanos 2, T933 171 829, www.teresacarles.com. A warm, modern interior and tasty, creative vegetarian cuisine make this a great bet for veggies. It's also good for breakfast or afternoon coffee and cakes.

Tapas bars and cafés

Bar Kasparo, Plaça Vincent Martorell 4, T933 022 072. Open 0900-2400. Metro Catalunya. A popular café-bar overlooking the playground in the square (it's a good place to bring your kids). Tasty sandwiches and hot dishes; friendly but unhurried service.

Suculent, Rambla de Raval 43, T934 436 579, www.suculent.com. Three of Barcelona's best chefs are behind this revamped gastrobar, which peps up classic tapas recipes with unusual ingredients and focuses on superb produce.

Eixample *p49, map p30*

€€€ Casa Calvet, C/de Casp 48, T934 134 012. Mon-Sat 1300-1530 and 2030-2300. Metro Urquinaona. Gaudí designed the building (for which he won an award in 1900) and it retains some beautiful Modernista touches inside, including exquisite stained-glass windows. Fresh, modern Catalan cuisine is on offer; try the smoked foie gras with mango sauce, and the fabulous desserts. Go for the set lunch (€34) if the à la carte options are too pricey.

€€€ Cinc Sentits, C/Aribau 58, T933 239 490, www.cincsentits.com. Canadian-Catalan chef Jordi Artal is at the helm of this charming, Michelin-starred restaurant, where exquisite, imaginative Catalan cuisine is served in a choice of set menus.

€€€ Tragaluz, Passatge de la Concepció 5, T934 870 621, www.grupotragaluz.com. Open 1330-1600 and 2030-2330. Metro Diagonal. In a very pretty side street off the Passeig de Gràcia, this is a very stylish, fashionable restaurant on 2 levels with a huge glass skylight (*tragaluz*), which slides open in summer. The food is fresh, elegant

Mediterranean-style fare, and the downstairs there's an oyster bar and Japanese dishes.

€€ Tickets, Paral·lel 164, www.ticketsbar.es. Albert Adrià, brother of Ferran, both formerly of El Bullí, are behind this colourful, fun restaurant, currently the hottest ticket in town. Reserve at least 2 months in advance online (no telephone number).

Tapas bars and cafés

La Bodegueta, Rambla de Catalunya 100, T932 154 894, www.labodegueta.es. Mon-Sat 0800-0200, Sun 1830-0100. A charming, old-fashioned little cellar bar lined with bottles, which serves a selection of excellent tapas and does a very good-value fixed-price lunch.

Laie Llibreria Café, C/ Pau Claris 85, T933 181 739. Mon-Fri 0900-2100, Sat 1000-2100. Metro Urquinaona. Barcelona's original bookshop café, with comfy armchairs, magazines to flick through, and a good range of tasty snacks and light meals including a good-value set lunch.

Monvínic, Passeig de Gràcia 38-40, T932 726 1 87, www.monvinic.com. A huge, glassy wine bar and dining room, serving elegant modern Mediterranean cuisine with an enormous selection of wines.

Montjüic *p53, map p30*

€ La Tomaquera, C/de Margarit 58, T934 418 518. Tue-Sat 1330-1730, 2030-2330. Metro St Antoni or Paral.lel. A resolutely no-nonsense restaurant serving up great grilled meats with garlic sauce, *torrades* with different toppings, and home made desserts. The snails are famous, as welkl as Catalan classics, such as pigs' trotters.

Tapas bars and cafés

Quimet & Quimet, C/ Poeta Cabañas 25, T934 423 142. Mon-Sat 1200-1600, Mon-Fri 1900-2230; closed Aug. Metro Paral.lel. A small, traditional *bodega* usually packed with crowds; it's got one of the best selection of

wines in the city, and a range of excellent tapas to match.

Gràcia and Parc Güell
p57, map p30

€€€ Botafumeiro, C/Gran de Gràcia 81, T932 184 230. Daily 1300-0100, metro Fontana. An outstanding Galician seafood restaurant, with a stunning array of sea creatures on the menu; the excellent value *menu de degustación* is highly recommended.

Tapas bars and cafés

Sol Solet, Plaça del Sol 21, T932 174 440. Mon-Fri 1900-0200, Sat and Sun 1200-0200. Metro Fontana. One of the prettiest bars in Gràcia, this has marble-topped tables, old tiles and paddle fans, and looks out on to the square. A good range of tapas are on offer, including several vegetarian options.

Port Vell, Barceloneta and Vila Olímpica
p58, maps p30 and p36

€€€ Els Pescadors, Plaça Prim 1, T932 252 018, www.elspescadors.com. Daily 1300-1545 and 2000-2400, metro Poble Nou. A charming whitewashed restaurant with a terrace overlooking a magical square surrounded by tumbledown buildings and shaded by 2 huge mulberry trees. It's way off the beaten track, but has a fine reputation for its seafood dishes.

€€ Agua, Passeig Marítim 30, T932 251 272. Sun-Wed 1330-1600 and 2030-2430, Thu-Sat 1330-1600 and 2030-0100. Metro Barceloneta. A slick, stylish restaurant with tables right on the beach, this specializes in rice dishes, often with an unusual twist but there are plenty of good meat and fish dishes.

€€ Kaiku, Plaça del Mar 1. T932 219 082, www.restaurantkaiku.cat. Beautifully fresh Medirreanean cuisine with the emphasis on seafood and rice dishes is served at this sea-front restaurant. Order the fabulous *arròs del xef* (their own paella, with smoked rice), and settle down on the terrace with some wine.

€€ Pez Vela, Passeig del Mare Nostrum 19, T932 216 317, www.grupotragaluz.com/rest pezvela.php. This modern update of the classic beach shack (*xiriinguito*) is located underneath the **W Hotel** right on the beach, and has a gorgeous interior, outdoor tables almost on the sand. The paella is outstanding.
€€ Set Portes, Passeig de Isabel II 14, T933 193 033, www.7portes.com. Daily 1300-0100, metro Barceloneta. A very famous old restaurant, with frilly net curtains, a piano and apronned waiters, the 'Seven Doors' has been dishing up traditional Catalan cuisine since 1836. The clientele is now fairly touristy, but the food retains its excellent reputation, particularly the house speciality, *paella de peix*.

Tapas bars and cafés
Xiringuito Escribá, Platja de Bogatell. Mon-Thu 1300-1600 , Fri-Sun 1300-1600 and 2100-2300 in winter, Tue-Sun 1100-0100 in summer. Metro Llacuna. This is run by the celebrated **Escribá** confectioners, and serves delicious seafood tapas and main dishes followed by truly mouth-watering desserts. Book well in advance.

🎧 Bars and clubs

La Rambla *p34, map p36*
Boadas, C/Tallers 1, T933 189 592. Mon-Thu 1200-0200, Fri-Sat 1200-0300. Metro Catalunya. Elegant, classy art deco cocktail bar which began life in 1933; celebrity drinkers, including Miró, have left sketches and mementoes along the walls.
Jamboree, Plaça Reial 17, T933 191 789, www.masimas.com/jamboree. Mon-Sat 220-0500. Metro Liceu. This jazz club (see page 71) becomes a night club when the sets end: after about 0100, the crowds pour in to enjoy the R&B, soul and funk which plays until dawn.

Barri Gòtic *p35, map p36*
La Macarena, DJ Zone, C/Nou de Sant Francesc 5, T933 175 436, www.macarena club.com. Daily 2300-0400, until 0500 on Fri and Sat. Small, intimate club playing electronica beloved by DJs from around the world. Buzzy, upbeat and very cool.
Malpaso, C/ Rauric 20, T934126005. Daily 2130-0230, until 0300 Fri and Sat. Metro Liceu. Just down an alley behind the Plaça Reial, this is a groovy, red-painted little bar with an eclectic soundtrack and a few punters dancing under the revolving disco ball.
Pilé 43, C/ d'Aglà 4, T933 173 902. Daily 1900-0200, until 0300 on Fri and Sat. Metro Liceu. A brightly-lit, fashionable bar filled with retro furniture, lights and knick-knacks – everything you see and sit on is for sale.
Sub Rosa, C/Rauric 23. If you're looking to impress a date, try this intimate and dimly lit cocktail bar just off the Plaça Reial. It's provocative decor was apparently inspired by the Stanley Kubrick film *Eyes Wide Shut*.

La Ribera and Sant Pere
p42, maps p30 and p36
El Mariatchi, C/Codols 14. Rumour has it that this hard-to-find little bar is owned by singer Manu Chao. True or not, it's still worth tracking down, to enjoy cheap drinks and great (often live) music, in a fun, colourful setting.
Gimlet, C/ Rec 24, T933 101 027. Mon-Sat 2000-0300. Metro Arc de Triomf. Classic, minuscule cocktail bar which draws the fashion crowd as well as plenty of celebrities (not that anyone would deign to notice).
Pitin Bar, Pg/ del Born 34, T933 195 087. Daily 1200-0300. Metro Barceloneta. **Pitin** has been going for years and years, unaffected by changes in fashion, and yet managing to stay cool without any effort. It's a split level bar with a tiny spiral staircase, decorated with all kinds of junk and lit with fairy lights.
Ribborn, C/ Antic de Sant Joan 3, T933 107 148, Wed-Sat 1900-0200, until 0300 on Fri and Sat, Sun 1800-0300, metro Barceloneta.

A relaxed, thoroughly unpretentious bar with simple tapas and DJ sessions at weekends.

El Raval *p46, maps p30 and p36*

Betty Fords, C/Joaquín Costa 56. A good choice all round, this laid-back joint serves coffee and snacks by day, then heats up at night when it adds cocktails and music to the mix. The funky, eclectic decor features fashionably mismatched furnishings and attracts an arty local crowd.

Marsella, C/ Sant Pau 65, T934 427 263. Mon-Thu 2200-0230. Metro Liceu. The big, dusty, bottle-lined **Marsella** was started by a homesick Frenchman more than a century ago. The smell of absinthe hits you as soon as you walk in; get there early to grab a battered, marble-topped table under the lazy paddle fans and soak up the atmosphere.

Moog, C/Arc del Teatre 3. A classic on the city's nightlife scene since the 80s, this club is still a big crowd-pleaser, with electronica on the main dance floor, and 80s hits and pop music upstairs.

Eixample *p49, map p36*

BeCool, Plaça Joan Llongueras. This club may be small, but it's got a big reputation. It regularly features some of the hottest DJs in town, particularly during the **Radar** mini-festival, held during **Sónar** (mid-Jun).

Nits d'Estiu (Summer Nights) at La Pedrera, Pg de Gràcia 92, www.lapedrera. com. Jul and Aug Thu, Fri and Sat 2100-2400. Metro Diagonal. Sip a cocktail and check out the live music and stunning views across the city from the undulating rooftop of **La Pedrera**.

Montjuic *p53, map p30*

La Terrrazza, Poble Espanyol, T934 231 285, www.nightsungroup.com. May-late Sep only Thu-Sun and days before bank holidays 2400-0600. Metro Espanya. The biggest summer party in the city, **La Terrrazza** is a hugely popular and posey outdoor venue, where you can chill out under the pine trees

or prance on the podiums to excellent dance music played by an impressive list of guest DJs. Massive queues and a strict door policy.

Sala Apolo, C/ Nou de la Rambla 113, T934 414 001, www.sala-apolo.com. Fri-Sat 2430-0600. Metro Paral.lel. This combined concert hall and nightclub is housed in a sumptuous old theatre. Now it's one of the best venues in town – great club nights and a very varied programme of live music.

Gràcia and Parc Güell *p57, maps p30 and p36*

Café del Sol, Plaça del Sol 16, T934155663. 1300-0200, Fri and Sat until 0230. Metro Fontana. This is a very mellow spot during the day, with creamy white walls showing changing art exhibitions. There's a good selection of tapas on Sun mornings and a delightful terrace out on the square in summer. DJ sessions on Fri and Sat nights.

Port Vell, Barceloneta and Vila Olímpica *p58, map p30*

Razzmatazz/The Loft, C/ Almogàvers 122, T933 208 200. Fri and Sat 0100-0500. Metro Bogatell, www.salarazmatazz.com. Perhaps the biggest and best nightlife venue in town, **Razzmatazz** is both a concert venue and club. There are 5 spaces, each with a different style.

Tibidabo and the outlying districts *p60, map p30*

Bikini, C/ Deu i Mata 105, (in L'Illa shopping centre), T933 220 800, www.bikinibcn.com. Tue-Thu 2400-0430, Fri and Sat 2400-0530. Metro Les Corts. The original legendary **Bikini** was bulldozed to make room for the L'Illa shopping centre. The club has been recreated in the shopping centre and offers 3 different spaces, hosting everything from live gigs (very big names) to Latin sounds and lounge.

Mirablau, Plaça Dr Andreu s/n, T934 185 879. Open 1100-0500. FGC Avinguida del Tibidabo then taxi uphill. Plaça Dr Andreu is where the Tramvia Blau stops and the funicular climbs up Tibidabo. The bar is a swanky, elegant spot with a terrace overlooking the whole city, perfect for a cocktail or some tapas.

🎭 Entertainment

Cinemas

Filmoteca de la Generalitat de Catalunya, Plaça Salvador Seguí, www.filmoteca.cat, T935 671 070. The Catalan government funds the **Filmoteca** which offers an overview of the history of cinema, with a constantly changing series of films devoted to themes, directors or countries.

Renoir-Les Corts, C/Eugeni d´Ors 12, Les Corts, T934 905 510, www.cinesrenoir.com. A well-equipped 6-screen cinema which offers at least 2 films in English.

Verdi, C/Verdi 32, T932 370 516 and **Verdi Park**, C/Torrijos 49, T933 287 900, www.cinemes-verdi.com. Both in Gràcia. These 2 cinemas in Gràcia show international and Spanish art and independent films. Yelmo Icaria, C/Salvador Espriu 61, T932 217 585. Www.yelmocineplex.es. The city's main vo (versió original) cinema and the place to see all the Hollywood blockbusters in English. Cheaper tickets on Mon.

Contemporary music

There's always plenty going on in Barcelona, from impromptu performances in shabby bars to huge concerts with all the big names.

The **Sónar festival** of multimedia music and art is fantastic (see page 73), and the **BAM festival** which runs at the same time as the **Festa de la Mercè** (see page 73), is a great way to catch some alternative sounds. Jazz is traditionally very strong in the city, and the Andalucían immigrants and their children ensure that the flamenco scene retains its energy.

Clubs like **Jamboree** and **Luz de Gas** (see above) offer a real mixed-bag of musical styles, and are always worth checking out. There are plenty of venues covering everything else, from tiny, ultra-hip bars with the latest in electronica to huge crowded *salas* with mainstream rock and pop. Pick up flyers at music shops to discover some of the less well-known venues.

Bikini, C/ Deu i Mata 105, T933 220 800. Metro Les Corts. See Bars and clubs, above.

Harlem Jazz Club, C/Comtessa de Sobradiel 8, T933 100 755. Metro Jaume I. Small but atmospheric, with very creative programming and inexpensive admission charges.

Jamboree, C/Plaça Reial 17, T933 017 564. Metro Liceu. A popular jazz club (see page 69), this turns into an even more popular nightclub after the live performances are over.

Jazz Sí Club, C/Requesens 2, T933 290 020. Metro Universitat. Impromptu performances from students of the music school who run the place, as well as a diverse programme of live music each night, ranging from Cuban folk to soul, and jazz to rock.

Luz de Gas, C/Muntaner 246, T932 097 711. FGC Muntaner. A stunning turn-of-the century music hall, with a wide selection of live music: everything from soul, jazz and salsa to rock and pop.

Razzmatazz, C/Almogavers 122, T933 208 200. See Bars and clubs, above.

Sala Apolo, C/ Nou de la Rambla 113, T934 414 001. Metro Paral.lel. See Bars and clubs, above.

Dance

Barcelona's contemporary dance scene is the best in Spain, with dozens of innovative dance groups producing some of the most striking and exciting dance in Europe. Names to look out for include **Cesc Gelabert**; **Danat Dansa**; **Mudances**, founded by Àngels Margarit; and **La Fura dels Baus**. Andalucían immigrants have kept the flamenco tradition alive, and there's a **Flamenco Festival** in early May and it's often possible to see some great visiting performers. The *tablaos* (flamenco shows) are touristy, but can be fun. Watch out for special events at some of the museums and cultural institutions like the **CCCB** and **MACBA** (see page 47). There are always dance events in the summer **Grec Festival** (see page 73), which usually feature the best of local talent.

The following theatres regularly host dance events: **El Mercat de les Flors**, the **Teatre Nacional**, **Teatre Lliure** and the **Sala Beckett** (see Theatres, below).

Classical music

The city's churches often offer concerts, particularly in the summer (details from the Palau de la Virreina, see page 34). The church of Santa Maria del Mar is one of the loveliest, with perfect acoustics, but the cathedral of la Seu, the churches of Santa Maria del Pi, Santa Anna, Sant Felip Neri and the Monastery in Pedralbes all offer a sporadic programme of concerts. **Festival de Música Antiga** (see page 73) is not to be missed, with early music in some of the city's most beautiful venues, like the *Saló de Tinell* in the Palau del Rei. Many of the museums also offer concerts: it's always worth checking out what's on at the **CCCB** (see page 47) and the Fundació Miró, and there is a series of concerts in the city parks during the summer.

Gran Teatre del Liceu, La Rambla 51-59, T934 859 900, www.liceubarcelona.cat. Metro Liceu. The (almost) faithful reincarnation of the celebrated opera house has become extremely popular, so getting hold of tickets can be difficult.

Palau de la Música Catalana, C/Sant Francesc de Paula 2, Barri Gótic, T932 957 200, www.palaumusica.org. The acoustics may be terrible, but the triumphant Modernista setting makes any performance worthwhile (see page 46).

Flamenco

Barcelona can't compare with Madrid, Seville or Granada on the flamenco front, but there are a few decent choices if you want to catch an act.

El Tablao de Carmen, Poble Espanyol, Montjüic, T933 256 895. Set inside the 'Spanish village', this is a pricey flamenco joint geared towards coachloads of tourists, but features very high-class acts, and if you book in advance you won't have to pay the entrance fee into the Poble Espanyol.

Los Tarantos, Placa Reial 17, Barri Gòtic, T933 183 067. Popular, touristy flamenco *tablao*, but this venue has the added attraction of a late-night club and other performances.

Theatres

Barcelona's theatrical tradition is both accessible and highly innovative, with several experimental theatre groups demonstrating the city's flair, verve and innovation. The widespread use of multi-media, mime and choreography means that theatre in the city can cross any linguistic barriers.

Mercat de les Flors, C/Lleida 59, Montjüic, T934 261 875, www.bcn.es/icub/mflorsteatre. This beautifully converted flower market has become one of the main venues for the **Grec Festival** (see page 73) and puts on productions from some of the city's most innovative performers. Excellent contemporary dance as well as cutting edge drama.

Sala Beckett, C/Alegre de Dalt 55 bis, T932 845 312, www.salabeckett.cat. Founded by the **Teatro Frontizero** group, which includes the eminent contemporary playwright José Sanchis Sinisterra. Interesting new theatre and contemporary dance.

Teatre Lliure, C/Montseny 47, T932 892 770, www.teatrelliure.com. One of the most prestigious theatres in Catalunya which has produced some of its leading actors and directors.

Teatre Nacional de Catalunya (TNC), Plaça de les Arts 1, Eixample, T933 065 707, www.tnc.cat Inaugurated in 1997, this Ricardo-Bofill designed building is the flagship of the city council's efforts to smarten up the grim Glòries district.

Performances range from high quality drama to contemporary dance.

Spectator sports

Basketball Basketball is massively popular throughout Spain. Barcelona's 2 biggest teams are **FC Barça** and **Club Joventut Badalona**. The season runs from Sep-May. **FC Barcelona Palau Blau Grana** (next to Camp Nou stadium), Av d'Arisitides Maillol, metro Collblanc, T934 963 675, tickets from €32-72, www.fcbarcelona.com.
Club Joventut Badalona. C/Ponent 143-161, Badalona (on the outskirts of the city), T934 602 040, metro Gorg, tickets from €20-30, www.penya.com.

Football The city has 2 clubs in La Liga: **FC Barcelona** and **RCD Espanyol**. Getting tickets for the Camp Nou stadium is difficult, but you stand a chance of seeing **Espanyol** play. The season runs from late Aug-May. **FC Barcelona Camp Nou**, Av d'Arisitides Maillol, metro Collblanc, T934 963 600, ticket hotline: T934 963 702, tickets from €20-90, www.fcbarcelona.com. An online ticket sales service is on the way, but for now you'll have to buy tickets from the stadium ticket office, available 2 days before a match. **RCD Espanyol**, Estadi Olimpic, Pg. Olimpic, 17-19, Montjüic, metro Paral.lel then funicular, or metro to Plaça Espanya then shuttle bus (match days only), www.rcdespanyol.com. Tickets for Barcelona's less famous team can be purchased near the stadium entrance.

Tennis **Barcelona Open**, a prestigious 10-day international tournament, takes place at Barcelona's smartest tennis club during the last week of Apr.
Reial Club de Tennis Barcelona-1899, C/ Bosch i Gimpera 5-13, T932 037 852, bus 63, 78, tickets €20-60. Bono-tickets give you admission to all 10 days and are better value, www.rctb1899.es.

⚙ Festivals

Contact the Palau de la Virreina (see page 34) for information on cultural festivals.
1 Jan Cap d'Any Street parties and carousing to bring in the New Year. Big club nights – with high prices.
5 Jan Cavalcada des Reis The Three Kings parade through the city throwing sweets to the kids.
Feb/Mar Carnestoltes Carnival has a great party atmosphere but is not such a big event as it is down the coast in Sitges.
23 Apr Sant Jordi Big celebration for the festival of the patron saint of Catalunya. Lovers traditionally exchange gifts on this day – books for men and roses for women (nowadays it's often the other way around).
Holy Week Setmana Santa Parades and religious processions.
Late Apr/Early May Feria de Abril Andalucían-style flamenco and carousing.
11 May Festa de Sant Ponç A street market on Carrer Hospital (Raval) to honour the patron saint of beekeepers and herbalists.
May Festival de Flamenco and Festival de Música Antiga Festivals of flamenco and early music.
May/Jun Corpus Christi See the 'ou com balla' (egg dancing on a fountain) in the cathedral cloister.
Early Jun Marató de l'Espectacle Non-stop alternative performances at the Mercat de les Flors (see Theatres, above). Includes the **Dies de Danza** festival.
23 and 24 Jun Festa de Sant Joan The most exuberant festival in the Catalan calendar: bonfires, fireworks, demons and *cava*.
28 Jun Dia per l'Alliberament Lesbià i Gai Gay pride parade though the city.
Jun Sónar Festival of Multimedia and Music (www.sonar.es).
Jun/Jul Classics als Parcs, classical concerts in the city's parks, www.bcn.cat/parcsijardins.

Jun/Jul Grec Festival The city's biggest performing arts festival.

Mid-late Aug Festa Major de Gràcia Gràcia's neighbourhood festival.

11 Sep Diada National de Catalunya Catalan National Day.

24 Sep Festes de la Mercè A massive week-long celebration, with dragons, fatheads, human castles, fire-running and fireworks, all kinds of free events, a swimming race across the harbour, as well as concerts and the BAM alternative music festival.

End-Sep Festa Major de la Barceloneta Barceloneta's neighbourhood festival.

Oct-Dec International Jazz Festival.

1 Nov Tots Sants (Castanyada) All Saints' Day; people visit family graves and eat traditional foods.

1-22 Dec Fira de Santa Llúcia The feast day of Santa Llúcia marks the beginning of the Christmas season and the Christmas market.

25-26 Dec Nadal and Sant Esteve Christmas and the Catalan equivalent of Boxing Day are low-key family affairs, with big family lunches; kids beat the Christmas Log, shouting '¡Caga Tio¡ ¡Caga¡' – Shit, log! Shit! The log bursts open to reveal a small gift. The main present giving doesn't happen until 6 Jan.

O Shopping

No other city makes shopping so easy, with more shops per capita than anywhere else in Europe. They range from tiny old-fashioned stores which haven't changed at all in decades, to grand glitzy shopping malls where you can get everything you could possibly want under one roof.

Bookshops, newspapers and magazines

The stalls along the Rambla all have a good selection of foreign newspapers and magazines and occasionally even a few novels in English.

Altaïr, metro Passeig de Gràcia. A travel specialist with a good selection of books, guides and maps, many in English.

Fnac, El Triangle, Plaça Catalunya 4, metro Catalunya. Enormous store with books, music, a concert ticket service, and an international news-stand and café on the ground floor.

Department stores

El Corte Inglés, Plaça Catalunya 14, metro Catalunya, www.elcorteingles.com. This huge department store is part of a vast Spanish chain. There's a basement supermarket and delicatessen, plus fashion, leathergoods, toiletries, electrical goods, and souvenirs. There's a café on the top floor with fabulous views, and look out for the 'Opportunidads' or bargains on the 8th floor. There's another branch just down the road at Av Portal de l'Àngel which has books, music and DVDs.

Design, decorative arts and household goods

BD Edicions de Disseny, C/Ramón Turro 126, www.bdbarcelona.com. In a restored warehouse, this is the showroom for one of Barcelona's most prestigious design firms. Exquisite, expensive furniture – both reproduction Modernista and contemporary designs – and other household goods from local and international designers.

Galeries Vinçon, Passeig de Gràcia 96, metro Diagonal, www.vincon.com. The best-known and most influential design emporium in the city, located right next to La Pedrera, with everything for the home from furniture and lighting to kitchenware and tableware.

Fashion

Barcelona has an excellent reputation for cutting edge design; there are hundreds of boutiques offering the unusual work of local designers, as well as plenty of others which feature the latest from the big international fashion houses. Carrer Portaferrissa in the Barri

Gòtic is lined with young fashion shops, and there are several new designers popping up almost daily in the trendy Born area. The Raval has lots of clubwear and vintage fashions, and the big, international fashions (**Chanel**, **Prada** and **Gucci** et al), can be found up in the Eixample.

Camper, El Triangle, C/Pelai 13, metro Catalunya, www.camper.es. Trendy, comfortable shoes at a reasonable price.

Furla, Pg de Gràcia 59, metro Pg de Gràcia. Flagship store offering very stylish bags and shoes in unusual colours and designs.

Giménez & Zuazo, C/ Elisabets 20, metro Catalunya. Ultra-hip women's fashions from this Raval-based designer shop. Gorgeous fabrics, a vintage feel and wonderful accessories make this a must for fashionistas

Jean-Pierre Bua, Av Diagonal 469, metro Diagonal. The original and best-known designer fashion shop, with the latest from names like **Jean-Paul Gaultier**, **Vivienne Westwood** and **Dries Van Noten**. There is also a selection of unusual, stylish bridal wear.

Mango, Pg de Gràcia 65, metro Pg de Gràcia, www.mangoshop.com. Catwalk fashion at affordable prices, with ranges for work, evening and casual wear, including shoes and accessories. Several branches.

Zara, Pg de Gràcia 16, metro Pg de Gràcia, www.zara.com. The flagship store has a little of everything – affordable fashion for men, women and children, as well as a selection of stylish homewear.

Food and wine

Escribà, Gran Via de les Cortes Catalanes 546, metro Urgell. Chocolate heaven, and it's worth coming just to see the incredible window displays. Wonderful cakes and beautifully packaged chocolates.

Queviures Murrià, C/ Roger de Llúria 85, metro Passeig de Gràcia. This old-fashioned grocery store is set in beautiful old Modernista premises with a tiled exterior featuring the famous monkey designed by Catalan painter Ramon Casas. You'll find a range of farmhouse cheeses, excellent hams, and a good selection of wines and *cavas*.

Vila Viniteca, C/Agullers 7-9, metro Jaume I www.vilaviniteca.es. This is a family-run wine store, with a dizzying selection of wines and *cavas* from all over Catalunya and Spain. It also has an adjoining grocery store with excellent hams, cheeses, olives and other goodies.

Malls

El Triangle, C/Pelai 39, metro Catalunya, www.triangle.es. This gleaming mall contains an enormous **Fnac** (books, music and concert tickets), **Habitat**, **Sephora** (perfumes and cosmetics), a **Camper** shoe store and several other smaller fashion shops.

L'Illa, Av Diagonal 545-557, metro María Christina, www.illa.es. The most upmarket mall in the city, this has all the fashion chains there are along with a **Fnac**, **Decathlon** sports shop, and several fancy designer boutiques.

Markets

Els Encants, Plaça de les Glòries Catalanas, metro Glòries. A sprawling flea market; get there early if you want a bargain and keep a close eye on your belongings.

La Boquería, La Rambla 91, metro Liceu. Barcelona's best-loved food market with hundreds of stalls. Stalls at the front have tourist prices – be prepared to browse and price check.

Mercat de Sant Antoni, C/Comte d'Urgell 1, metro Sant Antoni. Another wrought-iron Modernista market (currently being refurbished), the fresh produce stalls are replaced by a second-hand book and coin market on Sun. The stalls have moved into a nearby modern building while restoration is underway.

Plaça del Pi, metro Liceu. Plaça del Pi hosts several markets. On the first Fri and Sat of the month, there's a honey market, when you'll also find other things like cured hams and farmhouse cheeses for sale. There's an antiques market on Thu, and art is for sale on weekends in the adjoining **Plaça Josep Oriol**.

Music

Discos Castelló, C/Tallers 3 and 7, metro Catalunya, www.castellodiscos.es. You'll find everything at these stores from classical to hip hop. They also specialize in collectors' editions of classic rock and pop bands.

Etnomusic, C/Bonsuccés 6, www.etnomusic. com, metro Catalunya. Well-known world music shop with helpful staff.

Sports goods

Nus Esports de Muntanya, Plaça Diamant 9, metro Fontana, www.espeleonus.com. A mecca for mountaineers or anyone interested in adventure sports.

Tactic Surf Shop, C/Enric Granados 11, metro Universitat, www.tacticbarcelona.com. Clothes and equipment for surfers, windsurfers, snowboarders and skateboarders.

Tomás Domingo, C/ Rocafort 173, metro Tarragona i Entença, www.tomasdomingo. com. One of the best cycling shops in the city, with a wide range of models and accessories.

Unusual shops

Almacenes del Pilar, C/Boquería 43, metro Liceu. A stunning selection of traditional fringed Spanish silk shawls and elaborate fans.

El Ingenio, C/Rauric 6, metro Liceu. This magical old shop was founded in 1838. Inside you'll find everything you need for a fiesta – puppets, masks, carnival and fancy dress outfits.

El Rei de la Màgia, C/Princesa 11, metro Jaume I, www.elreydelamagia.com. An extraordinary shop devoted to magic and magicians, with walls papered with photographs of celebrated magicians.

▲ What to do

Barcelona Sports Information Centre: Servei d'Informació Esportiva, Av de l'Estadi 30-40, Montjuïc, T934 023 000. Leaflets and information on local sports centres.

Golf

Club de Golf El Prat, El Prat de Llobregat, T933 790 278, www.rcgep.com. This club is out near the airport (get a taxi). In past years, this club has been used for the **Spanish Open**. **Club de Golf Sant Cugat**, C/de la Villa s/n, Sant Cugat del Vallès, T936 743 908, FGC from Plaça Catalunya to Sant Cugat. 18-hole course with a bar, restaurant and pool.

Gyms and fitness clubs

Centres de Fitness DiR. There are several well-equipped (pools, saunas, weight rooms, etc) DiR fitness centres in the city; for location information call T901 304 030 or check out www.dir.cat. Bring your passport to sign up.

Jogging

Best places to jog include the boardwalk from Barceloneta to Mar Bella – run early before the crowds come. Parc de Collserola is another great place for a run (see page 61). The park information centre has maps. There are fantastic views along Carretera de les Aigües at the top of Av Tibidabo in the Collserola.

Sailing and watersports

Base Nàutica de la Mar Bella, Av de Litoral (between the beaches of Bogatell and Mar Bella), T932 210 432. Windsurf rentals, boat rentals, snorkelling equipment rentals and a wide range of courses. There's also the added bonus of DJ sessions in summer.

Centre Municipal de Vela, Moll de Gregal, Port Olímpic, T932 211 499, www.velabarce lona.com. Sailing courses for all levels.

Swimming
Club de Natació Barceloneta/Banys
de Sant Sebastià, Plaça del Mar 1, T932 210
010, www.cnab.cat, metro Barceloneta. Very
close to Barceloneta beach. Indoor and
outdoor pools, gym, sauna, restaurant
and café.
Piscines Bernat Picornell, Av de l'Estadi
30-40, T934 234 041, www.picornell.com,
metro Paral.lel then funicular, or metro to
Plaça Espanya then bus No 61. Magnificent
pools used in 1992 Olympics. Indoor and
outdoor pools, gym/weights room.

Tennis
Centre Municipal de Tennis Vall
d'Hebron, Psg de la Vall d'Hebron 178-196,
T934 276 500, metro Montbau. 17 clay courts,
7 asphalt courts and 2 open-air pools.

Yoga
Ujuyoga, T622 172 284, www.ujuyoga.com.
Yoga seesions in English at locations in Gràcia
and in the historic centre.
Centre de Ioga Iyengar de Barcelona,
C/ Pelai 52-3, T933 183 533,
www.iogabcn.cat. Metro Catalunya. Pure
Iyengar yoga in a convenient, central location.

⊘ Transport

Air
Air France: T902 207 090,
www.airfrance.com.
British Airways: T902 111 333, www.ba.com.
Delta: T902 810 872, www.delta.com.
easyJet: T902 599 900, www.easyjet.com.
Iberia: T902 201 214, www.iberia.com.
For further information, see page 28.

Bus
The main hub for local/city buses is the Plaça
Catalunya. The bus stops display clear,
user-friendly bus maps listing the stops made
on each route. Single tickets cost €2. Buses
on most routes usually run from Mon-Sat
0600-2230, with a less frequent service on

Sun. The night bus (*nit bus*) service runs from
2230-0400 daily and covers 18 routes. Most
pass through Plaça Catalunya, and arrive
roughly every half hour. The discount passes
like the **T-Dia** or the **T-10** are not valid; you
must buy a single ticket (€2). These are only
available on board the bus. The local bus
routes are clearly marked at bus stops, and
the TMB and tourist offices have a useful
transport map (or see online at
www.tmb.cat). It's unlikely that you'll need
buses to get around the old city, but useful
bus routes for tourists are: No 24 to the gate
of the **Parc Güell**; No 63, 64 and 78 for the
Palau Reial de Pedralbes and the **Monestir
de Santa Maria de Pedralbes** (plus a wide
choice of bus lines along La Diagonal,
including Nos 7, 33, 67 and 75); and Nos 17,
36, 39, 45 and 59 for **Barceloneta**. Bus
Nos 14, 59 and 91 runs the whole length
of **La Rambla**.

Car
Driving in Barcelona is not to be
recommended: the streets are small and
always clogged and parking spaces are
difficult to find. Cars with foreign plates or
hire cars are prime targets for thieves so
don't ever leave anything valuable in them
and use monitored underground car parks
when possible.
    Offices of the major car rental companies
can be found at the airport, and at
Barcelona-Sants train station. The best deals
are almost always available online, and you
should find out if the airline you fly with
offers special car rental deals.
Avis, T902 180 854, www.avis.com.
Europcar, T902 105 030, www.europcar.com.
National (a partner of the Spanish car hire
firm, **Atesa**), T902 100 101, www.national.
com, www.atesa.es.
Vanguard, T934 393 880, C/Villadomat 297,
www.vanguardrent.com. Local car hire firm,
which also rents out motorbikes and scooters.

Cycling

The city's network of bike lanes is being expanded all the time. Barcelona's bike rental system, **Bicing** (www.bicing.cat) is not really geared towards tourists, but it has certainly made the the city and its inhabitants considerably more bike-friendly.

Bikes are great if you want to do some off-road cycling in the wonderful Parc de Collserola (see page 61) behind Tibidabo. Cycling along the seafront, from Barceloneta, along the Port Olímpic and out to the beaches of Mar Bella is a great way to spend an afternoon. The tourist information centre at Plaça Catalunya has a free cycling map of the city.
Al Punt de Trobada, C/ Badajoz 24, T932 216 367, www.alpuntdetrobada.com. Bike rental and repairs.
Biciclot-Marítim, Pg. Marítim, Platja de Barceloneta, , www.biciclot.net. Bikes and tandems for rent – great location on the beach front if you want to cycle along the boardwalk. Also run bike tours.
Un Cotxe Menys, C/ Esparteria 3, T932 682 105. 'One car less' (in Catalan) do bike rentals, and offer guided tours.

FGC trains

Some city and suburban destinations are served by FGC trains (Ferrocarrils de la Generalitat de Catalunya), which are run by the Catalan government. They are mainly useful for getting to the less central sights like Gràcia or Tibidabo.

Metro

There are 8 metro lines (Mon-Thu 0500-2300, Fri 0500-0200, Sat 24 hrs, Sun 0600-2400) identified by number and colour. A single ticket costs €2 or you can get a T-Dia for €7, which allows unlimited transport on the bus, metro and FGC trains for 1 person during 1 day, or a T-10, which offers 10 trips on the bus, metro and FGC trains for €9.80 and can be shared. The T-10, handily, is also valid for the airport train.

Taxi

City taxis are yellow and black, and easily available. There's a taxi stand on the Plaça de Catalunya, just across the street from the main tourist information office. To call: **Barnataxi**, T933 222 222; **Fono-Taxi** T933 001 100; **Ràdio Taxi** T933 033 033.

Telefèric/cable cars

Telefèric de Monjüic The cable car from Av Miramar swings up to the castle at the top of the hill. Daily Jun-Sep 1000-2100; Oct and Mar-May 1000-1900; Nov-Feb 1000-1800. Tickets cost €7 single and €9.80 return.
Telefèric de Barceloneta (Aeri del Port) The cable car journey across the bay is one of the most thrilling rides in Barcelona, and definitely not for people suffering from vertigo. It closes intermittently for works. It runs from the Miramar station at the end of Av Miramar on Monjüic down to Passeig de Joan de Borbo in Barceloneta. Open daily mid-Oct to Feb 1000-1730, Mar to mid-Jun and mid-Sep to mid-Oct 1000-1900, mid-Jun to mid-Sep 1000-2000. Ticket prices are hefty: €10 single €15 return.

Tram and funicular

Tramvia Blau/Blue Tram A refurbished antique tram which is the first part of the journey up Tibidabo. It runs every 15-30 mins between from Plaça Kennedy (near FGC train station Av del Tibidabo) to the Plaça Andreu where it joins the funicular (see below). Runs 1000-1800, weekends only in winter (mid-Sep to mid-Jun) and daily in summer and over Easter (€3 single, €4.80 return).
Tibidabo funicular Take the funicular from the Plaça Andreu to the top of Tibidabo (return €7.50, or €4 if you show a park admission ticket). Opening times coincide with those of the Parc d'Atraccions de Tibidabo; generally speaking it's weekends only in winter, daily in summer.
Montjüic funicular Departs Paral.lel metro station and heads up to Av Miramar, close to

the Fundació Miró. Metro tickets and passes are valid, or a single ticket costs €2 (includes a mini-guide. Open spring and summer 0900-2200, autumn and winter 0900-2200. It connects with the telefèric/cable car to the top of Montjüic (see above).

Walking

Barcelona is a delightful city to walk around, and seeing it on foot is definitely the best way to appreciate its charms. The sights of the old city are all within easy walking distance, but those of the Eixample are quite spread out. There are free maps provided by the the big department store **El Corte Inglés**, but it's worth investing in the slightly better tourist office map (€1.5). There's also a great inter-active street map at www.bcn.es/guia.

❶ Directory

Cultural centres

British Institute, C/Amigó 83, T932 419 700, www.britishcouncil.org. English lessons, library, and a noticeboard full of accommodation ads.

Institute of North American Studies, Via Augusta 123, T932 405 110, www.ien.es. Useful reference library.

Embassies and consulates

There's a full list of embassies and consulates in the phone book under Consulats/Consulados. See also www.embassiesabroad.com.

Medical services
Dentist

Dr Nicholas Jones, Av Diagonal 281, T932 658 070. English dentist, trained at London's Royal Dental Hospital.

Hospitals

CAP 24 hr Perecamps, Av Drassanes 13-15, T934 410 600, metro Drassanes or Paral.lel. This clinic deals with less serious emergencies and injuries.

Hospital Clínic, C/ Villarroel 170, T932 275 400, metro Hospital Clinic.

Hospital de la Santa Creu i Sant Pau, C/ Sant Quintí 89 Sant Antoni María Claret 167, T932 919 000, metro Guinardó-Hospital de Sant Pau or Sant Pau-Dos de Maig.

Pharmacies

Farmàcia Clapés, La Rambla 98, T933 012 843, metro Liceu. 24-hrs.

Farmàcia Torres, C/ Aribais 62, T934 539 220, metro Universitat 24 hrs.

Useful addresses

Emergency numbers There is one number for all the emergency services (ambulance, fire and police): **T112**. To contact the emergency services directly, call: Ambulance/*Ambulància* T061; Fire service/*Bombers/Bomberos* T080; National Police/*Policia Nacional* T091; Municipal Police/*Policia Municipal* T092.

Police station The most central *comisaría* (police station) is at C/Nou de la Rambla 76-80, T932 904 849.

Contents

Footprint features

Catalunya & Andorra

South of Barcelona

The beaches south of Barcelona are long and golden. The prettiest seaside town is Sitges, which also has the wildest and most outrageous nightlife. The buzzy, easy-going city of Tarragona is crammed with Roman ruins, but also has a clutch of good beaches, and a port full of great seafood restaurants. The resorts of the Costa Daurada aren't for everyone, but fine if you are just looking for sun, sea and sand. At the southernmost tip are the wild, empty wetlands of the Ebre Delta, a paradise for birdwatchers. Inland, there are Modernista *bodegas* for trying out local wines and *cava*, the spectacular medieval monasteries of the 'Cisterican Triangle' and a smattering of fine old medieval towns and villages with some fantastic local festivals.

Costa Garraf → *For listings, see pages 95-100.*

Leaving the city the **Garraf Massif** drops dramatically into the sea, creating a spectacular coastline of steep cliffs overlooking tiny coves. Beyond the massif stretch sandy beaches and a couple bustling seaside towns known as the Costa Garraf. **Castelldefels**, which started out as a tourist resort, has effectively become a suburb of Barcelona, but it has long golden beaches and some fine seafood restaurants.

Just beyond Castelldefels is **Garraf**, a quietly pretty seaside town with a great beach, cacked by a delightful row of bottle-green-andwhite-painted beach huts and a colourful port packed with seafood *tascas*. Gaudí designed the striking **Celler de Garraf** (now a retaurant)for the Güell family in 1888, a pointy, fairytale *bodega* attached to an old keep.

Sitges → *Phone code: 938. Population: 19,583.*

The Belle of the whole coastline south of Barcelona is undoubtedly Sitges, a beautiful whitewashed town clustered around a rosy church out on a promontory, which gets packed with hip Barcelonins on summer weekends. Strictly speaking, it's not part of the Costa Daurada proper (which begins a few miles down the coast) but it does have some of the finest long sandy beaches on the coast. No one really comes to Sitges for the museums; beaches, bars and the certainty of a good time are what draw the hordes of trendy Barcelonins. Since the 1960s, it's also become a hugely popular gay resort who put the kick into its famously over-the-top celebrations for Carnival in early spring. The long sandy beaches are invariably crowded, and right at the westernmost end are a couple of pretty wild nudist beaches, one of which is gay.

Catalunya doesn't feel like the rest of Spain – probably because it doesn't really consider itself Spanish. Now an autonomous community, the Catalans consider themselves a nation apart, and talk of secession from Spain has intensified in the last few years. Post-Franco Catalunya has vigorously encouraged the re-emergence of its national language, traditions and culture, and Catalan, rather than Castellano, is the *lingua franca*.

Places in Sitges

Cau Ferrat ① *C/Fonollar s/n, T938 940 364, closed for renovation.* Sitges has a big reputation for partying, which began when the Modernista painter Santiago Rusiñol (one of the founders of Els Quatre Gats in Barcelona, see page 42) set up home here in the 1890s. Two little fishermen's cottages leaning over a sheer cliff in the heart of the old town were expensively and flamboyantly renovated, the walls painted a glowing azure blue and hung with paintings by all Rusiñol's friends including Picasso, and then the place was crammed with a fantastical hoard of Catalan ironwork; he called it the Cau Ferrat –'Den of Iron' – and it is now a fascinating museum. Rusiñol made the top floor into one huge neo-Gothic hall, which looks like a cross between a cathedral and a junkshop: it's stuffed full of ironwork, bric-a-brac, paintings and bits of ancient pottery and glass which Rusiñol dug up himself. There are also two minor paintings by El Greco, which were the star attraction of the 1894 Festa Modernista (Festival of Modernism), when they were brought from Barcelona by train and then hoisted aloft by four artists and taken in a solemn procession to their new home in the Cau Ferrat – for years, the residents of Sitges thought Señor El Greco was one of Rusiñol's relatives. Rusiñol's home was always filled with artists, musicians and writers, and he organised five Modernist Festivals between 1892 and 1899 to celebrate the new ideas that were being expounded – the wild antics which accompanied these festivals gained the town a heady reputation for bad behaviour which it has been cultivating ever since.

Museu Marice ① *C/Fonallar s/n, T938 940 364, closed for renovation.* Next door to the Cau Ferrat the Museu Maricel has a collection of art from the medieval period to the early 20th century displayed in a light-filled old mansion hanging over the sea.

Museu Romàntic ① *C/Sant Gaudenci 1, T938 942 969, visits by guided tour only: Oct-Jan Tue-Sat 0930-1400, 1530-1830, Sun 1000-1500, Jul-Sep Tue-Sat 0930-1400, 1600-1900, Sun 1000-1500, €3, concessions €1.50, free first Wed of the month.* The third of Sitges' museums is tucked away in a small street in the centre of the old town, set in an elegant townhouse and recreates the life of an affluent Sitges family at the end of the 19th century. Stuffed with knick-knacks, engravings, and period furniture and carriages, it also has an enormous collection of antique dolls.

Vilanova i la Geltrú → *For listings, see pages 95-100.*

Further down the coast and resolutely down-to-earth after flamboyant Sitges, Vilanova i La Geltrú is a busy working port with a large fishing fleet. The palm-lined Passeig Marìtim is crammed with restaurants where you can taste the day's catch, and there are two good beaches – the nicest is at the end of the Passeig Marìtim. There is also a handful of museums to keep you occupied on a rainy day.

Right by the train station is the **Museu del Ferrocarril** ① *Costat de l'estació, T938 158 491, www.museudelferrocarril.org, Tue-Fri and Sun 1030-1430, 1600-1830, daily in Aug 1030-1430, 1700-2000,* where fans of old trains can clamber over steam engines and play with model railways.

Nearby there's the **Biblioteca Museu Balaguer** ① *Av de Victor Balaguer s/n, T938 154 202,* with a surprisingly good collection of artworks including a couple of fine El Grecos and some pieces on loan from the Prado.

Museu Romàntic Can Papiol ① *C/Major 32, T938 930 382,* is linked to the Sitges Romantic museum (see above), and is housed in another fine mansion with an equally florid collection of 19th-century fripperies. The tourist office ① *Passeig del Carme s/n, T938 154 517, www.vilanovaturisme.cat.*

The Wine Route

Catalan *cava*, the delicious home-grown bubbly, is mostly produced in the valleys of the Alt Penedès region, just southwest of Barcelona and a short trip inland from Sitges. Well over half the land is given over to vines, which snake trimly across the hills as far as the eye can see. Many *bodegas* are open for visitors, but you'll have to check with the tourist offices in Sant Sadurní d'Anoia (the main centre of *cava* production) or in Vilafranca del Penedès for opening hours and times. Most *bodegas*, besides the really big producers like Freixenet, prefer visits to be arranged in advance. The hills become increasingly rugged beyond Falset, another big wine-producing town, and, lost among them, are some tiny medieval villages overlooked by ruined castles and monasteries. The **tourist office** ① *Plaça del Ajuntament 1, T938910325, st.sadurnia@diba.es.*

Sant Sadurní d'Anoia

The main centre for *cava* production is Sant Sadurní d'Anoia, where the two giants of the *cava* world, **Freixenet** ① *T938 917 000, www.freixenet.es, guided tours Mon-Thu 1000, 1130, 1530, 1700, Fri 1000 and 1130, Nov and Dec weekends only by prior arrangement,* and **Codorniú** ① *T938 183 232, www.codorniu.es, Mon-Fri 0900-1700, Sat-Sun 0900-1300,* have flung open their swirling Modernista doors for slick and professional tours and tastings.

Vilafranca de Penedès

This is the centre for the region's still-wine production and there are some interesting excursions around the town with dozens of small *bodegas* tucked away in the surrounding hamlets. Vilafranca de Penedès itself is a relaxed market town with a smattering of Modernista mansions and the odd Gothic church or townhouse, Vilafranca de Penedès is the perfect setting for an old-fashioned slap-up lunch on a square. In the centre of the old town, there's a slick, new **Vinseum** ① *Plaça Jaume I No 5, T938 900 582,*

Catalan wines

Catalunya has been making wine since the fifth century BC. The Romans thought of it as plonk (although it was popular in all corners of their empire) and it took almost 2000 years for its reputation to improve. Now Catalunya is one of the most up-and-coming wine-producing areas in Spain, with a very wide variety of red, white, and rosé wines. But of course it's best known for the sparkling wine, *cava*, produced locally by the methode champenoise.

There are nine main wine-growing area which have been designated as Denominació d'Origen (DO) like the French and Italian models, each producing distinctive wines. The Alella region makes mostly very good dry and sweet whites, but also some delicious reds. The Conca de Barbarà region produces excellent *cava*,

rosés and whites. In the Empordà region on the Costa Brava, you'll find simple reds and rosés. Around Costers del Segre, they produce a bit of everything – red, white, rosé and *cava* (but the reds are best known). Tarragona is known for its red and white wines, but it also has something unusual: Paxarete, a very sweet traditional chocolate-brown wine. The wines of the Priorat and neighbouring Montsant DOs are unusual and pricey, reflecting the difficulty of cultivating the hilly land, while the wine of the Terra Alta is usually light and fresh.

Undoubtedly the best-known wines come from the Penedès region, the largest and most important wine-producing area in Catalunya. These include the vast range of wines made by the enterprising Torres family.

www.vinseum.car, Tue-Sat 1000-1400, 1600-1900, Sun and public holidays 1000-1400, a high-tech temple to wine in a splendid medieval palace. At the end of the visit, you can enjoy some local wines and tapas in the museum's taverna.. The tourist office ① *Carrer Cort 14, T938 920 358*, has a list of *bodegas* which run tours and tastings.

Olèrdola

① *16 Mar-15 Oct Tue-Sun 1000-1400, 1500-2000, 16 Oct-15 Mar Tue-Fri 1000-1400, 1500-1800, Sat 1000-1600.*
A couple of kilometres towards the coast, the Iberian-Roman ruins of Olèrdola are clustered on a windswept hilltop which has been inhabited since around 1800 BC. Right at the top, a ghostly ancient church is still surrounded by strange body-shaped stone tombs dating back a thousand years. There is some fine, easy walking in the surrounding forested hills – the visitor centre at Olèrdola has a map.

Falset

Modernista architecture is not confined to the cities in Catalunya; many of the old *bodegas* were designed by fashionable architects at the end of the 19th century and most wine villages boast a an extravagant Modernista wine cellar or two. These villages are hidden in the folds of steep hillsides thickly laced with vines that produce some notoriously strong wines. The largest of the wine-producing towns of the Priorat is Falset, which has a swirling Modernista *bodega* by César Martinell, one of Gaudí's acolytes, which is known as the 'Catedral del Vino'. The remains of the 12th-century castle were renovated

-tech **Wine Museum** ① T655 043 370, summer 1100-1400, 1600-1900, ?30, 1600-1730, admission €3.50.

ains

wines were first produced in this region by the monks of the Cartoixa d'Escaladei (Charterhouse of Scala Dei), 25 km away in the Prades Mountains, who established the first **Carthusian monastery** ① Camí de la Cartoixa s/n, Escaladei, T977 827 006, Oct-May Tue-Sat 1000-1300 and 1500-1700, Jun-Sep Tue-Sat 1000-1330 and 1600-1930, Sun 1000-1330, €3, concessions €2, in the Iberian Peninsula in the 12th century. Little remains of the monastery's former splendour, but the ruins are hauntingly set just beneath the peak of Montsant, where there's some excellent walking.

Close to Montsant are several striking villages: tiny **Siurana**, with just 30 inhabitants, is dominated by the imposing ruins of an Arab fortress perched on the edge of a vertiginous cliff. It's a densely packed village of winding streets with ancient houses lined by stone archways, overlooked by a Romanesque church. Tourists, mainly Catalans, pile up here in the summer, but out of season it's very quiet and there is some very attractive walking in the surrounding area. **Prades**, a walled medieval city built of warm, rosy stone, has another ruined Arab castle, and an arcaded central square overlooked by the 13th-century Església de Santa María built in the transitional style between Romanesque and Gothic. Another little charmer is **Poboleda** with its rather grand 17th- and 18th-century mansions lining the pretty streets.

Tarragona → Phone code: 977. Population: 110,947.

Tarragona, imposingly perched on a rocky outcrop overlooking the sea, is one of the oldest cities in Spain and one of the most important in Catalunya. It's a brisk, industrious city with a picturesque old quarter curled around the unusual Gothic cathedral, and a busy working harbour lined with great seafood restaurants.

Arriving in Tarragona

Getting there Tarragona is well connected by train and bus to most Spanish cities and to inland cities. The train station is at the bottom of the hill, with the harbour located down the coast to the south. The AVE (high-speed traion) station is located 11 km from the city centre. ▸▸ For further details see Transport, page 100.

Getting around You won't need to use the local buses for getting around most of the main sights which are mainly located in the old quarter. To get to the (slightly) less crowded beaches along the coast, take bus No 1 or 9 from the Rambla Vella.

Orientation Tarragona is easy to negotiate on foot: right on top of the hill is the old quarter with the cathedral, where most of the sights are concentrated. The old quarter is divided from the newer extension which spreads downhill by the parallel avenues of the Rambla Vella and the Rambla Nova, two long avenues where many of the shops are located.

Tourist information The tourist office is near the cathedral ① Carrer Major 39, T977 245 064.

Background

The Romans established a military base here at the end of the third century BC which played an important role in the conquest of the Iberian peninsula. They liked it so much that they decided to make Tarraco the capital of Hispania Citerior, and built temples, baths, an amphitheatre, a circus and a forum, bequeathing a spectacular series of Roman monuments which are among the most extensive in Spain and were declared a UNESCO World Heritage Site. St Paul is said to have preached here and it became an important bishopric under the Visigoths in the fifth century AD. Like most of Catalunya, its fortunes

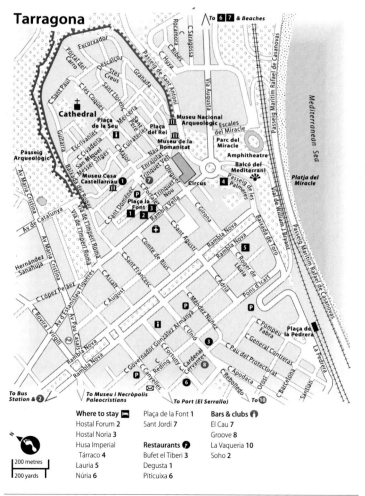

Tarragona

Mediterranean Sea

To 6 7 & Beaches

Cathedral

Museu Nacional Arqueologic

Plaça del Rei

Museu de la Romanitat

Parc del Miracle

Amphitheatre

Balcó del Mediterrani

Platja del Miracle

Passeig Arqueologic

Museu Casa Castellarnau

Circus

Plaça la Font

Rambla Vella

Rambla Nova

To Bus Station &

To Museu i Necròpolis Paleocristians

To Port (El Serrallo)

To

200 metres
200 yards

Where to stay 🛏	Plaça de la Font 1	Bars & clubs 🍸
Hostal Forum 2	Sant Jordi 7	El Cau 7
Hostal Noria 3		Groove 8
Husa Imperial Tárraco 4	**Restaurants 🍴**	La Vaqueria 10
Lauria 5	Bufet el Tiberi 3	Soho 2
Núria 6	Degusta 1	
	Piticuixa 6	

peaked in the middle ages, but it suffered once power was transferred from Catalunya to Castille and it became a backwater. Severely repressed after the Catalan rebellion of 1640, and then sacked by the French in 1811, the city sank into decline. That all changed in the 20th century, thanks to the growth of the wine and tourist industries, and 21st-century Tarragona is now one of Catalunya's most dynamic and prosperous cities.

Places in Tarragona
Cathedral and the Old City ① *Plaça de la Seu, T977 238 685, 17 Mar-4 Nov 1000-1900, Jun to 16 Nov Mon-Sat 1000-1900, 5 Nov-16 Mar Mon-Sat 1000-1400, closed Sun and religious holidays, €4, concessions €2.* At the heart of the old city stands the austerely beautiful Cathedral. Construction began at the end of the 12th century and was completed in 1331, and the cathedral is a perfect example of the transition from Romanesque to Gothic. A wide staircase sweeps up to the main façade with an imposing Romanesque portal surrounded by 13th-century sculptures of the Virgin and the Apostles surmounted by a vast rose window. The cloister has delicately carved pinkish columns featuring a world of fabulous creatures, including one which depicts 'La Processó de las Rates' (Procession of the Rats) – the story of the clever cat who outwitted the mice by playing dead and leaps up from his own funeral to gobble them up (get a custodian to point it out). Hidden in the medieval gloom of the church is a magnificent 15th-century alabaster altarpiece by Pere Joan, and the entrance ticket includes a visit to the small Museu Diocesano, with a dusty collection of ecclesiastical treasures (including a reliquary containing St John the Baptist's finger) and a 15th-century tapestry of medieval life, *La Bona Vida*.

Casa Castellarnan ① *C/Cavallers 14, T977 242 752, Tue-Sun 1000-1500, admission €3.15.* The main street of the old city, the Carrer Major, heads down from the cathedral; off to the right is the Carrer de Cavallers where sounds of pianos, opera singing and trumpets from the Conservatory of Music float across it. This was the city's most aristocratic address during the medieval period. A former mansion which dates back to the early 15th century has been beautifully refurbished to hold the Museu Casa Castellarnau with a graceful Gothic courtyard and rather patchy exhibits outlining the city's history. The second floor has retained its opulent 18th-century fittings, with vast chandeliers dripping from frescoed ceilings, and preserves the interior of a pretty 18th-century pharmacy, moved here when the original premises just down the street collapsed.

Les Muralles ① *Av Catalunya s/n, T977 242 220, Oct-May Tue-Sat 1000-1330, 1630-1830, Sun 1000-1500, Jun-Sep Tue-Sat 1000-2100, Sun 1000-1500, €3.15.* The old Roman walls which still ring much of the old city have been converted into an attractive walkway known as the Passeig Arqueològic which winds between the Roman walls and a stretch of 18th-century walls built by the British during the War of the Spanish Succession. There are stunning views out across the plains and around to the sea.

Museu Nacional Arqueològic ① *Plaça del Rei 5, T977 236 209, Jun-Sep Tue-Sat 0930-2030, Sun and holidays 1000-1400, Oct-Mar Tue-Sat 1000-1330, 1600-1900, €2.40, concessions €1.20.* On the edge of the old town, just off the Plaça del Rei, the huge, airy Museu Nacional Arqueològic holds an excellent collection of artefacts gathered from the archaeological sites which provide a vivid picture of life in Imperial Tarraco.

Circ Romà ⓘ *Rambla Vell, www.museutgn.com, Apr-Sep Tue-Sat 0900-2100, Sun 0900-1500, Oct-Mar 0900-1900, Sun 1000-1500, admission €3.15.* The Circus was largely used for chariot racing, which was enormously popular. Despite its age – it was constructed in the 1st century AD – it's incredibly well preserved.

Amphitheatre ⓘ *Parc del Miracle, T977 242 579, Jun-Sep Tue-Sat 1000-2000, Sun 1000- 1400, Oct-May Tue-Sat 1000-1300 and 1600-1700, Sun 1000-1400, €1.87.* The old city lies north of the Rambla Vell, a handsome promenade which culminates in the famous **Balcó del Mediterrani (Balcony of the Mediterranean)**, a mirador with beautiful views over the amphitheatre, the town's main beach (the Platja del Miracle) and out to sea. Take the path below the Balcó del Mediterrani to reach the ancient Amphitheatre, where gladiators and wild animals fought to the death. Three Christian martyrs were tortured to death here in AD 259, and a basilica was erected to them in the sixth century on the site of their martyrdom. The lower town holds the busy modern extension to the city, full of shops and restaurants.

Museu i Necròpolis Paleocristians ⓘ *Av Ramón y Cajal 80, T977 211 175, open 0930-1330, 1500-1730 (Jun-Sep until 2000), Sun 1000-1400.* Right out on the edge of town, there's another fascinating collection of Roman remains at this museum. Roman law forbade burials within the city walls, and the necropolis, still scattered with amphorae, plinths and inscribed tablets, was established well outside the ancient city. It was used for pagan and Christian burials, and the museum currently houses an extensive collection of sarcophagi and glimmering mosaics gathered from the site.

Port and Tarragona's beaches A good 20-minute walk from the old city is Tarragona's port, **El Serrallo**, a busy harbour crammed with fishing boats and densely packed with seafood restaurants. They are all good, and crowded at weekends, but it's worth heading into the streets behind the seafront to get a better deal. The **Platja de Miracle**, the city's main beach, falls short of its fancy name: it's a perfectly decent city beach but it can get very crowded. There are better, quieter beaches north of the city – such as Arrabassada – which you can reach by taking bus No 1 or 9 from the Rambla Vella, about 4 km from the centre, or Sabinosa (another 1 km beyond Arrabassada), which is for nudists at its northern end.

Around Tarragona
There are plenty more Roman ruins scattered across the plains around Tarragona, including the spectacular aqueduct, better known as the **Pont de les Ferreres (Devil's Bridge)**, which brought water to the Roman city all the way from the Río Gayo, about 32 km away. The aqueduct is about 10 minutes outside the city; take bus number 5 from Avenida Prat de la Riba. West of the city at **Centcelles** near the small town of Constantí, is the most important Paleo-Christian monument in Spain, a resplendent Roman villa which, during the fourth century, was converted into a **basilica** ⓘ *T977 523 374, Jun-Sep Tue-Sun 1000-1330 and 1600-1930, Sun 1000-1400, Oct-May Tue-Sun 1000-1330 and 1500-1730, Sun 1000-1400, €1.80.*

Other Roman sights are scattered along the coast along the ancient Vía Augusta but they are pretty much impossible to reach without your own transport; about 6 km northeast is the **Torre dels Escipions**, a massive 10-m-high funerary monument probably dedicated to the Scipio brothers who died in battle against the Carthaginians, and 2 km further north is the **Pedrera del Mèdol**, a Roman stone quarry with an impressive 'needle'. Near the town of Altafulla (see below), the triumphal **Arc de Berá** stands astride the ancient road, in memory of some long-forgotten battle.

Costa Daurada → *For listings, see pages 95-100.*

The 'Golden Coast' has been popular with visitors since the Romans ruled half of the Iberian peninsula from their base at Tarragona. It hasn't been developed quite as intensively as parts of the Costa Brava, but nor is it as striking, although the broad, sandy beaches still attract millions of families every summer.

Resorts north of Tarragona

The northernmost resorts of the Costa Daurada – **Cunit**, **Calafell** and **Torredembarra** – are low-key collections of seaside villas with decent beaches but little else. Lively **Altafulla** has a picturesque walled old quarter tucked back from the sea which is dominated by a sturdy castle, spectacularly floodlit at night, and a handsome 17th-century church. There are more good, if busy, beaches along the modern seafront, and plenty of bars and restaurants. Nearby **Tamarit** has another castle out on a small promontory jutting into the sea. On the outskirts of Altafulla at **Els Munts**, a magnificent **Roman villa** ① *Barri Marítim d'Altafulla, T977 562 806 Jun-Sep Tue-Sun 1000-1330 and 1600-2000, Sun 1000-1400, Oct-May Tue-Sun 1000-1330 and 1500-1730, Sun 1000-1400, €1.80, concessions €1.35*, has been discovered; it probably belonged to a prominent official from Roman Tarraco who spared no expense on the fine mosaics and elegant decoration.

Salou and around

Just southeast of Tarragona, **Salou** is the Costa Daurada's main resort, a cheerful, neon-lit mini-Benidorm with high-rise developments, fish and chip shops and cafés advertising 'tea just like your mum makes'. Between Salou and Tarragona is **PortAventura** ① *T902 202 220, www.portaventura.es, opening hours vary (check the website); admission adults €45, juniors €39; 2 days €56/46; 3 days €69/56*, a massive theme park with heart-stopping rollercoasters, such as the Shambhala (the tallest in Europe), log flumes and a great virtual underwater ride called the Sea Odyssey.

Cambrils, just down the coast from Salou, is smaller and less hectic. It's an unassuming resort town set back from a large harbour which still has a working port and an excellent selection of seafood restaurants. Cambrils has an excellent gastronomic reputation. The award-winning **Can Bosch**, is one of the finest restaurants in Catalunya, see Restaurants, page 98.

If you want a break from the beach, spend a day in **Reus**, which is just a couple of miles inland and stuffed with Modernista mansions and plane-shaded squares. It was the birthplace of Antoni Gaudí, but he never designed any buildings for his home town. Many of the finest houses in Reus were designed by Domènech i Montaner – who built the Palau de la Música in Barcelona, see page 46 – including the resplendent Casa Navàs (a private house, admission by guided tour only, see below) which overlooks the arcaded Plaça del Mercadal. The tourist office has a useful map marked with all the Modernista highlights, and offers guided tours around the city which are often the only way to see the interiors. Reus makes a less hectic base than the coastal resorts.

Costa Daurada is easy to get to by public transport. There's a regular local train service between Barcelona, Tarragona and all the other resorts: one way €7 (regional, one hour 18 minutes) or €21 (high-speed, 52 minutes). Do not take the AVE to Tarragona; the train station is 11 km from the city centre.

Parc Natural del Delta de l'Ebre

At the southernmost tip of Catalunya are the wide, flat marshlands of the Delta de l'Ebre, where the huge River Ebre finally meets the sea. The area has been designated a natural park in order to protect the 300 species of bird which have made these wetlands their home, including flamingoes, herons, marsh harriers and a wide variety of ducks. There's a spellbinding if harsh beauty in the immense expanse of wetlands, the vast sky, and the wild beaches scattered with driftwood, and even in the height of summer you are almost guaranteed to find yourself alone. One of the best ways to see it is to rent a bike, but it's important to stick to the marked trails – the birds won't return to their nests if they are disturbed. The trails and birdwatching hides are marked out on a map available from the park information office. Boat-trips down the river and out to sea are offered from Amposta and Deltelebre. Amposta, the largest town in the region, is also the least attractive but it's a hub for local bus routes: quiet little Deltelebre or seaside Sant Carles de la Ràpita make more attractive bases. There's a park information office and a small **eco-museum** ① *C/Dr Martí Buera 20, Deltelebre, T977 489 679*. **Tourist information office** ① *C/Sant Isidre 128, T977 744 624*.

Up the Río Ebre

Tortosa
Just inland, the fortified city of Tortosa straddles the River Ebre, surrounded by lush farmland. It's southern Catalunya's largest town and main transport hub. It was in the front line for several months during the Civil War, until the Republicans were ousted in a bloody battle that cost 35,000 lives and is commemorated by a monument by the river. War took its toll and Tortosa's medieval streets suffered extensive damage. Among the survivors are the Gothic cathedral, built on the site of a mosque, which has a delightful cloister, and a rich collection of Modernista townhouses which are sprinkled throughout Tortosa's Eixample and are marked on the tourist office map. The most spectacular sight is the lofty Arab fortress, La Zuda, which bristles from the highest point in the town; it's now a luxurious parador, but you can still stroll around the ancient walls for wonderful views across the plains.

Miravet
There's another castle upriver at Miravet; built by the Arabs, it was given to the knights of the Templar by Ramon Berenguer IV in 1153 after the reconquest of Catalunya. The fortress is balanced heartstoppingly on a cliff above the Río Ebro, reached by a steep, narrow path. It's a quiet, even ghostly, spot, not least in the Patio de la Sang (Patio of Blood) where the last Templars of Miravet were beheaded in 1308. A winding staircase leads to the top of the tower for far-reaching views along the river and down to the pretty village beneath. An old-fashioned ferry – powered only by the river's current – takes cars and passengers across the water.

Cistercian Triangle → *For listings, see pages 95-100.*

Lost in the barely visited expanses of southern Catalunya, the three medieval monasteries of the Cistercian Triangle offer a tranquil alternative to the giddy social life of the coastal resorts. The most important is Poblet, which inspired Gaudí, and is surrounded by beautiful forest with some great walking trails. Santes Creus and humble Vallbona de las Monges are both close to quietly charming villages which rarely see visitors.

Background

The Monestir de Santa María de Poblet was founded in 1151 by Ramon Berenguer III in gratitude for the success of his campaign to rid Catalunya of the Moorish invaders. Poblet and its sister monasteries Santa Creus and Vallbona de las Monges became known as 'the Cistercian Triangle', imposing reminders of the power of Christianity and the sovereign. From the 16th century, their influence waned and the final blow was struck in 1835, when the Mendizabel laws were enacted, depriving the Church of vast swathes of its land and properties. All three suffered attacks, but Poblet, the first and most important of the three, was suspected of harbouring Carlist sympathisers, and an angry mob rampaged through its halls, destroying everything they could find and torching its celebrated library. The ruins mouldered for decades, but became a haunting symbol of an empire lost to the romantic innocents of the late 19th century. Gaudí was one of many who dreamed of its reconstruction, which was finally carried out after the Civil War.

ReialMonestir de Santa María de Poblet and around

ⓘ *T977 870 089, www.larutadelcister.info, Tue-Sun 1000-1240 and 1500-1725, until 1755 in summer, €7, concessions €4, a combined ticket to all 3 monasteries of the Cistercian triangle is available for €9, entrance by guided tour only.*

The monastery is spectacularly set in a tranquil, golden valley, a vast complex sprawling behind glowering battlements and fortifications. The main entrance into the Monastery is through the Porta Dorata (Golden Gate) where kings would dismount to kneel and kiss the crucifix proffered by the Abbot, and above it is the sumptuous 14th-century Gothic palace. It was a favourite retreat and resting place of a long line of count-kings, many of whom were buried here; Alfonso II was the first, as early as 1196, but the monastery was officially declared a Royal Pantheon in the 14th century. A community of monks now live here, and one of them will guide you around the monastery's stirring collection of beautifully renovated buildings.

At the heart of the complex is the peaceful Romanesque cloister, flanked with delicate arcades and the stone tombs of long-forgotten monks, and containing an octagonal pavilion with a huge stone fountain. Leading off the cloister is an echoing vaulted Gothic chapter house with the tombs of the monastery's abbots laid into the stone-flagged floor, the library with its brick parabolic arches which must have inspired Gaudí, an enormous wine cellar, the old kitchens lined with copper pots and pans, and the austere wood-panelled refectory. Steps lead up to the vast dormitory, with a screen behind which the present-day monks have their humble cells, and you can look down over the cloister from the upper gallery. The glorious main church is austerely unadorned in the Cistercian tradition apart from a tremendous Renaissance alabaster retable which fills the apse behind the main altar. But the prize here is the collection of royal tombs exquisitely wrought in alabaster which flank the altar; they were desecrated by the rampaging mob in 1835, but Frederic Marés, the eccentric sculptor and obsessive collector, see page 39, was responsible for their reconstruction in 1850.

Behind the monastery, Poblet forest stretches up to the peaks of the Prades mountains, a craggy, wild landscape where eagles wheel overhead. There are some beautiful walking trails, including a scenic route up to the Pic de l'Àliga (1052 m), which begins and ends in the tranquil village of Poblet (information on the trails from Poblet tourist office, by the monastery gates). The delightful town of L'Espluga de Francolí makes a good base for walkers and vists to the monastery. There are **tourist offices** ① *L'Espluga de Francolí, Torres Jordí 16, T977 871 220, and Poblet monastery, Passeig Abat Conill 9, T977 871 247.*

Montblanc

Montblanc, about 5 km from Poblet, is an enchanting medieval town completely encircled by turreted walls which time seems to have passed by. Montblanc prospered during the Middle Ages, when it had a substantial Jewish community who lived in the tangle of streets between the grand Gothic **Església de Santa Maria** and the humble little Romanesque **Església de Sant Miquel** lower down the hill. The best time to come is during the **Setmana Medieval**, which kicks off on the feast day of Sant Jordí (23 April) and is a week-long festival of medieval song and dance. Plaça Major is always busy, particularly during the evening *passeig*, when families gather at the lively cafés spilling out on to the square. **Museu Frederic Marès** ① *Jun-Sep Tue-Sat 1000-1400 and 1600-2000, Sun 1000-1400, Oct-May, Sat and Sun only, free,* holds a typically eccentric selection of painting and sculpture from the 13th to the 19th centuries, including some beautiful carved polychrome statues from the 14th century. **Tourist information** ① *Antiga Església de Sant Francesc s/n, T977 861 733.*

Monestir de Santa Maria de Vallbona, Vallbona de les Monges

① *T973 330 266, Tue-Fri 1030-1330, 1600-1845, 1730 in winter, Sat and Sun 1200-1330.*
Almost 30 km north of Poblet, the humblest of the three Cistercian monasteries is the Monestir de Vallbona de les Monges, which has housed a community of nuns for eight centuries. Catalan queens made it a place of retreat and some, including Violant of Hungary, wife of Jaume I, are buried here. There's a delightful Romanesque cloister with prettily carved capitals covered in vines and flowers and the church is a fine example of the Transitional style between Romanesque and Gothic. It was built between the 13th and 14th centuries, and is quiet, contemplative and almost unadorned but for Violant's tomb and a stone Virgin. You will need your own transport. The **tourist office** ① *Passeig Montesquin s/n, T973 330 567.*

Monestir de Santes Creus, Aignamurcia

① *T977 638 329, Oct-May 1000-1730, Jun-Sep 1000-1900, closed Mon, €4.50, concessions €3, free entry on Tue.*
Like Poblet, the monastery of Santes Creus has had a colourful history; the favourite of many of the Catalan count-kings, both Pedro the Great and Jaume II chose to be buried in its magnificent church. After 1835, the monks were ousted and the monastery's buildings were sacked, only to suffer further ignomiy when the Tarragon prison was shifted here

for fear of the plague in 1870, finishing off the job begun in 1835. The honey-coloured village grew up when locals moved into the abandoned monks' residences in the early 19th century, and is surrounded by ancient fortified walls. Now part of the Museu d'Història de Catalunya (see page 59), visits to the monastery begin with an audio-visual presentation which gives a 3D glimpse into the life of a medieval monk, after which visitors can wander around the semi-ruined complex. The highlight is the lacy Gothic cloister with its tracery and carved capitals, which was created by the English master mason Reinard de Fonoll, and contains an elaborate Gothic stone fountain. There's a small **tourist office** ① *Santes Creus in the Plaça Sant Bernat s/n, T977 638 141*.

Valls
The nearest town of any size to Santes Creus, Valls doesn't look much on the outskirts but contains a neat little medieval hub, with crooked streets and a fine old Gothic church. It's famous for two things, both close to the Catalan heart; the daring of its *castellers* (it has the best regarded team of human castle builders in Catalunya, Els Xiquets de Valls – see page 99) and the tastiness of its *calçots*. The *castellers* are commemorated with a huge statue in the centre of town which shows a complicated human tower presided over by the *enxaneta*, the nimblest, littlest kid who waves from the top. *Calçots* are a kind of onion, a cross between a shallot and a spring onion, which are roasted on a charcoal grill and served with a nutty romesco sauce. They are traditionally accompanied by lamb cutlets, and are a favourite springtime dish when every bar and restaurant hangs out a sign advertising the '*calçotada*'. The **tourist office** ① *C/de la Cort 61, T977 612 530, www.ajvalls.org*.

South of Barcelona listings

For Where to stay and Restaurant price codes and other relevant information, see pages 11-20.

🛏 Where to stay

Sitges *p82*
Sitges plenty of good accommodation options oozing character. That said, there never seem to be enough rooms to go round in the high season or over Carnaval, so book well in advance. Sitges also gets very crowded in Jul and Aug, when finding accommodation is virtually impossible.

€€ Hotel Romàntic, C/Sant Isidre 33, T938 948 375. Set in a graceful 19th-century mansion with a garden terrace, this is one of the most popular hotels in Sitges, particularly with gay visitors, and gets booked up very quickly.

€€ La Pinta, Passeig de la Ribera 52, T938 940 999. Run by same owners of **Santa Maria**, more modern.

€€ Santa Maria, Passeig de la Ribera 52, T938 940 999. Bright, modern rooms in a 19th-century mansion right on the seafront; there are 2 good, busy seafood restaurants downstairs with a pavement terrace.

€ El Xalet, Isla de Cuba 33-35, T938 110 070. Delightful quirky hotel set in a Modernista villa, with a garden and pool. Rooms are surprisingly simple, but always booked up well in advance.

Camping
There are a few campsites in Sitges. **El Garrofer**, T938 941 780, which has shady sites off the main road into Sitges. **Camping Sitges**, T938 941 080, www.campingsitges.com.

Vilanova i la Geltrú *p84*
€€€-€€ César, C/Isaac Perel 4-8, T938 151 125, www.hotelcesar.net. Best place to stay, in a quiet area close to the beach. It's good value most of the year, but prices leap a couple of categories in Jul and Aug.

€€-€ Hotel Ricard, Passeig Maritim 88, T938 157 100. A simpler choice close to the beach. It's cheap unless you come in Jul and Aug.

Camping
There are 2 campsites in Vilanova i la Geltrú: Raco de Mar, T938155245, www.campingel racodemar.com. The smaller and humbler of the 2.
Vilanova Park, T938 933 402, www.vilanova park.com. Large, well equipped and right on the beach. Also rents bungalows.

The Wine Route *p84*
€€ Sol i Vi, Ctra San Sadurni, and Vilafranca Km 4, T938 993 204. This is the best place to stay. Set in a beautifully converted stone farmhouse, 4 km outside Sadurni in Lavern, it has a pool and friendly owners who can organize tours to the surrounding vineyards.

Tarragona *p86, map p87*
€€€€ Husa Imperial Tárraco, Paseo de las Palmeras 43000, T977 233 040, www.hotel husaimperialtarraco.com. Magnificent panoramic views from the 'balcony of the Mediterranean' are the principal attraction of this large, slightly dated hotel with pool, tennis, and restaurant.

€€ Hotel Núria, T977235011, F977244136. A large modern hotel next to the Arabassada beach, with a café downstairs. It's also a 5-min bus journey (No 1 or No 9) to the city.

€€ Hotel Plaça de la Font, Plaça de la Font 26, T977 240 882, www.hotelpdelafont.com. Sdimple hotel on a charming square in the historic quarter – get a room with a balcony overlooking the square if you can.

€€ Hotel Sant Jordi, Via Augusta 185, T977207515, www.hotelsantjordi.info. One of several large, modern hotels lining the busy N-340, this one offers spacious rooms with large terraces and is just a short walk

from the Sabinosa beach, popular with Tarragona's trendy crowd. It's a 5-min bus journey (take the No 1 or the 9) into the city.
€€ Lauria, Rambla Nova 20, T977236712, www.dormicumhotels.com/en/hote-lauria. Accommodating staff, and a central location close to all the sights of the old city, plus a pool and café.
€ Hostal Forum, Plaça La Font 37, T977 211 333. On the corner of the delightful Plaça la Font, the Forum has basic en suite rooms at a bargain price.
€ Hostal Noria, Plaça La Font 53, T977238717. Set in a narrow, creaky house overlooking one of the prettiest squares in old Tarragona, this has small, but attractive, rooms and a busy (and noisy) bar downstairs. Upper floors are quietest.

Camping
There are plenty of campsites along this coast.
Caledonioa, Ctra N-340, Km 1172, T977 650 098. A good option for families, close to great beaches (800 m) and with pool.
Torre de la Mora, Ctra N-340, Km 1171, T977 651 277, www.torredelamar.com. Nerar the sea, but far enough away from the coastal train line to guarantee a good night's kip.

Costa Daurada *p90*
€€ Hotel Gaudí, C/ Arrabal Robuster 49, Reus, T977 345 545. A decent modern option in the city centre.
€ Hostal Santa Teresa, C/Santa Teresa 1, Reus, T619 245 642, www.hostalsanta teresa.com. A simple, family-run *pensión* on a little pedestrian street.

Parc Natural del Delta de l'Ebre *p91*
€€ Delta Hotel, Av del Canal, Camino del Illeta s/n, T977 480 046, www.ddeltahotel.es. A traditional local house, set in wilderness in the middle of the natural park, which can organize different excursions and rent out bikes. It's also got one of the best restaurants, mid-range priced, in the area.

€€ Hotel Mas Prades, Ctra T-340 Km 8, Deltebre, T977 059 084, www.hotelmasde prades.com. A contemporary hotel with stylish rooms, a stunning location amid the rice fields of the Ebro Delta, and an excellent restaurant.
€€ Hotel Rull, Av del Canal, T977 487 728, right by the park information office, this new hotel offers large, comfortable rooms and a restaurant.
€€ Juanito Platja, Passeig Marítim s/n, Sant Carles de la Ràpita, T977 740 462. A welcoming, low-key resort hotel close to the beach.
€€ Masia Tinet, Barri Lepanto 13, Deltebre, T977 489 389, www.masiatinet.com. An eco-friendly hotel in a restored farmhouse, with just a handful of pretty rooms and a good restaurant.
€ Hostal La Panavera, Plaça del Forn 25, El Perelló, T977 490 318. A charming option in a delightful little village about a 10-min drive from the beaches, with rustically decorated rooms.

Camping
There are 2 official campsites in the Delta de l'Ebre.
L'Aube, Urbanització Riumar, T977 267 066, **Riumar**, Urbanització Riumar, T977 267 680, slightly more expensive and better equipped than **L'Aube**, has a launderette and rents bungalows. Both have pools.

Up the Río Ebre *p91*
€€€ Parador de Tortosa, Castillo de la Zuda, Tortosa, T977 444 450, www. parador.es. The huge 10th-century fortress is now a beautifully appointed parador with gardens, a pool and a good, but expensive, restaurant (open to non-residents).

Cistercian Triangle *p92*
€€ Del Senglar, Plaça Montserrat Canals, L'Espluga de Francolí, T977 870 121, www.hostaldelsenglar.com. A real charmer,

with old wooden beams and a garden with a pool. The restaurant is excellent, and they hold barbecues in summer.

€€ Hostal Grau, C/Pere III, Monestir de Santes Creus, T977 638 311, www.hostel-grau.com. Just outside the old walls. Welcoming and traditional. Also has a restaurant.

€€ Masia del Cadet, Les Masies de Poblet, T977 870 869, www.masiadelcadet.com. A beautifully renovated 15th-century farmhouse in a hamlet outside Poblet, with a fine, mid-range, restaurant and welcoming owners. There's a small, cheap family-run restaurant with a terrace, the **Hostal Fonoll**, right opposite the monastery entrance, T977 870 333, which offers a good *menú del día* at less than €10.

€ Fonda dels Àngels, Plaça Àngels, Montblanc, T977860173. An attractive little inn in the heart of the town, with a reasonably priced restaurant.

€ La Masoveria del Bosc, Plaça de l'Estació, Valls, T977 6000 941, www.lamasoveriadel bosc.com. Attractive rooms in an old farm-house; also has self-catering apartments.

❷ Restaurants

Costa Garraf *p82*
€€ Las Botas, Av Constitución 326, Castelldefels, T936 651 824. A good, traditional roadside restaurant serving typical Catalan dishes. Just outside town.

€€ Xiriniguito del Garraf, Platja de Garraf s/n, Garraf, T936 320 016. A classic, beachside restaurant overlooking a very pretty beach with fresh fish and other local dishes. Cheaper dishes too. Recommended.

Sitges *p82*
If you've got the money, there's plenty to choose from in Sitges, including good seafood restaurants and lots of places to pose. Unfortunately, cheaper places are few and far between.

€€€ Maricel, Passeig de la Ribera 6, T938 942 054, www.maricel.es. Probably the best seafood restaurant in town; right on the beachfront with a pale, elegant dining room full of floral prints and oil paintings. Closed Tue and second two weeks in Nov.

€€ El Celler Vell, C/Sant Bonaventura 21, T938 111 961, www.elcellervell.com. Good Catalan food and a laid-back atmosphere. The *menú del día* is good value at less than €15.

€€ El Velero, Passeig de la Ribera 38, T938 942 051. Another classic seafood restaurant on the main drag, with a loyal, local clientele and an excellent *menú degustación* (tasting menu) for €23.

€€ Bon Estar, C/ Parellades 63, T938 943 493. This chic little eaterie offers a great lunch deal for €10 and a set evening menu for €15. A fantastic bargain in pricey Sitges.

Vilanova i la Geltrú
€€ La Fitorra, C/Isaac Peral 4, T938151125, is a pretty restaurant serving big portions of fine fresh fish and tasty paella.

The Wine Route *p84*
€€ Cal Ton, C/Casal 8, T938 903 741. You can try delicious, contemporary Catalan cuisine accompanied by an extensive wine list.

€€ El Cairat, C/Nou 3, Falset, T977 830 481. You can enjoy more classic, moderately priced, Catalan cooking (including home-made pasta) a welcoming spot which uses the freshest local produce.

€ Casa Joan, Plaça Estació 8, Vilafranca del Penedès, T938 903 171. Exquisite, modern Catalan dishes and great regional wines.

€ El Pigot de Arbolí, C/Trinquet 7, Arbolí, T977 816 063. Close to Siurana, this is a friendly and cheap restaurant. The staff are happy to recommend dishes.

Tarragona *p86, map p87*
€€ Degusta, C/Cavallers 6, T977 220 652. Chic, fashionable restaurant in a Modernista townhouse with an airy interior, and tasty contemporary cuisine. Great-value set lunch for €15.

€€ La Cuineta, Baixada del Patriarca, T977 226 101. Tasty Mediterranean dishes in this delightful spot in Tarragona's historic quarter.

€€ Piticuixa, C/Cardenal Cervantes 14, T977 230 649. A traditional, comfortable eaterie, good for grilled meats and traditional dishes, such as *cargols a la llanna* (oven-baked snails).

€ Bufet el Tiberi, C/Martí d'Ardenya 5, T977 235 403, www.eltiberi.com. Stuff yourself Roman style for around €12.

Costa Daurada *p90*

€€€ Can Bosch, Rambla Jaume I, Cambrils, T977 360 019. An excellent seafood restaurant with a fine reputation, serving a range of local delicacies including *arròs negre*: try the fabulous *carpaccio de gambes* if it's on the menu.

Parc Natural del Delta de l'Ebre *p91*

Plenty of restaurants offer rice dishes made with rice grown in the Delta.

€€ Casa Ramón Marines, C/Arsenal 16, Sant Carles de la Ràpita, T977 742 358. Family run, this has been going since 1948 and serves excellent seafood. Also has rooms.

Up the Río Ebre *p91*

See also Where to stay.

€€ Berenguer IV, C/Cervantes 23, Tortosa, T977 249 580. A reasonable option in the town centre.

Cistercian Triangle *p92*

See also Where to stay.

€€ El Molí de Mallol, Muralla Santa Anna 2, near Montblanc, T977 860 591. One of the best places to eat, a converted watermill clinging to the ancient walls serving delicious, traditional dishes.

€€ Fonda Cal Blasi, C/Alenyà, T977 861 336, www.fondacalblasi.com. Charming inn and restaurant in a pretty 19th-century building.

€€ Masia Bou, Ctra Lleida km 21.5, Valls, T977 600 427. Known as the 'Palace of Calçotadas', is the best place to try Valls' speciality.

🎵 Bars and clubs

Sitges *p82*

You'll find dozens of bars and clubs on and around the **C/ Marqués de Montroig** and the **C/ 1er de Maig**, and many have small summer terraces. One of the biggest and best known clubs in Sitges is **Atlantida**, a gay mecca at the southern end of the beach.

In the quieter streets near the church, you'll find less raucous bars with big terraces to kick back and relax. Most of the gay bars are concentrated on and around the Carrer Sant Bonaventura. For the best gay bars and restaurants, pick up the gay map of Sitges/ Barcelona from almost any bar in town.

Vilanova i la Geltrú *p84*

While Sitges is the main focus for nightlife on this strip of coast, there's still plenty of action on the Passeig Marítim and around.

Tarragona *p86, map p87*

Tarragona is always pretty buzzy, with plenty going on across the city.

In the old town, there's **El Cau**, C/ Trinquet Vell 2, www.elcau.net, with alternative music and live bands at weekends; **Groove**, C/Cervantes 4, in the new part of town, showcases a wide range of music, from indie to funk, with DJs on Fri nights.

There are dozens of clubs around the port, including **Soho**, Port Esportin, serving well-priced cocktails, and **La Vaqueria**, C/ Rebolledo 11, which has live jazz, blues, rock and pop as well as art exhibitions and theatre performances.

Giants, dragons and castles in the air

After years of repression during the Franco era, Catalunya is celebrating its traditional festivals with ever-greater verve and exuberance, resuscitating centuries-old customs and traditions in an outpouring of national pride and optimism. These are some of the most popular traditions, which you'll almost certainly see at any village 'festa'.

Correfoc

'Fire-running' goes back hundreds, if not thousands, of years. Parading drummers beat a pulse-quickening march through the streets, heralding the arrival of *dracs* (dragons), surrounded by leaping *demonis* (demons) setting off fireworks. Youths step out from the crowd to prevent the dragons passing, standing or kneeling in their path and getting showered with sparks as they shout ¡No pasaran¡ (You will not pass). Fire-running can be dangerous, and the tightly packed mass of the crowd means escape isn't easy – wear protective, cotton clothing if you want to join in.

Gegants and Capsgrossos

The *gegants* (giants) first appeared at Catalan festivals in the Middle Ages. They are enormous figures made of wood and papier-mâché who lumber along in the festival parades. The *capsgrossos* (fatheads) are squat leering versions, who accompany the giants on the mischievous little figures, some of the modern ones bear the faces of famous celebrities and politicians.

Castellers

The art of building human towers dates back to the 1700s, and has undergone a major revival in recent years. It's a perfect example of the civic pride which marks the Catalans, each person having an important part to play, and the whole depending on the co-operation and steadiness of each individual. The bottom layer with its central sturdy knot of people known as the pine cone or *pinya* looks like a rugby scrum, upon which, gradually, carefully, the layers are built up. An *aixedor* (child) provides the support for an *anxenata* (an even smaller child) who nimbly scampers to the top and grins like a gargoyle, waving to the crowd below.

Sardana

The grave, stately circle dance of the Catalans is a world away from the flamboyance of Andalucían flamenco. It's an ancient folkloric tradition which can be seen most weekends in towns and villages, where you will probably be encouraged to join in. But beware – it's not as easy as it looks. The cobla (band) strike up, and a knot of people, sometimes as few as four, will link hands and circle with slow sedate steps, interspersed with longer, rising ones. The circles get bigger and bigger as more and more people join in. True aficionados will wear espadrilles tied with coloured ribbons.

⚙ Festivals

Sitges *p82*
There is something going on in Sitges almost every month, and the best time to visit is when a fiesta is in full swing.

Feb/Mar Carnestoltes (Carnival), among the biggest and wildest celebrations in Spain, largely thanks to the gay community who have taken the event into their own hands.
Jun The streets are carpeted with flowers for **Corpus Christi**.

End Aug The town's **Festa Major** dedicated to Sant Bartomeu, is a riot of traditional parades with Giants, Fatheads and Dragons, see box, page 99.

Tarragona *p86, map p87*
Mid-Jun to mid-Aug Festival d'Estiu (FET), a huge, city-wide performance arts festival featuring theatre, dance, cinema and music events, many of which are held outdoors and for free. Pick up a brochure from the tourist office.
End Sep Festa de Santa Tecla, held for 10 days, with parades featuring Catalan *gegants*, and popular dance and music.

⛰ What to do

Parc Natural del Delta de l'Ebre *p91*
Carlos Cid Centre Hípic, Amposta, T649 509 392, www.hipicadomasclasica.com. This riding school; also offers excursions on horseback around the Ebro Delta.
Creuers Delta de l'Ebre, T977 481 128. For information on boat tours.

⊘ Transport

Costa Garraf *p82*
There are regular local trains from **Estació-Sants** down the coast south of Barcelona but not all of them stop at **Castelldefels** and **Garraf**. For the beaches at Castelldefels, get off at Castelldefels-Platja just after the town stop.

Sitges *p82*
Sitges is on the main coastal train line between **Murcia**, **Valencia** and **Barcelona**, although not all the high-speed trains stop here. There are regular regional trains between Barcelona-Sants and Tarragona. There are regular daily bus services (T939 937 511) to Barcelona, but the train is more reliable and the views are fantastic.

The Wine Route *p84*
There are regular local trains from Barcelona-Sants to **Vilafranca de Penedès** and **Sant Sadurní d'Anoia**. Many of the *bodegas* are scattered outside the main towns, and you'll need your own transport as few are on bus routes. There are twice-daily buses between Reus and Prades, stopping at some villages on the way. The tourist offices have details of local bus routes.

Tarragona *p86, map p87*
Tarragona is linked by bus to most major Spanish cities, including **Barcelona**, **Madrid**, **Seville**, **Alicante** and **Murcia**, and there are services inland to **Lleida**, **Reus** and **Poblet**.
   There are very frequent local and express trains from **Barcelona-Sants** down the coast to Tarragona and onwards to **Tortosa**, **Valencia** and **Alicante**. The more expensive, plusher Euromed trains are hardly any faster unless you are travelling longer distances.
   Don't take the AVE train to Tarragona: the station is 11 km from the city centre. However, the AVE is a fast – if pricey – option for getting to **Lleida**. There are also train services inland to Lleida via **L'Espluga de Francolí** and **Montblanc**, and express services to **Madrid** and **Seville**. See www.renfe.com.

Parc Natural del Delta de l'Ebre *p91*
Hilario Pagò, T646 069 186, and **Tornè**, T977 408 017, both in the nearby village of Goles de l'Ebre, rent out bikes.

Cistercian Triangle *p92*
The nicest way to get to **Poblet** is by train from **Barcelona-Sants** to **L'Espluga de Francolí**, and walk the final attractive 3 km to the monastery. Otherwise, there are regular buses between **Tarragona** and **Lleida** which will drop you right outside the monastery gates. To **Montblanc**, trains leave **Barcelona-Sants**, from here you can pick up a bus to **Poblet**. There are infrequent local buses from **Valls** to **Santes Creus**.

Along the coast north of Barcelona

Heading north towards the French border from Barcelona, you'll pass some small towns with long, sandy beaches, largely popular with locals, before hitting the former fishing village of Blanes, now a huge resort, which marks the start of the spectacular Costa Brava. Swathes of this ravishing stretch of coast, characterised by steep, reddish cliffs plunging into turquoise bays, have been blighted by thoughtless over-development, but some stretches have been preserved miraculously untouched. Whitewashed Cadaqués, out at the tip of the rugged Cap de Creus headland, remains one of the most enchanting towns on the Mediterranean.

Costa Maresme → *For listings, see pages 109-113.*

Costa Maresme (recently rechristened **Costa de Barcelona**) runs for about 50 miles north of Barcelona; despite the grand title, it's really just a string of small towns joined up by a railway. The narrow beaches, an almost unbroken sandy strip from Barcelona to Blanes (official starting point of the Costa Brava, see page 102), have the railway line running right behind them but they are hugely popular with Barcelonin day-trippers and are always packed out on summer weekends.

Caldes d'Estrac
Fly past the dreary sprawl which extends northwards as far as ugly, industrial Mataró and continue on to Caldes d'Estrac (also known as Caldetes), a smart resort spread attractively over pine-forested hills which has been celebrated for its hot springs since Roman times. As a result, the streets are lined with graceful villas and it boasts fewer ugly developments than some of the concrete ex-fishing villages that sprouted like toadstools during the 1960s.

Arenys de Mar
Caldetes is joined by 4 km of sandy beaches to Arenys de Mar, which has an excellent reputation for its local cuisine and you can escape the crowds in a hill-top seafarer's cemetery, with fabulous views and some over-the-top Modernista headstones. There isn't much in the way of nightlife along this coast (with the exception of Mataró, which is packed with blaring *bacalao* discos), but Arenys has a couple of decent bars especially around the fishing harbour and around Carrers Ample and D'Avall in the old part of the town.

Canet de Mar
The Modernista architects were especially fond of Canet de Mar, just up the coast, and built a smattering of summer houses there a century or so ago. Most are private but you can visit the **Casa Museu del Lluis Domènech i Montaner** ① *T937 954 615, check for*

opening times; a guided tour of the town's Modernista villas is offered on the first Sat of every month, a winsome, pointy pavilion which is stuffed full of memorabilia relating to the architect of the extraordinary Palau de la Música, see page 46, in Barcelona. Canet's beachfront is a bit more down-to-earth, with the usual souvenir shops and cafés lined up behind the long sandy beaches.

Sant Pol de Mar

Beyond Canet is delightful Sant Pol de Mar, with a few fishing boats pulled up on to the sands and a colourful tumble of old houses (behind the inevitable apartment blocks). Easily the prettiest town on this stretch of the coast, most of the old cottages have been spruced up and belong to wealthy Catalan second-homers – it's a chi chi little spot, where even the train tracks deferentially head inland, leaving the lovely coves in peace.

Calella

The biggest resort along this strip of coast, Calella is a shrimp compared to the big boys up the coast on the Costa Brava proper, but still a sizeable tourist town, especially popular with families, with ranks and ranks of apartment buildings running along its endless sandy beaches. The **tourist office** ① *C/Sant Jaume 231, T937 690 559.*

Costa Brava → *For listings, see pages 109-113.*

The former fishing villages of Blanes and Lloret de Mar have become two of the biggest resorts on the Costa Brava, with ever-growing suburbs of apartment blocks and long, sandy beaches which teem with crowds of northern European tourists on package holidays. If you are looking for sun, sea, sand and a decent English breakfast, this is the place to come. If not, keep heading up the coast to the resorts further north where package tourism has yet to take such a determined hold. The stretch from Sant Feliu de Guíxols to L'Estartit is one of the most varied. While there are plenty of huge, anonymous resorts, it's also possible to find some ex-fishing villages like Tamariu which, while not exactly off the beaten track, are still refreshingly low-key. There is a clutch of beautifully preserved medieval towns just inland, and the prosperous fishing town of Sant Feliu de Guíxols has a smattering of Modernista mansions and a colourful harbour.

Blanes

The Costa Brava starts officially in Blanes, at the rock called Sa Palomera which divides its lengthy golden beach. It is the first of a string of towns devoted to package tourism on a grand scale. The small fleet of fishing boats in the harbour, a tiny old quarter of narrow streets and a lively daily produce market evoke faint memories of its former life as a prosperous fishing town, but it's the unending stretch of concrete apartment blocks, with their neon-lit bars and cafés, which bring in the business nowadays. If you aren't here for the beaches, the only other things to do are climb up to the old watchtower for stunning views, or visit the botanical garden, the **Jardí Botànic Mar i Murtra**, which has more than 7000 species of Mediterranean and tropical plants. The gardens are located on top of the cliff at the Passatge Karl Faust 10. A special bus service leaves from the Plaça Catalunya near the tourist office if you can't face the stiff walk.

There are also a couple of pretty coves to explore, like the one at **Sant Francesc**, beyond the old watchtower, and the cove of **Santa Cristina**, with a series of well-marked botanical trails and a crumbling hermitage. There's a smart hotel and a couple of beachside cafés which are open in summer only. It's a steep walk down if you come by road but the summer boat service (from Blanes or Lloret de Mar) will take you there effortlessly.

Lloret de Mar

A few kilometres up the coast is Lloret de Mar, a brash, brassy resort dedicated wholeheartedly to package tourism. It's not for everyone so, if you're not looking for a few days of unabashed hedonism, give Lloret a miss. The tourist information office has leaflets which mark a couple of walks and mountain-bike itineraries along the rocky coastline, passing some truly delightful coves (best, obviously, out of season). But Lloret's raison d'être is to give its foreign visitors a good time and it does a reasonable job, with its fish and chip shops, theme parks, go-kart tracks, and unapologetically tacky nightlife.

Tossa de Mar

Tossa de Mar, hugging a small cove dotted with small boats, and overlooked by the ruins of a fortified village, is generally considered to be the first truly charming town along the Costa Brava. But even Tossa has succumbed to the big bucks offered by property developers – it's worth squinting to avoid the sight of the dreary new section of the town which has taken over one end of the harbour. Despite that, the narrow streets lined with whitewashed houses and the perfectly curved bay, are still among the prettiest sights of the Costa Brava. The Villa Vella ('Old Town'), perched high on the Cap de Tossa, is the only medieval fortified village left standing in Catalunya, with a crumbling church and several old stone houses contained within an amazingly intact circle of walls and towers. In July and August, the crowds descend in droves and there isn't an inch of free sand on its beach (clamber around the headland to find less crowded bays). In summer, a glass-bottomed boat, *Fonda de Cristal*, makes a tour of the surrounding coves. From the 1930s, Tossa began to draw a stream of artists including Marc Chagall who described it as a 'blue paradise' and the **Municipal Museum** ① *Plaça Roig i Soler 1, T972 340 709, Jun-Sep Tue-Sun 1000-2100, Oct-May 1000-1330 and 1600-1900 €1.80*, was inaugurated to house some of their works along with a collection of archaeological findings gathered over the centuries. The town is quieter, prettier and infinitely more atmospheric out of season.

Sant Feliu de Guíxols and around

Sant Feliu de Guíxols is a pleasant old port with a long sandy beach and a handsome Passeig Marítim dotted with the odd Modernista mansion. Sant Feliu made its fortune in the cork industry in the 19th century and still has an agreeable air of doing-very-nicely-thank-you. The town has managed to keep the worst excesses of the tourist industry at arm's length, and the harbour hasn't yet been blighted by high-rise apartment blocks. The narrow streets of the old town make a delightful stroll, skirting the 10th-century **monastery**, is currently being refurbished to house an impressive art collection on loan from the Thyssen-Bornemisza. The **Espai Carmen Thyssa** ① *T972 820 051, daily 1000-2100, €6, concessions €4.50*, shows regular temporary exhibitions; the economic crisis has put a halt to the expansion plans for the moment.

Overlooking the town is the little hermitage of **Sant Elm**; it's a stiff climb up but worth it for the fantastic views. The tourist office has information on various walking and biking itineraries in the area, including one which leads past several dolmens. The **tourist office** ① *Ctra Sant Feliu a Polanids, T972 820 074, www.guixols.cat.*

S'Agaró to Palamós

There is a string of big, beach resorts north of Sant Feliu de Guíxols; first up is **S'Agaró**, the smallest and prettiest with a fine, shallow beach spread around a horseshoe-shaped bay. **Platja d'Aró** is neon-lit and very built-up with dreary apartment blocks, but it's worth exploring the little coves outside the town to the north, where there is a beautiful enclave of century-old villas, and a fine coastal path, the **Camí del Ronda**. Platja d'Aró was the port for the medieval town of **Castell d'Agaró**, a couple of kilometres inland, with a much-restored castle and a handsome late-Gothic church. **Calonge** is even lovelier, a dense medieval town of narrow streets twisted tightly around another church and castle. Its port, now another bland resort spread around a small bay, is **Sant Antoni de Calonge**. The monster along this part of the coast is **Palamós**, which still has a busy, colourful harbour full of fishing boats at one end, but has otherwise been swallowed up in a grim sea of apartment blocks overlooking the long, sandy beaches.

Palafrugell

A lively cork-manufacturing town, with a slew of **Modernista buildings**, Palafrugell has a little 16th-century **church** and a colourful **Sunday market**. Set a couple of kilometres back from the sea, it's not over-run with tourists and retains a refreshingly authentic Catalan village atmosphere. There's an engaging little museum to the cork industry, **Museu del Suro** ① *Plazeta del Museu s/n, T972 307 825, www.museudelsuro.cat, open 1000-1300, 1400-1900 (until 2000 on Sat and in summer*, which is more interesting that it sounds.

Villages around Palafrugell

This is one of the prettiest and least spoiled stretches of the Costa Brava. From Palafrugell, there are frequent bus connections to a handful of fishing villages which have grown into bustling resorts squeezed between some delightful coves. This charming stretch of the coastline is a favourite with wealthy Barcelonins, whose villas and seaside apartments line the bays. There are plenty of foreign visitors too, but, so far at least, these seaside towns are still unblighted by concrete monstrosities. In whitewashed **Calella de Palafrugell**, a former fishing village which still has a harbour full of brightly painted boats, you can listen to the old sea shanties (*havaneras*) brought back from Cuba, and try *cremat*, coffee flambéed with rum and spices. Little **Tamariu**, tucked around a tiny bay, is a favourite with families and sufficiently cut off to feel undiscovered (at least in Costa Brava terms), unless you are here in July or August. **Llafranc** is larger, a chic resort set around a yacht-packed marina, surrounded by pine forests and gleaming villas. There are great views from the Sant Sebastià lighthouse, which you can reach on foot via a spectacular coastal path from Llafranc or Tamariu.

Villages inland

To escape the coastal fleshpots, head inland to these relatively unspoiled villages and market towns with a clutch of historical attractions. Lofty **Begur**, with its fancy

19th-century mansions built by local boys who made good in the Americas (known as *Indianos*) and its old walls studded with grim stone keeps, is set just inland. It's a stiff, steep climb down to the beaches and there's no public transport. Just north is the striking fortified village of **Pals**, with spectacular views across the surrounding countryside and an over-preserved old quarter known as El Pedró which has been colonized by affluent second-homers. Despite the relentless prettification, it's hard not to be charmed by the warm stone houses spilling over with flowers. The nearby beaches are among the least known on the coast – although don't expect them to be empty: **Sa Riera** has broad sands and good views across to the Illes Medes (see below), and little **Sa Tuna** has been saved from package tours because of its remote, pebbly cove.

The unfinished Gothic castle of Montgrí stands in ruins on a hillside above **Torroella de Montgrí**; it's worth the climb to enjoy the amazing views. The tranquil, arcaded Plaça de la Vila is the setting for concerts during the annual **International Music Festival** held in July and August.

Northwest, **Verges** is famous for its unsettling medieval Dansa de la Mort (Dance of Death) performed in the narrow streets the night before Good Friday, and Foixà has a magnificent medieval castle. **Ullastret**, with a neat winding medieval hub, has a small **museum** ① *Puig de Sant Andreu s/n, T972 179 058, Tue-Sat Jun-Sep 1000-2000, Oct-May 1000-1400 and 1500-1800, €2.30, concessions €1.60* (part of the Museu de Arqueologia de Catalunya), devoted to the remains of the ancient Iberian city (third-fourth century BC) discovered in its outskirts in the 1940s, and still being excavated.

Charming **Peratallada**, one of the most attractive and least visited of these villages, boasts its own fine collection of sturdy medieval buildings, and is famous for its local pottery. It's also close to the little village of **Púbol**, home to the third point of the so-called Triangle Dalinià (Dalí Triangle). Dalí gave the **Castell de Púbol** ① *T972488655, 15 Mar-14 Jun and 16 Sep-1 Nov 1030-1800 daily except Mon, 15 Jun-15 Sep 1030-2000, €8, concessions €4*, also known as the Castell Gala Dalí, to his wife and muse Gala, who would frolic here with her young lovers and demand that her husband made appointments to see her. The castle houses a collection of the paintings and drawings which Dalí gave Gala to decorate it, and there's a selection of Gala's haute couture finery upstairs. The beautiful gardens are filled with elephant sculptures, another gift from Dalí to his wife.

There are tourist offices in most of the villages including **Begur** ① *Av Onze de Setembre s/n, T972 624 520*, and **Pals** ① *Plaça Major 7, T972 637 380*; both have information on the numerous excellent walks in the area, including parts of the GR92.

Golf de Roses → *For listings, see pages 109-113.*

The huge, curving bay of the Golf de Roses stretches for about 25 km, tipped at both ends with a craggy cape. In the middle is a vast expanse of flat wetlands, part of which have been set aside as the Parc Natural dels Aiguamolls de l'Empordà, a paradise for birdwatchers. This area was among the first to be settled on the Iberian peninsula when Greek and Phoenicians established trading posts along the coast more than two and a half thousand years ago. The remains of one of the most important Greek settlements have been found near Empúries. Just off the southern cape is another natural park, the tiny islands of the Illes Medes, a very popular diving destination, and the gulf is rounded off with Roses, a family resort lined with long sandy beaches.

Illes Medes and L'Estartit

The small archipelago of the Illes Medes was once a haven for pirates and smugglers; now a marine reserve with a wealth of aquatic creatures living in and around the rare coral. It hit the news in 2002, when a group of Catalans 'took' the island for Catalunya: the leader called himself 'Pere Gil', a tongue-in-cheek reference to the island of Perejil which was briefly occupied by the Moroccans and caused a furore in Spain. The islands have become very popular – perhaps too popular – for water sports, and there are several diving companies based in the mainland resort of L'Estartit. L'Estartit is well known for its preserved anchovies, jars of which are sold in every shop in town. This area is the heartland of the Empordà region, well known for its fine regional cuisine which often combines meat and seafood in unusual ways – pig trotters stuffed with prawns is a local favourite.

The **tourist office in L'Estartit** ① *Passeig Marítim 47-50, T972 751 910, www.visitestartit.com*, and **Illes Medes park information office** ① *Passeig del Port s/n, Espigó de Llevant, T972 751 701*, can provide a list of the dozens of diving companies which offer trips and diving courses around the Illes Medes. It's best to come in the off season – May or September – when the waters aren't so crowded.

L'Escala and Empúries

L'Escala was home to Caterina Albert (1869-1916), the author of *Solitude*, a novel published under a *nom de plume* in 1905 which scandalized the public with its frank portrayal of female sexuality. Nowadays, there isn't a whiff of decadence in this comfortably low-key seaside resort, which is popular with Spanish families and renowned for its excellent seafood, still brought in each day by the small fishing fleet.

Close by L'Escala are the ancient ruins of Empúries, founded around 600 BC and possibly the first and certainly one of the most important Greek colonies in Iberia. It's a beautiful setting: a quiet headland, with pine forests and a dazzling curved bay. The first settlement was built on what was then a small island, now the site of the small, walled village of **Sant Martí d'Empúries** (now a pretty village tucked behind crumbling medieval walls which gets over-run with tourists in the summer), where the Greeks erected a temple to Artemis, the goddess of the moon and hunting. They built a new city ('Neapolis') on the mainland, where you can stroll among the old market, streets, cisterns and temples clustered along the shore. The Roman town established a couple of centuries later just inland has been excavated, and you can visit two fine **Roman villas** with beautiful mosaics floors, and the remnants of the forum and amphitheatre. Many of the artefacts discovered on the site are displayed in the small **museum** ① *T972770208, www.mac.cat, Jun-Sep 1000-2000, Oct-May 1000-1800, €3, concessions €2.10*, but most of the important ones have been taken to the Museu d'Arqueologia in Barcelona. There's a wild expanse of sand dunes to stretch out on after a visit.

Parc Natural dels Aiguamolls de l'Empordà to Roses

When the Greeks were around, much of the land curving around the Golf de Roses was marshy and waterlogged, popular with birds but no use to the human population, who subsequently drained much of it to grow rice and other crops. Another chunk was drained when the mad scrabble for holiday properties erupted in the mid-20th century, but finally sense prevailed and the remaining marshlands with their important bird and animal life were given legal protection and became the **Parc Natural dels Aiguamolls de l'Empordà**.

These wetlands are home to about 330 species of birds (and mosquitoes – don't forget repellent) and there are plenty of walking trails and hides for bird or animal watching. There's a **park information office** ① *El Cortalet, Ctra de Sant Pere Pescador Km 13.6, Castelló d'Empúries, T972 454 222.*

Squeezed between the two protected sections of the marshes is **Empuriabrava**. It's little more than an overgrown housing estate with canals instead of roads and its own nightclubs and shopping malls. A couple of miles inland, **Castelló d'Empúries** makes a much nicer base and has a vast Romanesque-meets-Gothic church known as the 'Cathedral of the Empordà', with an accomplished sculptural *Adoration of the Kings* around the door. The biggest town on the Golf de Roses is **Roses** itself, big, blowsy and overpriced, but with an interesting *ciutadella* (fortress) to stroll around, and a fine, sandy beach which is crammed in summer. Kids will enjoy **Aqua Brava** ① *Bahi de Roses, Ctra de Cadaqués,T972254344, www.aquabrava.com,* a huge new water park with an enormous wave pool.

Cap de Creus to the French border → *For listings, see pages 109-113.*

The Cap de Creus is one of the wildest and most beautiful stretches of coastline in Catalunya. A narrow road twists across the cape and out to whitewashed Cadaqués, spilling prettily down to a curving bay right out on the tip of the cape. The Cap de Creus has also been designated a natural park, and offers some spectacular hiking and diving. More whitewashed fishing villages dot the coast all the way to Portbou on the French border, but only Llança can lay claim to being a sizeable resort. If you've got your own transport, finding a quiet beach should be pretty straightforward but public transport can be sketchy.

Cap de Creus Natural Park
Behind Roses, the flat wetlands of the Empordà suddenly rear up into the jagged peaks of the Cap de Creus, formed by the final thrust of the Pyrenees, its slopes narrowly ridged with olives, cork trees and low stone walls which once supported rows of vines. The cape, severe, wild and beautiful, has been designated a natural park and offers a variety of activities from hiking and scuba diving to fishing and birdwatching: artificial platforms have been introduced to try to coax back the ospreys which vanished two decades ago, but there are plenty of other species – more than 200 – of bird life to enjoy. From the Verdera watchtower at the tip of the peninsula, there are stunning views back over the Cap's twisted rocks stripped of plants and moulded into surreal shapes by the winds. The **park information office** ① *El Port de la Selva, T972 193 191,* is in the Monestir de Sant Pere de Rodes (see Port de la Selva, below).

Cadaqués and Portlligat
The sheer inaccessibility of remote, arty Cadaqués, and the fact that the determined residents wouldn't allow massive building projects, means that it has managed to hang on to its old-fashioned charm. Steep crooked streets lined with gleaming whitewashed cottages meander down to the bay, and it's stuffed full of smart restaurants, art galleries and craft shops. A simple white church seems to float above the highest part of the old town, where there's a small square which offers beautiful views across the bay. The town was once known as the St Tropez of the Costa Brava and you can see why. Nearby is Cadaqués' quirky **municipal museum** ① *C/Narcís Monturiol 15 (behind the church), T972*

258 877, mid-Sep to mid-Jun 1030-1330, 1530-1830 (winter Wed 1000-1500), mid-Jun to mid-Sep 1000-2000 (Wed 1000-13000, 1500-2000), closed Sun, with works by Picasso and Dalí. There's a **tourist office** ① *C/Cotxe 2, T972 258 315, www.visitcadaques.org.*

Cadaqués is an excellent base for exploring the remote coves and walking trails of the Natural Park, and the magnificent trans-Pyrenean walking trail, the GR11, begins here too. Hire a boat to find a tiny, pebbly bay all for yourself around the cape: the water is so clear that the starfish creeping along the sea bed 50 ft below are clearly visible. There's a celebrated classical music festival in the summer.

The tiny bay of Portlligat, a mile or so around the cape from Cadaqués, is where the area's most famous resident, Salvador Dalí, chose to settle during much of his life at **Casa-Museu Salvador Dalí** ① *T972 251 015, www.salvador-dali.org, Tue-Sun 1030-1800, summer (mid Jun to mid-Sep) daily 0930-2100, closed early Jan to mid-Feb; reservations essential, €11, concessions €8.* Long abandoned but now partly refurbished, it can be visited in small groups but you must reserve in advance. The house is a surprise; furnished mainly by Gala, his wife and muse, it is a very private series of simple, whitewashed rooms and terraces linked with stairways. It was obviously conceived as a refuge and doesn't even have a spare bedroom. There are some touches of Dalí's imperious surrealism, like the enormous stuffed polar bear dripping with medals and jewellery which greets visitors at the main entrance, but these are largely confined to the entranceway and swimming pool – the most public areas of the house. In private Dalí was obviously less of showman than might have been expected, but he did insist that Gala's private boudoir was to be constructed in the same shape as a sea urchin. The bizarre acoustics mean that even the dullest conversation is given a purring, sensuous edge. The swimming pool is shaped like a keyhole, overlooked by surreal artworks including a statue of the Michelin man, and there's a fat, stuffed boa over the canopied seating area.

Port de la Selva

Around the coast, comfortable whitewashed Port de la Selva is refreshingly humble after all the glitz of Cadaqués. A twisting road winds up and up to the lofty **Monestir de Sant Pere de Rodes** ① *T972387559, Oct-May Tue-Sun 1000-1730 Jun-Sep 1000-2000, €4.50, concessions €3*, clamped grimly against the mountainside and often lost in wreaths of mist. When the Moors were finally driven back, the lands were distributed between the victors and the Church; this was once a Dominican monastery with lands stretching across the whole peninsula and beyond during the height of its influence in the 13th century. An entire town grew up on the outskirts of the monastery but nothing remains besides the graceful, ruined church of Santa Helena resting on the horizon. A thousand years ago, the monks who lived among these lonely peaks began to cultivate grapes; the vines eventually covered the entire region, until phylloxera killed them off in the 19th century. These narrow walls snaking palely across the slopes are all that remain. Try to come in the morning when the sun is on the monastery; it can be cold and gloomy in the afternoon. There's a great restaurant (€) if you want to stay for lunch.

There is some excellent walking to be had around the complex; a 20-minute scramble up the steep hillside will take you to the solid remnants of the **Castle of Sant Salvadera de Verdera**, commanding the highest peak and offering more breathtaking views, or there are more extensive hikes around the Cap de Creus natural park (the information office, with a book shop selling maps and guides, is in the monastery).

Llança to Portbou

Next up on the coast from Port de la Selva is **Llança**, a cheerful harbour town which is the nearest this stretch of coast has to a full-blown resort, but is often overlooked in the charge towards better-known Cadaqués. It's popular with Spanish and French families, and there are plenty of wild beaches to be discovered close by. Then comes **Colera**, another small-scale resort, overlooked by the romantic ruins of a Romanesque Benedictine monastery Santa Qirze de Colera. Right on the border (3 km from Cerbere in France) is **Portbou**, an agreeable little town, with narrow plane-shaded streets, a handful of good but reasonably priced seafood restaurants, and a small promenade around a tiny, pebbly bay.

Along the coast north of Barcelona listings

For Where to stay and Restaurant price codes and other relevant information, see pages 11-20.

● Where to stay

Costa Maresme *p101*

€€ El Romaní B&B, C/Santa Teresa l, T937 910 553. Simple, great-value rooms, some with their own terrace in a charmingly old-fashioned house.

€€ Hostalet l, C/Manzanillo 9, Sant Pol de Mar, T937 600 605. A welcoming, old-fashioned *pensió*. Good value.

€€ Hostal Mar Blau, Canet de Mar, C/Sant Domènec 24, T937 940 499. Basic but close to the beach.

€€ Pensió El Pekinaire, C/ Colón 57, Calella, www.elpekinaire.com. A great-value modern guesthouse with lovely owners.

€ Mitus, C/Riera de la Torre, Canet de Mar, T937 942 903. A basic cheapie right on the beach.

€ Pensió Pinzón, C/el Callao 4, Caldes d'Estrac, T937910051. A friendly, simple option.

Costa Brava *p102*

€€€€ Hostal de la Gavina, Plaça de la Rosaleda s/n, S'Agaró, T972 321 100, www.lagavina.com. For a real treat stay here. The perfect setting for an Agatha Christie novel, **Gavina** has antique-furnished rooms, a stunning seawater pool, 2 excellent restaurants (**€€€-€€€**) and superb facilities. Closed in winter.

€€€€ Mas de Torrent, Alfueras de Torrent s/n, Torrent (just outside Pals), T972 303 292, www.mastorrent.com. This stunning 18th-century country house, set in gardens, has an award-winning restaurant, an outdoor pool, and all kinds of activities on offer including mountain-biking or a ride in a hot-air balloon.

€€€ Hotel Sa Punta, Platja de Pals, Pals, T972 636 410, www.hotesapunta.com. A very comfortable seafront option with pool and fabulous restaurant.

€€€ Parador Costa Brava, Platja d'Aiguablava, in Aiguablava, T972 622 162, www.parador.es. This parador in a modern building is surrounded by woods and gardens right out on the cliffs. There is also an excellent restaurant and bar, open to non-residents.

€€ Hostal Celimar, C/Carudo 12, Llafranc, T972 301 374. Small but attractive rooms, some with balconies.

€€ Hostal Sa Tuna, T972622198, Playa Sa Tuna, www.hostalsatuna.com. This cosy, family-run hotel has an excellent, mid-range seafood restaurant.

€€ Hotel Aiguaclara, C/Sant Miguel 2, T609 118 087, www.hotelaiguaclara.com. Enchanting little hotel in an elegant 19th-century building, with a garden and fine restaurant.

€€ Hotel Diana, Plaça d'Espanya 6, Tossa de Mar, T972 341 116, www.diana-hotel.com. The nicest accommodation option in Tossa, a 19th-century mansion with some original

Modernista decor, including a fireplace designed by Gaudí, the Diana offers great discounts out of season, but book well in advance. Closed mid-Nov to Mar.

€€ **Hotel Guitart Monterrey**, Arda de la Vila de Tossa 27, Lloret de Mar, T972 346 054, www.guitarthotels.com. Fancy, 5-star chain hotel with a wide range of amenities, including a restasurant, spa, pools and gardens.

€€ **Hotel Plaça**, Plaça de Mercat 22, Sant Feliú de Guíxols, T972 325 155, www.hotel plaza.org. Simple family-run option with an excellent restaurant.

€€ **Hotel Sant Roc**, Plaça Atlàntic 2, Calella de Palafrugell, T972 614 250. A fabulous place to stay, surrounded by gardens with a panoramic terrace overlooking the bay. Prices jump dramatically in Aug. Closed Nov-Mar.

€€ **La Marina**, C/Ciutat de Palol 2, Platja d'Aró, T972 817 182. Great little guesthouse near the beach.

€€ **Pensió Cap d'Or**, Passeig del Mar 1, Tossa de Mar, T972 340 081. This friendly option right on the seafront has spotless, if simple, accommodation. Book rooms with sea views weeks in advance. Closed Oct-Feb.

€€ **Planamar**, Passeig del Mar 82, Platja d'Aró, 972 817 177, www.planamar.com. On the beach, and with excellent watersports facilities.

€€ **Rosa**, Carrer Pi I Ralló 19, Begur, T972 623 015, www.fondacanev.com. Friendly, family-run hotel, where prices drop considerably out of season.

€€ **Sa Barraca**, Ctra de Fornells, Begur, T972 623 360. Each room has a terrace with views over the bay.

€ **Fonda L'Estrella**, C/ de les Quatre Cases 13, Palafrugell, T972 300 005. Just off the Plaça Nova, this popular budget option offers simple rooms around a sunny courtyard.

€ **Fonda Lluna**, C/Roqueta 20, Tossa de Mar, T972 340 365, is the best budget choice, tucked in a narrow street in the old quarter. Rooms are small, but made up for by the fabulous roof terrace.

€ **Hostal Kiku**, C/Sant Andreu de Sa Palomera, Blanes, T972 332 727. Right by the beach and the rock of Sa Palomera, and with a very decent, cheap restaurant.

Camping

Cala Llevado, Tossa de Mar, T972 340 314, www.cala llevado.com. One of the nicest campsites on the coast, overlooking a breathtaking cove.

Càmping Moby Dick, C/Costa Verde 16-28, Calella de Palafrugell, T972 614 307, www.campingmobydick.com. Shady sites just 100 m from the beach.

Camping Pola, Ctra de Sant Feliu, Tossa de Mar, T972 341 050, www.campingpola.es. This is the best campsite, with a pool, super-market and other facilities 4 km out of town. Take the bus for Sant Feliu and ask them to drop you off.

Golfo de Roses *p105*

€€€ **Almadraba Park**, Platja de Almadraba, Parc Natural dels Aiguamolls de l'Empordà to Roses, www.almadrabapark.com, T972 256 550, perched on a cliff above an excellent beach. Glitzy and modern.

€€ **Hostal Empúries**, Platja de Portitxol s/n, L'Escala, T972 277 207, www.hostal empuries.com. An eco-friendly hotel in a wonderful location by the beach near the Greco-Roman ruins of Empúries.

€€ **El Roser**, Plaça Església 7, L'Escala, T972 770 219, www.elroser.com. This attractive, old-fashioned hotel has a popular restaurant and during the summer you can join in the *sardana* dancing on the seafront on Wed evenings.

€€ **Hotel les Illes**, C/Illes 55, T972 751 239, L'Estartit. A modern hotel near the port which is geared towards divers.

€€ **Hótel-Restaurante La Cala**, C/Sant Sebastià 61, Roses, T972 256 171. Down-to- earth comforts, simple rooms and a good Catalan restaurant. Prices drop out of season.

Cap de Creus to the French Border *p107*

There are plenty of places to stay in Cadaqués.

€€ Hostal Cristina, C/Riera 1, T972 258 138, www.hostalcristina.com. One of the nicest places to stay in Cadaqués. On the beach. Best rooms have a terrace.

€€ Hostal Maria Teresa, C/Pintor Terruella 22, Llança, T972 380 125. Surrounded by olive trees between the old town and the beach.

€€ Hostal La Tina, C/Major 15, Port de la Selva, T972 387 149. Family-run affair, pristine and with a great restaurant.

€€ Hostal Marina, C/Riera 3, next door to **Cristina**, T972 159 091. Closed Jan-Mar. Another nice place to stay in Cadaqués, also on the beach.

€€ Hotel Masia, Passeig de la Sardana 1, Portbou, T972 390 372. The best rooms have views across the bay.

€ Pensión Vehi, C/Església 5, Cadaqués T972 258 470. With simple rooms in the old town near the church, and a very decent and cheap restaurant.

❷ Restaurants

Costa Maresme *p101*

€€€ Els Tinars, Ctra Sant Felina Girona, Llagostera, T972 830 626, www.elstinars.com. Fantastic contemporary cuisine in supremely elegant surroundings.

€€€ Portinyol, Puerto de Arenys s/n, Arenys de Mar, T937 920 009. Good place to splash out on some fine dining: beautiful sea views and food.

€€€ Sant Pau, C/Nou 8-10, Sant Pol de Mar, T937 600 662. One of the most acclaimed restaurants in Spain, with 3 Michelin stars. Carme Ruscalleda is one of the most famous female chefs in the world.

€€ Marola, Passeig del s Anglesos 6, Caldes d'Estrac, T937 910 700. Great local seafood good for paella, going since the 1940s.

Costa Brava *p102*

The food is pretty ordinary in all these resorts unless you've got money to burn. In

Palafrugell you'll find plenty of places around the Plaça Nova. For eateries in the villages around Palafrugell look around the port and harbour areas and note that many of the hotels have very decent restaurants which offer good-value set lunch.

€€€ Cau del Pescador, Carrer Sant Domènec 11, Sant Feliu de Guíxols, T972 324 052, www.caudelpescador.com. Set in a charming fishermen's cottage, this is now an upmarket seafood restaurant which specializes in classic local dishes.

€€€ Restaurant El Far, next to the Faro de Sant Sebastià, Calella de Palafrugell, T972 301 639. Offers excellent seafood and is attached to a sumptuous hotel.

€€ Bahía, Passeig del Mar 19, Tossa de Mar, T972 340 322, www.restaurantbahia tossa.com. A long-established restaurant on the seafront, where you can tuck into local favourites such as *cim-i-tomba* (a rich stew of monkfish and potatoes).

€€ Can Flores II, Esplanada del Port s/n, Blanes, T972 332 633. A classic, over-bright, 60s-style restaurant which makes up for what it lacks in atmosphere with excellent seafood. The house speciality is fish baked in a salt crust, and the paellas are also good.

€€ Fonda Caner, Fonda Caner, Pi i Ralló 10, Begur, T972 622 391, www.fondacaner.com. A local favourite in the historic centre, this is a good place to try traditional Catalan dishes and seafood.

€€ Marabú Grill, Passeigeo del Mar 35, Sant Feliu de Guíxols, T972 321 023. For freshly caught sardines and a well-priced set lunch menu.

€ Casa Andrés, Av da la Palma 19, Tossa de Mar, T972 341 909. Serves a good-value fixed-price menu at lunchtimes and evenings (€11) which includes wine. You can eat out on the pretty flower-filled terrace.

€ El Sorrall, Passeig de S'Abanell 6, Blanes, T972 333 420. A good bet in the new part of town, serving local dishes, and offering a good-value set lunch.

€ Pomodoro, Paseo de Sa Caleta, Lloret de Mar, T972 369 023. Serves great, cheap, oven-baked pizzas right by the seafront.
€ Tragamar, Playa de Candell, Calella de Palafrugell, T972 615 189. Seafood right on the beach.

Cap de Creus to the French Border p107
€€ Casa Anita, Cadaqués, T972 258 471, for tapas or good home-cooking, crammed with locals.
€€ Casa Nun, Plaça Port Ditxos (at the end of Passeig Marítim), Cadaqués, T972 258 856. Housed in a romantically rickety, narrow old house, this serves freshly caught seafood and delicious desserts; go for the minuscule terrace in summer.
€€ La Vela, Av Pau Casals 23, Llança, T972 380 475. A classic from the 1960s which has a big reputation for its seafood.
€ Restaurante L'Àncora, Passeig de la Sardana 3, T972 390 025, Portbou. Serves freshly caught seafood to go with the sea views.

🍷 Bars and clubs

Costa Brava p102
In Blanes, there are dozens of bars and clubs along the Passeig Marítimo, afterwards finishing up at **Arena**.

Cap de Creus to the French Border p107
There's plenty of nightlife in Cadaqués, at least during the summer. There are a few nice bars along the harbourfront and the casino is a good spot for a coffee while you watch the old men fleece each other at cards). There are also a couple of popular spots, like **L'Hostal**, on the Passeig Marítim.

✷ Festivals

Costa Brava p102
Late Jul The town of Blanes explodes for the stunning **International Fireworks Festival**.

⛰ What to do

Costa Brava p102
Lloret is well set up for activities.
Club Hípic Lloret, Sant Pere del Bosc, T972 368 615. Horse riding.
Dirt Bike, Av del Rieral 87, Lloret del Mar, T972 108 331. For bike rental.

Cap de Creus to the French Border p107
Boats and Bikes Cadaqués, T972 258 027. To rent a zodiac, scooter or kayac.
Creuers Cadaqués, T972 159 462, offers cruised around the cape which leave from the harbour (€9 per adult, for 1½ hrs around Cap de Creus).
Els Caials, T972 258 841, rent diving and snorkelling equipment.

🚍 Transport

Costa Maresme p101
Bus Regular buses leave from the Estació d'Autobuses **Barcelona-Nord** for most resorts.
Train *Rodalíes/cercanías* (local trains) depart very regularly (at least every 30 mins) from **Estació Sants** via Plaça Catalunya, for all the coastal towns north of **Barcelona** to **Blanes**. Return fares to Blanes: around €12; Barcelona to Castelldefels: €2 (or 1 trip on your T-10, see page 78).

Costa Brava p102
Boat **Dofijet Boats**, T972 352 021, run a summer boat service between **Blanes**, **Lloret de Mar**, **Tossa de Mar**, **Sant Feliu de Guíxols** and **Palamós** (it also makes stops at smaller villages and coves).

Bus SARFA, T902 302 025, www.sarfa.com, run a regular bus service from **Girona** to most coastal resorts including **Blanes**, **Lloret de Mar** and **Tossa de Mar**. Tossa doesn't have its own train station; take a bus from Blanes, or from Girona. There are at least 10 departures daily. **TEISA**, T972200275, also runs a service between **Sant Feliu de Guíxols** and **Girona**.

Car If you are driving, the coastal road is beautiful but expect long, delays in summer.

Cycle You can rent bikes and motorbikes in all the resorts along the Costa Brava; ask at tourist information offices for details or visit www.costabrava.org.

Train There are regular *cercanías* from **Barcelona's** Plaça Catalunya station to **Blanes**; the station is 2 km out of town, and services are met with buses to Blanes proper and **Lloret de Mar**.

Golfo de Roses *p105*
Bus SARFA, T902 302 025, www.sarfa.com, run regular bus services to **Roses**, **Castelló d'Empúries** and **L'Estartit** from **Figueres**. There are also less frequent services to **L'Estartit** and **Roses** from **Barcelona**, but it's usually quicker to get the train to **Figueres** and take a bus from there. There are also bus connections with L'Escala and Empúries via **Toroella de Montgri** from **Palafrugell**.

Cap de Creus to the French Border *p107*
Bus SARFA, T902 302 025, www.sarfa.com, run services to **Cadaqués** from **Figueres** 4 times daily except Sun; €11 return, a daily service from **Girona** (weekdays only), and a twice-daily service from **Barcelona**. There are buses from **Llança** to **Port de la Selva**, and **Cadaqués**. There's a beautiful coastal hiking trail (part of the GR11)

Train There are regular trains from **Barcelona**, **Girona** and the French border at **Cerbere** to **Llança** and **Portbou**.

Inland Catalunya

This area contains some of the most visited and least visited attractions in all of Spain. The haunting monastery at Montserrat is the most popular day trip from Barcelona with many visitors arriving via the knee-trembling cable car ride or the rack-and-pinion railway. Further north in Figueres is the Teatre-Museu Dalí, a museum as flamboyant and bizarre as one would expect from the master of the absurd, which doubles as the artist's mausoleum. However, lurking further inland are isolated corners well worth exploring: the rugged landscape of Parc Natural del'Albera and the lava-stripped cliffs of La Garrotxa, for example, are both wonderfully remote.

Terrassa → *For listings, see pages 129-136. Phone code: 937. Population: 213,941.*
Terrassa, on the way to Montserrat, is a strikingly unattractive industrial city wreathed in puffs of acrid smoke. The Japanese once voted it the 'Ugliest City in Europe', but they obviously didn't get past the outskirts because the centre has managed to hang on to a unexpectedly delightful and unusual core of ancient churches and Modernista factories and mansions. Terrassa is not a popular tourist destination, so it's never overcrowded.

Places in Terrassa

A walk down the Carrer de Sant Pau will give you a taste of Terrassa's Modernista heritage; the former **Teatre Principal** is a frilly, domed confection with plenty of murals and stained glass, and nearby is a covered **market**, and the grandiose **Institut Industrial** in a former wool warehouse with a huge glass dome. There are also three delightful **Modernista shops** at Nos 17, 11 and 9, including one built by Domènech i Montaner (No 11).

Terrassa was at the forefront of Spain's industrial revolution in the mid-19th century and there are a couple of museums dedicated to its unique industrial heritage. The excellent and slickly designed **Museu Nacional de la Ciència i de la Tècnica de Catalunya (MNACTEC)** ① *T937 368 966, www.mnactec.cat, Tue-Fri 1000-1900, Sat and Sun 1000-1430; Jul and Aug Tue-Sun 1000-1430 only, €3.50, concessions €2.50, free first Sun of the month*, is set in a stunning Modernista 19th-century fabric factory and features all kinds of interactive gizmos. **Museu Textil** ① *C/Salmerón 25, T937 314 980, www.cdmt.es, 0900-1800, Thu 0900-2100, Sat and Sun 1000-1400, closed Mon and holidays, €3.50, concessions €2.50*, has a vast collection of fabrics, clothing and original designs.

Out in the **Parc del Vallparadís**, on the edge of the city, there's a remarkable complex of pre-Romanesque churches set in quiet gardens which were built on top of the old Roman settlement of **Ègara**. The largest, the Església de Sant Pere, has a Romanesque sarcophagus pressed into service as a font, and some Byzantine-inspired murals. **Església de Santa Maria** has a glittering retable by Jaume Huguet, and the smallest church, **Església de Sant Miquel**, was begun in the fifth century using Roman columns, and odds and ends, found on the site to prop up the dome. The park has a boating lake and swimming pool, especially popular at weekends.

Around Terrassa

Astonishingly close to industrial Terrassa, it's possible to lose yourself completely in the forests, jagged peaks and narrow ravines of **Sant Llorenç del Munt i l'Obac**. There are well-marked walking trails for people of all fitness levels, including a wonderful circular walk which passes over the peak of La Mola (where there is a great restaurant in an old monastery – perfect for lunch) and through the ravine of Santa Agnès (about four hours). The **park information office** ① *T938 317 300, www.diba.es*, and starting point for most of the trails, is near Matadepera, down a small track leading off the main road from Terrassa to Talamanca Km 10.8.

Montserrat → *For listings, see pages 129-136. Phone code: 938.*

One of the most popular day trips from Barcelona (about 40 km) is the Monastery of Montserrat, clamped high to a dramatic reddish massif (Montserrat means 'jagged mountain') and home to a miraculous statue of the Virgin known as La Moreneta ('the little brown one'). The Montserrat mountains erupt surreally from the surrounding plain, as unreal as a painted backdrop. The most dramatic way to arrive is by cable car, which sways on a tiny thread across the valley and up to the monastery, although you could choose the less terrifying rack-and-pinion railway, La Cremallera. The area around the monastery itself gets unpleasantly crowded, but you can escape to the surrounding Parc Natural Montserrat which offers fantastic hiking trails linking tiny half-forgotten hermitages.

Arriving in Montserrat

Getting there The monastery is easily accessible from Barcelona. A daily bus departs from Sants, or you can choose the rack-and-pinion railway, La Cremallera. Good-value all-inclusive tickets are available. ▸▸ *For further details, see Transport page 134.*

Best time to visit Montserrat is a hugely popular pilgrim destination, and it's always packed at weekends and in July and August. It's less crowded on weekdays in spring or autumn. The biggest annual pilgrimage takes place on 27 April and there's another on 8 September. Try to catch the children's choir in the basilica Monday to Friday at 1300 and 1845.

Tourist information ① *Plaça de la Creu, T938777724, www.montserratvisita.com.* They can provide information on accommodation, as well as plans and walking itineraries of the natural park of Montserrat.

Background

The mountain of Montserrat has long been sacred to Catalans: there were already five hermitages tucked between its peaks by the ninth century, and monks would hole themselves up in remote caves to fast and pray. The Benedictine monastery clamped daringly beneath a peak was established in the 10th century, but was largely demolished during the Napoleonic wars and most of the current grim, prison-like building was erected in the 19th and 20th centuries. The monastery vied with Santiago de Compostela as a place of pilgrimage during the middle ages, thanks to the sacred statue of *La Moreneta* (The Brown One), the miraculous polychrome wooden statue of the Black Virgin and Child which still presides over the altar of the basilica and is Catalunya's Holy of Holies. Legend has it that it was carved by St Luke and that St Peter later hid the statue in a cave, where it was discovered by shepherds in 880. Floods of pilgrims, particularly newly-weds, still pour in to touch the statue, and, even now, Montserrat is one of the most popular names for a girl in Catalunya.

Places in Montserrat

Basilica ① *0730-2000, free.* The heart of the monastery complex is the gloomy basilica, built in the 19th century, and very dark and solemn. A passage on the right (with flashing neon-lights) leads to the statue of La Moreneta encased in glass above the altar, and you can join the queue to touch it. The Escolania, one of the oldest children's choirs in Europe, sings Monday to Friday at 1300 and 1845 in the basilica. The monastery's **museum** ① *Plaça del Monestir, T938 777 745, open 1045-1745,* is divided into six sections, which include a dull collection of Catalan art from the 19th and 20th centuries, a more interesting selection of Spanish, Flemish and Italian Old Masters, and a collection of archaeological treasures from Mesopotamia, Egypt and Palestine. There is also a beautiful display of burnisherd icons. The **Interactive Exhibition** ① *T938 777 777, open 0900-1745,* €6, is an audio-visual display offering a glimpse into the daily life of the community of monks who still live here.

Parc Natural de Montserrat The bus-loads of tourists and souvenir stalls allow little peace or room for contemplation. But if you head out from the monastery into the surrounding natural park it doesn't take long to lose the crowds. There are two funiculars: the funicular Sant Joan heads up to the top of the massif for spectacular views, and another drops down to the tiny chapel of Santa Cova, built to celebrate the discovery of La Moreneta. Trails of various lengths and difficulties lead from both of them and wind across the park (maps and information available from the tourist information office); one visits each of the abandoned 13 hermitages and chapels which are scattered around the mountain. Experienced rock climbers can tackle some of the sheer cliffs.

Vic and the Parc Natural de Montseny → *For listings, see pages 129-136.*
Phone code: 938. Population: 40,900; Altitude: 484 m.

The handsome market town of Vic is set on a plain just 70 km from Barcelona, just north of the gentle mountains of Montseny. The old town is curled around one of the largest and finest squares in Catalunya, where twice-weekly markets are still held in a tradition which dates back several centuries. Vic may have lost the political prominence it boasted back then, but it remains a prosperous and genial town with a smattering of decent museums and vestiges of its Roman past.

In late 2012, Vic (like many other Catalan towns) proclaimed itself a 'Free Catalan Territory'.

Arriving in Vic and the Parc Natural de Montseny

Getting there and around Vic is accessible from Barcelona by train and there are several bus connections to other local villages, but it is difficult to explore fully the region without your own transport. The town itself is small and easy to get around on foot. ►► *For further details, see Transport page 135.*

Tourist information The **tourist office** ① *Plaça del Pes, Llotja del Blat, T938 862 091, www.victurisme.cat,* provides a useful map marked up with a 'tourist itinerary' and has a list of multilingual guides offering tours in the town and region. It is the main park information office for the Parc Natural de Montseny. Guided tours of the park are available and information is provided on the hiking trails, as well as opportunities for birdwatching, balloon rides, and horse riding.

Vic

Vic's famous markets still take place on Tuesdays (a small version) and Saturdays (huge) beneath the arcades of its grand old **Plaça Major**. Stalls are piled high with the local *embutits*, cured meats made from local pork, which are considered among the finest in Catalunya. If you miss the market, there are plenty of shops devoted to them lining the narrow streets. To see the sausage in its original incarnation, come during the week before Easter, when the traditional livestock market, the **Mercat del Ram**, is held. There's another great market held in early December – the **Mercat Medieval**. The buildings which surround the square are mainly Baroque or Modernista, some with curly sgraffito and wide, elegant façades. There are plenty of cafés around the Plaça to sit back and enjoy the scene.

Back when the Romans were in charge, at least nominally, they built a temple at the city's highest point, the ruins of which were discovered more than a century ago in the rubble of a 12th-century castle built by the ruling Montcada family. Since the sixth century, the town has been a bishop's see but much of its original Romanesque **cathedral** ① *Plaça Catedral s/n, T938 864 449, 1000-1300 and 1600-1900, free admission to the nave, €2 to the crypt and cloister,* was destroyed during a banal neoclassical refurbishment during the 18th century: the Romanesque crypt, the original belltower and fragments of the original cloister (which was shifted during the refurbishment) are still on view. Other highlights include a monumental Gothic alabaster altarpiece and colourful murals in the nave by the Barcelonin artist Josep María Sert. **Museu Episcopal** ① *Plaça Bisbe Oliba T938 869 360, www.museuepiscopalvic.com, Apr-Sep Tue-Sat 1000-1900, Sun 1000-1400, Oct-Mar Tue-Fri 1000-1300 and 1500-1800, Sat 1000-1900, Sun 1000-1400, €7, concessions €5,* holds an excellent collection of Romanesque murals and artworks gathered from rural churches and has just moved into brand new premises.

All these sights, as well as the Romanesque Porta de Queralt and the sturdy remnants of the city walls raised under Pedro III the Ceremonious, form part of a useful 'tourist route' marked out on a map by the tourist office which is clearly signposted around the town.

Les Guilleries and Pantà de Sau

Northeast of Vic, heading deeper into the mountains along the C-153, lies the region known as Les Guilleries with a string of especially lovely villages; surrounded by rolling hills, cliffs and secret waterfalls, this is a landscape to linger in, although you'll only manage it with your own transport as bus services are infrequent.

Closest to Vic is **Tavèrnoles** (population: 273), with a Romanesque church and the remnants of a medieval castle; then there's **Tavertit**, a minuscule and perfectly preserved 17th-century village of fewer than 150 souls (outside the tourist season) clinging to the edge of the mountain; and finally **Rupit** (population 309), so picture-postcard-perfect that it was reproduced in the Poble Español in Barcelona, see page 54. They are all best visited during the week, particularly in spring and autumn, when you can enjoy them in peace.

Some 15 km east of Vic is the **Pantà de Sau**, an attractive lake surrounded by forested hills where you can rent boats or swim. When the lake was dammed, the little village of Sant Romà de Sau was abandoned to the waters and the top of an old belltower sometimes appears when the water levels are low.

Parc Natural de Montseny and spa towns

The charming spa town of **Viladrau**, is a handy starting point for the Parc Natural de Montseny which has a particularly rich diversity of flora and fauna thanks to the range of habitats it offers, and provides excellent opportunities for walking (GR4 and GR5 cross the park) and horse riding as well as balloon tours. Spring and autumn are the best times to visit the park.

More spa towns are dotted around the hills to the east: **Sant Hilari Sacalm**, perched on a hilltop, is a prosperous little town where the pace of life is pleasingly slow. It's well known for its Easter passion plays (Via Crucis Vivent), some of the oldest and most dramatic in Spain. Southeast of Montseny lie the densely forested peaks of the La Selva region, brooded over by the immense Gothic ruins of Montsoriu castle. There are a host of villages lost in its folds, from **Breda** with its long tradition of ceramic-production and lofty Romanesque belltower to **Arbúcies**, dreaming on a mountain top. **Hostalric**, on the southern edge of the natural park, is just off the main A-7 motorway to France; it's corseted with a ring of ancient houses squeezed against the remarkably intact city walls.

Cardona

If you are looking for a place to break your journey to the Pyrenees, medieval Cardona, piled up on a rock in the middle of a plain, isn't a bad option if only for its famous parador. This is set in a spectacular castle clamped to the very top of the hill and was founded in 789 by Louis the Pious. Cardona is known as the 'Capital of Salt', for its nearby Salí, a ghostly mountain of pure salt that sits beside the river and has been mined since Roman times. It's easiest to get to Cardona by bus from Manresa (on the train line).

Solsona

West of Cardona is another fortified medieval town, Solsona, tightly packed behind a ring of walls studded with crenellated towers and topped with a ruined castle. It's an elegant town, packed with noble mansions dating back to the 16th and 17th centuries, and the cathedral houses a much-venerated 12th-century Virgin made of black stone. **Museu Diocesà i Comarcal** ① *Plaça Palau 1, T973482101, Jun-Sep 1000-1300 and 1630-1900, Oct-May 1000-1300 and 1600-1800, €3*, is housed in the archbishop's palace and contains an eclectic collection, which includes some beautiful medieval artworks.

Girona

→ For listings, see pages 129-136. Phone code: 972. Population: 96,722.

Girona, Catalunya's second city, is an unexpected charmer, sprawling languidly around the confluence of the Rivers Ter and Onyar. The expansive modern part of the city, with its leafy avenues lined with galleries and a handful of Modernista mansions, lies on the west side of the Onyar; on its eastern bank is the shadowy huddle of the ancient city which grew up around an early Iberian settlement. A ribbon of yellow-, orange- and ochre-painted houses, once attached to the city walls, hang over the river and behind them lies a medieval web of crooked alleys and narrow passages built on top of the Roman colony. A long-established university town, the big student population means the city's nightlife is almost as buzzy as Barcelona's, at least during the week, and the arcaded streets and placid squares of the old city are lined with trendy shops, bars and restaurants.

Arriving in Girona

Getting there Girona's airport is 12 km from town; for airport information, see www.aena.es. There's an hourly bus service from the airport with TEISA, T972 204 868, from outside the terminal to the bus station. Taxis (from outside the arrivals hall) cost around €20. Girona is very well served by buses and trains from Barcelona; for general bus information, call the bus station on T972 201 591. ➤ *For further details, see Transport page 135.*

Getting around The bus and train stations are next to each other, 10 minutes' walk from the old city where you'll find most of the sights. If driving, note that much of the old city is pedestrianized, so you'll have to park in the new part and walk. You won't need to use the bus system in Girona as the sites are all together in the old part of the city by the banks of the river.

Best time to visit Girona keeps a very full festival calendar (see below) so there's something going on for most of the year. The city's biggest festival is the Fires de Sant Narcís held at the end of October or beginning of November, when devils, dragons and giants parade though the streets. The old stone streets are always cool, even in the height of summer.

Tourist information The helpful **tourist office** ① *C/Juan Maragall 2, T872 975 975, www.girona.cat*, has informaton on guided walks around the Call (Jewish Quarter). They can also provide a leaflet on the 40 km-long former railway line which has been converted into a walking/biking path between Girona and Sant Feliu de Guíxols. If you are staying a few days, invest in the **Tiquet M5**, which offers a 50% discount to Girona's museums.

Background

An Iberian settlement, then a Roman colony and eventually a Moorish city for almost two centuries, Girona was also the medieval centre of one of Spain's largest and most influential Jewish communities. An important school of Jewish mysticism, the *Cabalistas de Girona*, was established during the 12th and 13th centuries, and the undisputed master of the Cabala was Moses Ben Nahman, or Nahmanides, who was born in Girona in 1194 and became the Grand Rabbi of Catalunya. The Jews suffered increasing persecution throughout the 14th century; 40 inhabitants were killed during the pogrom of 1391, and the Jewish quarter, or Call, was gradually sealed off and became a ghetto. Finally, by decree of the Catholic Monarchs (Ferdinand and Isabella), all Jews were expelled from Spain in 1492. The city's strategic location at the confluence of three rivers meant that it would always be in the front line of the seemingly endless wars which ripped across Europe and divided Spain for much of the following three centuries: by the

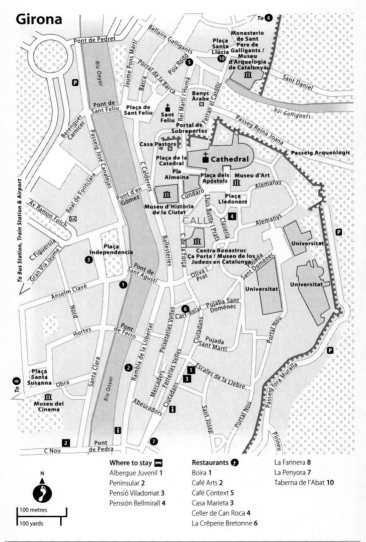

Girona

Where to stay ▣	Restaurants ⏺	
Albergue Juvenil 1	Boira 1	La Farinera 8
Peninsular 2	Café Arts 2	La Penyora 7
Pensió Viladomat 3	Café Context 5	Taberna de l'Abat 10
Pensión Bellmirall 4	Casa Marieta 3	
	Celler de Can Roca 4	
	La Crêperie Bretonne 6	

N

100 metres
100 yards

time Napoleon's armies came south of the Pyrenees in 1809, it had already been besieged more than 20 times. It held out against the French for nine months, gaining the nickname 'The Immortal'.

Places in Girona
El Call (the old Jewish Quarter) The old core of Girona has barely changed in centuries. **Carrer de la Força** follows the line of the Vía Augusta, and was the main artery of the medieval Jewish quarter, or Call, which remains astonishingly intact. Halfway up it, the Centra Bonastruc Ça Porta is built over the old Synagogue of Girona and houses an institute of Jewish learning, as well as the fascinating **Museu d'Història dels Jueus** ① *T972 216 761, May 15-Nov 14 Mon-Sat 1000-2000, until 1800 in winter, Sun and holidays 1000-1400, €4, concessions €2*, which describes the development of the Jewish community from the first mention of the Call in 898, and offers an interesting insight into the beliefs and practices of the Cabalistas.

Further up, the **Museu d'Història de la Ciutat** ① *C/de la Força 27, T972 222 229, www.girona.cat, Tue-Sat 1000-1400 and 1700-1900, Sun 1000-1400, closed Mon, €4, concession €2*, is housed in a sturdy 18th-century mansion with well laid out exhibits documenting the history of the city from prehistoric times to the introduction of electricity and the computer age. The most gruesome sight is the Capuchin cemetery (the room just inside the entrance on the right); the Capuchins dissected the bodies of dead monks on perforated benches and buried them in vertical tombs.

Cathedral and around Just beyond the museum, the street opens up on to the lovely **Plaça de la Catedral**, flanked by the 18th-century Casa Pastors (law courts) and the imposing Gothic Pia Almoina (almshouse). A broad flight of steps sweep up to the Cathedral ① *Plaça de la Catedral s/n, T972 214 426, www.lacatedraldegirona.org, Apr-Oct 1000-2000, Nov-Mar 1000-1900 (note that the nave is closed at Mass times); admission €7, concessions €5 (includes audioguide), free Sun*, one of the grandest in Catalunya, with an elaborate Baroque façade topped with a frilly belltower. The present cathedral was begun in 1312, but a century later Guillem Bofill added a single, daring nave in defiance of a committee of architects who swore it wouldn't work; it's still the largest in Europe, with an audacious 23-m span. The delicate Romanesque **cloister** with its intricately carved capitals was left over from the previous cathedral which occupied the spot, as is the Romanesque belltower, the Torre de Carlemany which was incorporated into the new construction as a buttress. **The Treasury** holds a fine collection of religious art, including a powerful 12th-century tapestry of the Creation (the best preserved Romanesque tapestry in Europe), and the *Còdex del Beatus* exquisitely illuminated by Mozarabic miniaturists during the 10th-century.

The former Episcopal Palace tucked behind the cathedral now houses Girona's excellent **Museu d'Art** ① *T972 203 834, www.museudart.com, May-Sep Tue-Sat 1000-1900, Sun 1000-1400, Oct-Apr 1000-1800, Sun 1000-1400, €2*, an eclectic collection of painting, sculpture, furniture, glass and gold and silver-work from the Visigothic period until the 19th century, displayed in cavernous vaulted halls. There are two notable Gothic retables, including a particularly fine piece from Bernat Martorell, and paintings from Joaquim Vayreda of the Olot school and the bohemian dandy, Santiago Rusiñol.

Beyond the Portal de Sobreportes Below the cathedral is the Portal de Sobreportes, the ancient Roman entrance to the city, and the final exit for condemned prisoners who went to their deaths in the square beyond. To the left stands the **Església de Sant Feliu** which was built over an old Christian cemetery where legend has it that the city's martyred patron saint, Sant Narcís, met a sticky end and contains some finely carved Roman and paleochristian sarcophagi. The Gothic belltower had its spire blasted off by a bolt of lightning in 1581, but still manages to poke its head above the red-tiled rooftops.

Behind the church of Sant Feliu are the **Banys Àrabs** ① *C/Ferran El Catòlic, T972 213 262, Apr-Sep Mon-Sat 1000-1900, Sun 1000-1400, Oct-Mar daily 1000-1400, €2, concessions €1,* which were built on the the-fashionable Arab model, perhaps by Moorish craftsmen in the 12th and 13th centuries, and are among the most well preserved in Spain. The loveliest area is the *frigidarium* (cold water pool), which is subtly illuminated by a skylight supported by a ring of slim columns. The niches are filled with changing contemporary art exhibitions and there's a little walkway across the rooftop.

Across the empty riverbed of the tiny Riu Galligans is **Monestir de Sant Pere de Galligants** ① *C/de Sant Llúcia, T972 202 632, www.mac.cat, Jun-Sep Tue-Sat 1030-1330, 1600-1900, Oct-May 1000-1400, 1600-1800, €2.30, concessions €1.60,* a sober 12th-century monastery with an unusual octagonal belltower and a fine cloister, which now houses an outpost of the Museu d'Arqueologia de Catalunya. The holdings date from the Paleolithic to the medieval period, attractively displayed in the former church and scattered around the overgrown cloister, and include Roman monuments and everyday objects like lamps and vases, a lead plaque inscribed with Iberian writing, and Iberian and Greek memorial stones. From just behind the museum you can climb up to the **Passeig de la Maralla** ① *1000-2000, free,* for a panoramic stroll across the top of the old city walls, with sweeping views out across the rooftops and the Ter Valley.

Museu del Cinema ① *C/Sèquia 1, T972413047, Tue-Fri 1000-1800, Sat 1000-2000, Sun 1100-1500, €3.* Over on the other side of the river, in the 19th-century extension to old Girona, this lively museum with an excellent collection of film memorabilia gathered by local film-maker Tomas Mallol: the 25,000 exhibits cover everything from 15th-century shadow puppets and magic lanterns to a rare piece of original film by the Lumiere brothers.

Around Girona

There are a couple of popular excursions from Girona: you could escape the heat of summer out at the lake of Banyoles, where local families come to eat picnics and mess about in boats, or visit nearby Besalú, an immaculate, perfectly preserved medieval town.

Banyoles Some 18 km north of Girona, Banyoles is a quiet town sitting peacefully beside a placid lake full of plump carp. Chosen to host the rowing competitions during the 1992 Olympics which sparked a host of new developments along the lake side. The new areas are not particularly attractive – although you can hire a boat, take a cruise, or potter about in a pedalo – but the old town has remained largely unspoilt, and there is some pleasant walking around the lake to pretty villages.

The hub of the old town (called the Vila Vella) is the arcaded **Plaça Major**, an agreeable leafy square with plenty of cafés, where a lively local market (on Wednesdays) has been held for almost a thousand years. The maze of narrow streets which surround the square still contain some fine medieval buildings, including the **Pia Almoina** (Almshouse) on the Plaça del Font which is now the local **Museu Arqueològic** ① *Jul-Aug 1130-1430 and 1600-1900, Sep-Jun 1130-1400 and 1600-1830, Sun and holidays 1030-1400; combined entrance ticket with the Museu Darder d'Historia, €3*. The museum's prize exhibit, the famous Banyoles jawbone, has been replaced with a replica but the original dates back to the paleolithic period, and is a reminder that this region is where the earliest human remains in Catalunya have been found. **Museu Darder d'Historia Natural** ① *T972 574 467, same hours and price as the Museu Arqueològic, above, but visits must be requested in advance*, has a limp display of flora and fauna.

The town first grew up around the **Monestir de Sant Esteve** which was established in 812; now sadly neglected on the eastern edge of town, it is rarely open, but if you manage to get in, it has a peaceful cloister and a remarkable 15th-century altarpiece. There's another attractive Romanesque church at the nearby village of **Porqueres**, an enjoyable half-hour walk around the lake.

Besalú Some 14 km north of Banyoles, Besalú is a perfectly preserved medieval town with a handsome 11th-century bridge complete with fortified gatehouse; so artful are its immaculate streets and picturesque houses that it looks suspiciously like a stage set. No matter who was invading or ruling Catalunya, Besalú seemed to prosper, even briefly becoming the seat of a small independent principality. Its fortunes declined from the 14th century, when it sank into genteel obscurity before being 'discovered' by zealous excursionists a century or so ago. Like Girona, Besalú also had an important Jewish community, and the most substantial relic of their time here is the **Miqwé**, or bath house, near the river, which was once attached to a synagogue, the remains of which are currently being excavated. Cobbled streets meander prettily between medieval squares, overlooked by Romanesque churches, such as the handsome 11th-century **Monestir de Sant Pere**, and the more elaborate 12th-century **Església de Sant Vicenç**, which overlooks a flower-filled square.

Figueres and around → *For listings, see pages 129-136.*
Phone code: 972. Population: 34,573.

Figueres is a likeable, down-to-earth provincial town which would be entirely unremarkable but for its most famous son: Salvador Dalì, who was born here at No.6 C/Monturiol on 11 May 1904. Thanks to its links with the celebrated artist, and the spectacular Teatre-Museu Dalí which he established in the centre of the city, it has become one of the most popular tourist destinations in Spain. Few visitors, however, make it to the wild, windswept corner of Catalunya north of Figueres, strewn with dolmens and home to the endangered Mediterranean tortoise. There are unspoilt villages to discover as well as excellent hiking in the wilds of the Albera Natural Park on the eastern end of the Pyrenees.

Arriving in Figueres
Getting there and around Frequent bus and train services travel to Figueres from Girona and Barcelona. You'll need your own transport if you are exploring the Albera and around, as most of the region is covered by buses that only make the trip to the bigger towns on market days. ▶▶ *For further details, see Transport page 135.*

Tourist information The **tourist office** ① *Plaça del Sol s/n, T972 503 155, www.figueres.cat*, has plenty of maps and guides to the area, and they offer guided walks of the town, including a two-hour guided walk of Dalí's Figueres. Outside Figueres, there are tourist offices in **Maçanet de Cabrenys** ① *T972 544 297*, and in **Sant Llorenç de la Muga** ① *T972569167*; both provide a leaflet called *Turisme Actif* (also available in English) which has lists of walks, nature trails, watersports and other activities in the Albera region.

Teatre-Museu Dalí

① *T972 677 500, www.salvador-dali.org, Jul-Sep Tue-Sun 0900-1915, Nov-Feb Tue-Sun 1030-1800, Mar-May Tue-Sun 0930-1800, Jul-Sep daily 0900-2000, night visits (2200-0100) in Aug only (ticket office closes 45 mins before closing time), €12, concessions €9 (includes admission to Dalí-Jewels).* Dalí's bizarre Teatre-Museu Dalí strikes a flamboyant pose in the centre of the city. Other Catalans have always suspected that the Tramontana wind which rages through the city has affected the Figuerans in the head, but Dalí was undoubtedly the battiest of them all. The Teatre-Museu is topped with a huge glass latticed dome like a fly's eyeball, and surrounded by giant boiled eggs and leaping figures; the walls are covered in squidgy protuberances, which, from a man who had a special toilet installed in order to better inspect his excrement and then wrote a book about it, can only be turds. His scatalogical obsessions have their roots in the earthy Catalan culture which puts a *Caganer* ('Crapper', see page 38) just downwind of the manger in the traditional Nativity scene which decorates good Catalan homes at Christmas.

Inside, the museum twists around a central courtyard strewn with old bones and skulls, in which a naked singing diva sprouts out of a Cadillac with a snake and a thorny rose; rooms and passages lead off into unexpected dead ends, and recesses hold classical statues with drawers for stomachs, or a velvet curtain providing a lush backdrop to an old fish skeleton. Surrealism demanded the participation of its viewers, and Dalí delighted in optical tricks; in the **Mae West room**, a sofa and a fireplace suddenly melt into the features of the great screen actress when viewed through a special eye-piece (suspended over a ladder supported by a plastic camel). In the **Palau del Vent**, a vast ceiling fresco depicts the ascension of Dalí and Gala (his adored wife and muse) into heaven, their enormous feet flapping as their bodies disappear into clouds. Dalí retired to the **Torre Galatea** (attached to the museum) at the end of his life and died here in 1989; he is buried behind a granite slab, so plain and simple that it's impossible not to suspect some kind of trick.

Next door, the **Dalí-Joies** exhibition contains a collection of jewels and jewellery designs by the eccentric artist.

Dedicated Dalí fans will want to make the trip to the other two corners of the Dalí Triangle: his whitewashed house overlooking a beautiful little cove near Cadaqués, page 107, and Gala's former home at the Castell de Púbol (Castell Gala Dalí), near Peratallada, page 105.

Other sights

The Teatre-Museu Dalí may be the top crowd-puller in Figueres, attracting almost as many visitors as the Prado in Madrid, but there are a couple of other museums which are worth a glance on a rainy day. The **Museu de L'Empordà** ① *Rambla 2, T972502305, www.museuemporda.org, Tue-Sat 1100-1900, Sun 1100-1400, closed Mon except holidays, €4, concessions €2*, has a collection of Roman artefacts, ceramics from the monastery of

Sant Pere de Rodes and a surprisingly good collection of 19th- and 20th-century art, including works by Sorolla, Nonell, Vayreda and Tàpies, as well as pieces by Dalí himself.

The **Museu del Joguet de Catalunya** ① C/Sant Pere 1, T972 504 585, www.mjc.cat, Jun-Sep Mon-Sat 100-1900, Sun and holidays 1100-1890; Oct-May Tue-Sat 1000-1800, Sun and holidays 1100-1400, €5, concessions €4, is a privately owned museum with more than 4000 delightfully old-fashioned toys – including some owned by Dalí, Miró and Lorca – from train sets and Meccano, dolls and dolls houses, to balls and spinning tops.

To the north of the city is the huge 18th-century **Castell de Sant Ferran** ① T972 506 094, www.castillosanfernando.org, visits by prior request, which is still owned by the military but you can walk around the star-shaped walls and bastions. It was the last stronghold of the Republicans during the Civil War, and was used as a barracks for new recruits to the International Brigade before they were sent to Barcelona.

Around Figueres

Sant Llorenç de la Muga Northwest of Figueres is this peaceful fortified village overlooking the River Muga and close to the **Pantà de Boadella**, a large reservoir surrounded by forest, with good hiking and mountain-biking trails. There's an excellent trail skirting the western edge of the reservoir which leads to the handsome medieval town of **Maçanet de Cabrenys**, with a maze of lively, narrow streets. Close by is **Darnius**, quieter and altogether less charming thanks to haphazard modern developments, but at least it's handily placed for the Club Nàutic which offers a range of watersports on the Pantà de Boadella.

Parc Natural de l'Albera The rugged landscape northeast of Figueres forms part of the Albera, the easternmost Pyrenean range, a wild and sparsely populated region scattered with dolmens and menhirs which is still home to the Mediterranean tortoise, or Herman's tortoise. There's a **Conservation Centre** ① Santuari del Camp, Garriguela, T972 552 245, www.tortugues.org (call to arrange a visit), near Garriguela, where an audio-visual account is given of the birth and development of these highly endangered creatures. Heading north towards the French border is the little stone village of **Espolla**, which is where the park information office ① Parc Natural Albera, Centre d'Informació del Paratge Natural, C/Amadeu Sudrià 3, 17753 Espolla, T972 545 079, is located with plenty of maps and leaflets on the various activities in and around the park. The countryside around Espolla is strewn with megalithic monuments dating back five millennia or more; the most important is the **Dolmen de la Barranc**, 3 km from the village, which dates to around 3000 BC.

Olot and La Garrotxa → *For listings, see pages 129-136.*
Phone code: 972. Population: 26,713.

Olot is a surprisingly vibrant market town lined with handsome mansions from the 18th and 19th centuries. It's also the main town and transport hub of the Garrotxa region, a strange landscape pocked with peculiar stubby eruptions. These are the grassy craters of long-extinct volcanoes, now part of the Parc Natural de la Zona Volcànica de la Garrotxa. Olot makes a good base for hiking and horse riding in the natural park, with plenty of bars, shops and restaurants on hand. The park is at its best in spring, when the streams are full and the woods are full of flowers, or in autumn, when the leaves change. Your own transport is pretty much essential for exploring the surrounding area.

Places in Olot and La Garrotxa

Jardi Botànic The information office ① *Ctra de Santa Coloma, T972 266 202, www.garrotxa.com*, for the Parc Natural de la Garrotxa is set in a tranquil mansion in a pretty duck-filled Jardi Botànic on the edge of town. It has plenty of maps and information on the walking trails which criss-cross the forested park. Medieval Olot was flattened by a volcano in the 15th century, and you can relive it in a dramatic audio-visual display at the excellent little **Museu dels Volcans** ① *Tue-Fri 1000-1400, 1500-1800 (Jul and Aug 1500-1900), Sat 1000-1400, 1600-1900, Sun 1100-1400 €3, concessions €1.50 (includes admission to Museu Comarcal)*.

Museu Comarcal de la Garrotxa ① *C/Hospici 8, T972 279 130, Jul-Sep Tue-Fri 1000-1300, 1500-1800, Sat 1100-1400, 1600-1900, Sun 1100-1400; Oct-May Tue-Sat 1100-1400, 1600-1900, Sun 1100-1400, €3, concessions €1.50 (includes admission to Museu dels Volcans*. The surrounding, hazy landscape of forested, misty cliffs and green fields edged with neat stone walls inspired the 19th-century artists of the Olot School, and you can check out their work at this excellent museum. The founder of the movement was Joaquim Vayreda i Vila (1843-1894), who visited Paris in 1871 and was spellbound by Millet's celebrations of rural life and scenery. On his return to Olot he began to paint lyrical landscapes suffused with a soft green light and developed an important following of painters and sculptors including Modest Urgell, Josep Armet and Joan Llimona. The collection is not entirely restricted to the works of the Olot school; one of the most dramatic paintings here is Ramon Casas' powerful *La Càrrega* (The Charge, 1899), in which mounted policemen viciously charge at a crowd of fleeing workers.

The museum also runs the **Casa-Museu Can Trincheria** ① *C/Esteve 29, T972 266 762, Tue-Fri 1000-1400, 1700-1900, Sat 1000-1400, 1700-1900, Sun 1100-1400, free*, which belonged to an aristocratic family in the 18th century. Filled with period furniture and decorations among them a very enthusiastic *caganer*, see box, page 38.

Around Olot

Close to Olot is the sleepy medieval town of **Santa Pau**, tucked behind crooked walls. Narrow streets hung with flower-filled balconies lead to the arcaded Plaça Major, overlooked by the Romanesque church of Santa María. There's a gentle walking path (about three hours) through the beautiful **Fageda d'en Jordà beech forest** from Olot and plenty more easy trails in the surrounding area. Information on walking trails can be obtained from the park information office in Olot, see above.

La Garrotxa

The villages scattered in the wilder reaches of northern Garrotxa are perfect bases for trekking among the lava-striped cliffs. Medieval **Castelfollit de la Roca** is perched on a sheer cliff overhanging the river Fluvià, and boasts one of the only museums dedicated exclusively to sausages in the world in the world devoted to sausages, the **Museu de l'Embotit** ① *C/Girona 10, T972294463, Mon-Sat 0930-1330 and 1600-2000, Sun 0630-1400 and 1630-2000, free*.

Just west is **Sant Joan les Fonts**, ringed by shabby industrial development, but with a handsome medieval bridge and an interesting Romanesque monastery. Just below the walls, a path leads to spectacular waterfalls cascading powerfully over a dam – the perfect spot for a dip.

Ripoll → *For listings, see pages 129-136. Phone code: 972. Population: 10,913; Altitude: 691 m.*

Ripoll is now a nondescript little town west of Olot where nothing seems to happen; quiet during the week, it is absolutely dead at the weekends, when everyone leaves for their second homes in the mountains. And yet it has a legendary place in Catalunya's history: this was the heart of the original Pyrenean fiefdom of Guifré el Pilos (Wilfred the Hairy), who created the foundations of modern Catalunya. He is buried in the Monestir de Santa Maria de Ripoll, which he founded in the ninth century, and which survives – at least in part – in the centre of the town. The portal is one of the finest examples of Romanesque sculpture in Catalunya. The pretty stone village of Gombrén, about 15 km from Ripoll, is worth a visit.

Places in Ripoll

Monestir de Santa Maria de Ripoll ① *Plaça Abat Oliba, 1000-1300 and 1500-1800 (Apr-Sep until 1900), €3, concessions €2*, was once a supremely important centre of learning, with one of the finest libraries in the world, but the whole thing went up in flames in 1835. The irreplaceable library, luckily, was saved and so too was the magnificent 12th-century portal, one of the most sublime works of the Romanesque period. A dense profusion of exquisitely wrought sculptures fan out from the doorway and on to the surrounding walls: Christ in Majesty presides at the highest point over the door, guarded by the Evangelists, and accepting the homage of the Ancients of the Apocalypse and saints. A host of biblical events, from the decapitation of Sant Paul to Jonah being swallowed by the whale, are played out in gory detail on the panels below. Around the door, the passing seasons are marked by charming depictions of the month's tasks: harvesting wheat in June; grape-picking in September, slaughtering a pig in November, and enjoying the sausages in December. Much of the delicate two-storeyed cloister also survived the fire, with more intricate carving around the capitals. After the fire of 1835, the church was restored to late 19th-century tastes, and is dull and gloomy. Lost in the shadows you'll find the tombs of Berenguer III and Wilfred the Hairy.

Next door to the monastery is the little **Museu de Ripoll** ① *Plaça Abat Oliba, T972 703 144, www.museuderipoll.org, Jul-Sep Tue-Sun 0930-1900, Oct-Jun Tue-Sun 0930-1330 and 1530-1800, €2.50*, set in part of the winsome 14th-century church of Sant Pere. Most of the church is closed, but, if you are lucky, one of the museum custodians might let you in. The museum itself is small and rather endearing, with exhibits covering everything from cooking pots to guns. Elsewhere, you can visit **Farga Palau**, an iron factory, in use from the 17th to 19th centuries, which is surprisingly interesting (ask at the tourist office for opening times).

Northeast of Ripoll to the French border → *For listings, see pages 129-136.*

Beyond Ripoll, the Pyrenees begin to loom dramatically. The mountain towns are stuffed full of Romanesque churches and monasteries, and make good bases for hikers in summer and skiiers in winter.

Sant Joan de les Abadesses

A few kilometres northeast of Ripoll, Sant Joan de les Abadesses grew up around a convent founded by Wilfred the Hairy, who shrewdly learned to get the Church on his side early on. The old train line between Ripoll and Sant Joan has been tarmaced over to create an easy and enjoyable walk (the 'Ruta del Ferro') through the countryside. A fine Gothic bridge spans the Riu Ter, but, like Ripoll, Sant Joan's days of glory are long gone. Unlike Ripoll, however, Sant Joan has become an attractive, relaxed market town with some gently worn old stone houses; the 15th-century bishop's palace which houses the tourist information office is especially pretty and has a peaceful cloister.

Close to San Joan, the hulking Romanesque **monastery** ① *Plaça de la Abadia s/n, T972 722 353, May, Jun and Sep daily 1000-1400 and 1600-1900, Jul-Aug daily 1000-1900, Mar, Apr and Oct daily 1000-1400, 1600-1800, Nov-Feb Mon-Fri 1000-1400, Sat and Sun 1000-1400, 1600-1800, €3, concessions €2*, built to withstand earthquakes, was established by Wilfred as a gift to his daughter Emma who was the first abbess here. Inside, it's a shadowy, cavernous space, which, on a dark afternoon before the lights are switched on, is still charged with the awe it must have inspired in medieval worshippers. The church's sole adornment is a sublime 12th-century wooden Descent from the Cross, a group of seven almost life-size figures; in 1256 a miraculously uncorrupted host was discovered inside the head of Christ and the statue has been an object of veneration ever since. The monastery museum (included in entrance ticket) has a rich collection of ecclesiastical treasures dating back a millennia, including gilded Gothic retables, and jewel-encrusted chalices.

There are more Romanesque churches scattered around the countryside. The tourist office has a leaflet describing a stiff but enjoyable walk, **Sender de les Quatre Ermites**, PRC60, to a few of them which joins up with the GR1.

Camprodon

Beyond Sant Joan de les Abadesses is the little mountain town of Camprodon, which straddles the confluence of two rivers, the Ter and the Ritort, and is prettily criss-crossed with stone bridges, including the sturdy 12th-century Pont Nou, still guarded by a tower. A century ago, this was a popular weekend excursion for affluent Barcelonins who would arrive here by train (sadly, long defunct) and stroll along the leafy promenades beside the river. It's a still a delightful, if slightly time-worn town, with bustling streets crammed with old-fashioned shops selling *embutits* (local cured meats) and leather crafts, a neglected Romanesque monastery tucked behind the showier parish Església de Santa Maria, and ornate townhouses boasting a Modernista flourish or two.

The composer Isaac Albéniz (1860-1909) was born in Camprodon and led a spectacularly adventurous life: he gave his first piano recital aged three, ran away from home aged nine, and, after touring Spain as a musical prodigy, stowed away on a boat heading to Port Rico. He is commemorated with an annual music festival and a chubby bust on the Plaça de Santa María.

North to the French Border

Twisting roads follow the river valleys northwards from Camprodon: the Ritort heads into France through a relatively bleak valley, but it's worth turning off to see the medieval monuments in the nearby villages of **Beget** and **Rocabruna**: Beget's church, with its lofty belltower, is especially handsome, and Rocabruna is overlooked by a crumbling castle. Neither town has anywhere to stay.

The local road which curves through the prettier **Ter Valley** culminates at the small **Vallter 2000** ski resort which is surrounded by a glacial cirque reaching 2702 m (8865 ft). There's no public transport directly to the resort – it's best to get a package with a Barcelona travel agency or take the daily bus from Barcelona to Campodon, then get a taxi. Vallter 2000 has 14 pistes and a slalom course and there are several hotels and restaurants in nearby Setcases. The excellent website, www.acem-cat.com, has complete information on all the facilities available in all Catalan ski resorts, as well as snow reports, news and a calendar of events. For information and to book accommodation in Vallter 2000 call T972136057, www.vallter2000.com.

Villalonga, a few kilometres from Camprodon, is a pleasant, down-to-earth town with another sturdy Romanesque church overlooking the main square, but just beyond it is tiny **Tregurà**, perched winsomely on a hillside and the starting point for some excellent hikes. Just beneath Vallter 2000 is the picturesque town of **Setcases**, but unfortunately its glossy reputation as a beauty spot has meant that most of its attractive stone houses have been snapped up by weekending Barcelonins.

Inland Catalunya listings

For Where to stay and Restaurant price codes and other relevant information, see pages 11-20.

⊝ Where to stay

Terrassa *p114*
Terrassa is too close to Barcelona to make staying overnight a particularly attractive option and most hotels are expensive and geared towards business travellers anyway.
€€ **Don Candido**, Rambleta Pare Alegre 98, T937 333 300. A modern hotel which offers 4-star comforts including a pool and gym for a surprisingly reasonable price.

Montserrat *p115*
There are 2 options (with the exception of the *refugi*), both run by monks at the monastery.
€€ **Abat Cisneros**, T938 777 701, www. montserratvisita.com. Where newly weds stay on a visit to get La Moreneta's blessing.
€ **Cel.les Abat Marcet**, T938 777 701, www.montserratvisita.com. Self-catering apartments ideal for families.
€ **Refugi Sant Benet**, T615 122 435. Mountain shelter on the GR172 long-distance path.

Camping
Càmping de Sant Miquel, accessible on foot, down the path between the funiculars, T938 777 777, which has a terrace and costs around €8-10 for 2 people and a tent.

Vic and the Parc Natural de Montseny *p116*
Note that much of the accommodation in the spa towns is only open in summer. If you fancy a visit to a spa – check out the website www.balneario.org for lists of spas and their facilities.
€€€€ **Parador de Vic-Sau**, Paraje El Bac de Sau, Vic, T938 122 323, www.parador.es. The plushest place to stay, is set in a luxurious stone farmhouse with beautiful views overlooking the Pantà de Sau (see page 117), 15 km from Vic. There's an excellent restaurant, a pool and facilities for watersports, horse riding, trekking, and mountain biking.
€€€ **Can Cuch**, Can Cuch 35, Montseny, T931 033 980, www.cancuch.com. A sumptuous hotel in a beautiful stone *masía* (a traditional country house), with lovely garden, a pool and blissful views.
€€€ **Hotel Sant Roc**, Plaça Sant Roc, Solsona, T973 480 006, www.hotelsant roc.com. An elegant hotel in a ravishing

Modernista mansion in the town centre, with a spa and a fine restaurant.

€€€ Hotel Urbisol, about 20 km southwest of Vic in the little town of Calders, T938 309 153, www.hotelurbisol.com. A beautifully converted farmhouse set in rolling hills. The ultra-chic interior is filled with sleek minimalist decoration, and each room has wooden floors, exquisitely simple wooden furniture, and beautiful views. There's also a gym, jacuzzi, outdoor pool and a fine restaurant, and the owners can arrange mountain-bike trips, horse riding and balloon rides. A real treat.

€€ Estació del Nord, Plaça Estació 4, Vic T935 166 292, www.estaciodelnord.com. A charming little hotel in the pretty restored rooms above the train station in the city centre.

€€ Estrella, Plaça Bisbe Font I, Rupit, T938 522 005. A friendly *hostal* with an old-fashioned bar and inexpensive restaurant.

€€ Hotel Sant Bernat, Ctra de Sta María de Palautordera a Seva Km 20.7, T938 473 011, www.hotelhusasantbernat.com. This traditional, stone hotel in the heart of the natural park has beautiful views over the wooded hills from the terraces and good hiking and mountain-biking on the doorstep.

€€ Hostal Torras, Plaça Gravalosa, Sant Hilari Sacalm, T972 868 096. A reasonable option that is open all year and has a decent restaurant.

€€ La Riba, Vilanova de Sau, T938 847 023, www.hotellariba.com. A family-run place with pretty rooms, an excellent restaurant and a swimming pool.

€€ Masia del Montseny, Pg de la Pietat 14, Viladrau, T938 848 014, www.masiadel montseny.com. In the centre of a pretty village with just 10 simple rooms.

€€ Parador Nacional Duques de Cardona, Cardona, T938 691 275, www.parador.es. This dramatic parador has antique-furnished rooms in an 8th-century castle. There's also a good, expensive restaurant serving local specialities.

€ Hotel J Balmes, C/Francesc Pla 6, Vic, T938 891 272, www.hoteljbalmes.com. A modern hotel on the edge of town with functional but bright rooms and friendly service.

Girona *p119, map p120*

€€€ Mas Salvanera, Beuda (8 km from Besalú), T972 590 975, www.salvanera.com. A lovely 17th-century stone farmhouse on a sunny hillside with just 8 thoughtfully decorated rooms and a pool.

€€ Hotel Peninsular, C/Nou 3, T972 203 800, www.novarahotels.com. A modern hotel close to the river with well-equipped rooms (no a/c, though, which can be a problem in summer) at a reasonable price.

€€ Mirallac, Paseo Darder 50, Banyoles, T972 571 045, www.hotelmirallac.com. Located right on the lake with large bright rooms and a pool (prices jump a category in summer).

€€ Pensión Bellmirall, C/Bellmirall 3, T972 204 009, www.bellmirall.cat. One of the nicest places to stay in Girona and almost always booked up as it has just 7 rooms: behind the cathedral, the artist owner has filled the medieval stone house with all kinds of knick knacks and plants. Rooms without bathrooms are cheaper. Closed Jan-Feb.

€€ Pensió Viladomat, C/Ciutadans 5, Girona, T972 203 176. Call ahead to get rooms at this friendly little *pensión*, which is perfectly located in the old town.

€ Albergue Juvenil, C/Ciutadans 9, T972 218 003, www.xanascat.cat. Well-equipped youth hostel in a great location in the old town. It functions as a university residence during the academic year, but still keeps a few rooms for visitors.

€ Ca La Flora, C/Llibertat 91, Banyoles, T972 582 480, www.calaflora.com. Enchanting little B&B in the town centre; each room is named after a different flower.

€ Fonda Comas, C/ Canal 19, Banyoles, T972 570 127. Nicely located in the old town and has a good, cheap restaurant downstairs.

€ El Turrós, Gloria Mota, Argelaguer (7 km from Besalú) T972 687 350. Lost in the middle of a forest, **El Turrós** has just 4 rooms; sit around an old wood-burning stove, and enjoy a home-cooked meal.

€ Hotel Siqués, Av President Companys 6-8, Banyoles, T972 590 110, www.grupcal parent.com. A large, traditional stone guest-house on the edge of town with a pool and an excellent restaurant. Best budget choice.

Figueres and around *p123*

There aren't too many accommodation options around the Parc Natural de l'Albera.

€€€ Mas Pau, Ctra de Figueres–Besalú Km 4, T972 546 154, www.maspau.com. 4-star comfort in a converted 17th-century stone farmhouse, with lovely gardens and a pool.

€€ Finca Paraiso, Camí del Club Nàutic, Darnius, T972 535 662, www.darnins.net. A traditional, rustically decorated guesthouse set in gardens close to the Boadella lake with facilities close by for horse riding, watersports, fishing, hiking and tennis.

€€ Hostal La Quadra, C/Rectoria 11, Maçanet de Cabrenys, T972 544 032, www.laquadra.com. A delightful little hostel with rooms decorated in stylish muted colours and quirky art. It's on the edge of town with a popular vaulted restaurant in the cellar (which offers a lunchtime set menu at around €10 during the week).

€€ Hotel Ángeles, C/Barceloneta 10, Figueres, T972 510 661. Good value, modest hotel in the centre of town with flouncy rooms equipped with TVs and phones.

€€ Hotel Durán, C/Lasauca 5, T972 501 250, www.hotelduran.com. A classic Empordan hotel with an exceptionally good, expensive restaurant specializing in regional cuisine.

€€ Hotel Empordà, Cra N-II, Km 763, Figueres, T972 500 562, www.hotel emporda.com. Lots of chintz and dowdy decor in the rooms, but it's the expensive restaurant that draws the crowds; one of the best in Catalunya.

Olot and La Garrotxa *p125*

Most of the villages in the Garrotxa have a few eating and sleeping options.

€€€ Les Cols Pavellons, Av de les Cols, Olot, T699 813 817, www.lescolspavellons.com. Spectacular, glassy cubes for sleeping, and an outstanding restaurant serving inspired contemporary cuisine.

€€ Hotel Cal Sastre, C/ Cases Noves 1, Santa Pau, T972 680 049, www.calsastre.com. Tucked into the ancient walls and surrounded by gardens, with an excellent restaurant and lots of old-fashioned charm. A fantastic option for hikers.

€ Alberg Juvenil, Passeig de Barcelona, Olot, T972 264 200, www.xanascat.com. Set in a graceful turn-of-the-20th-century mansion close to the centre, with dorm rooms sleeping 4 to 10.

€ Casa Paula, Plaça Santa Roc 3, Castellfolit de la Roca, T972 294 032. Overlooks the main square and has a nice little restaurant and bar.

€ Hostal La Perla, Av Santa Colona, T972 262 326. A modern hotel close to the botanic gardens with rooms or mini-apartments, some with views of the park.

Ripoll *p127*

Ripoll has little to offer besides the monastery and surrounding villages like Sant Joan de las Abadesses make more attractive bases.

€€ Solana de Ter, T972 701 062, www.solanadeter.com. On the outskirts of town the **Solana de Ter** has a pool, tennis facilities, a range of other sports activities and even a campground. The restaurant is very good and fairly priced.

€€ Fonda Xesc, Plaça del Roser 1, Gombrèn, T972 730 404. A delightful option just outside Ripoll; a picturesque stone guesthouse with an excellent restaurant.

€€ Hostal del Ripollès, Plaça Nova 11, Ripoll, T972 700 215, www.elripolles.com/hostal delripolles.com. A well-located, reasonable *hostal* above a good pizza joint and bar.

Northeast of Ripoll to the French Border *p127*

€€ Hotel La Coma, Prat de la Coma s/n, Setcases, T972 136 073/4, www.hotel lacoma.com. This modern chalet-style place is a fancy option with a sauna, jacuzzi, gym, swimming pool and the friendly staff will happily give you tips on on local hiking and mountain-biking trails.

€€ Hotel Sant Roc, Plaça Carme 4, Camprodon, T972 740 119, www.hotelsantroc.info. A charming, family-run hotel in the town centre, with simple rooms and a good restaurant.

€€ Mas Janpere, Esteve Dorca i Mara Navarro, 2 km from the centre of Sant Joan de les Abadesses, T972 720 366. A traditional Catalan *mas* (farmhouse) with comfortable rooms and self-catering apartments. Rates vary according to season and number of occupants.

€ El Janpere, Sant Joan de les Abadesses, T972 722 210. A pretty *casa rural* with apartments near the river, just outside te town centre and with a reasonably priced restaurant.

€ Hostal Nati, C/ Pere Rovira 3, Sant Joan de les Abadesses, T972 720 114. A basic *hostal* with a cheap café-bar just outside the centre.

❶ Restaurants

Terrassa *p114*
There are a few pleasant cafés with terraces on the Plaça Vella in the old quarter.

€€ Hostal del Fum, Ctra de Montcada 19, T937 888 337. This classic restaurant serves traditional Catalan dishes and is one of the best in town.

€ La Mola, Parc Sant Llorenç del Munt i l'Obac, T937 435 454. The only way to get to this restaurant perched on top of La Mola's peak, is on foot; supplies are brought up by donkey. Beans and sausages and other classic fare is served in an old monastery with fantastic views.

Montserrat *p115*
Bring a picnic or pick up supplies from the small shop near the monastery. The *cafetería* food on Montserrat is dire and overpriced.

Vic and the Parc Natural de Montseny *p116*
See also Where to stay.

€€ La Taula, Plaça Don Miquel de Clariana 4, Vic, T938 863 229. This is a local favourite, a traditional stone-walled restaurant serving classic local dishes.

€€ Rectoria d'Oris, Ctra de Torrelló a St Quirze de Bisora Km 83, T938 590 230. This converted rectory (5 km from Vic) houses a well-reputed restaurant serving the freshest cuisine made with local produce.

€€-€ Sau Vell, next to the sailing club, T937 447 130, www.sauvell.com. Good fish and lighter snacks overlooking the Pantà de Sau.

€ Amaranta, C/Güell, T972 940 832. Tasty vegetarian sishes and a good-value set lunch.

€ El Basset, C/Sant Sadurni 4, Vic, T938 890 212. Comfortable, traditional restaurant serving Catalan dishes. You can fill up on the lunch menu for around €15.

€ Coqueria Cuca Fera, C/Canyelles 3, Vic, T938 861 278. A great place for a cheap lunch, this offers the local *cocas* – bread – topped with anchovies, hams, cheese and all kinds of goodies. It's always packed so book in advance.

Girona *p119, map p120*
€€€ Celler de Can Roca, Ctra Taialà 40, T972 222 157. One of the finest restaurants in the world, with 3 Michelin stars to prove it.

€€ Casa Marieta, Plaça Independencia 5, T972 201 016. A classic, this traditional restaurant offers Catalan dishes prepared from seasonal ingredients.

€€ La Farinera, Passatge Farinera Teixidor 4, T972 220 220. Delicious Catalan and Basque dishes in a stylish setting.

€€ La Penyora, C/Nou del Teatre 3, T972 218 948. This is a local favourite and with good reason: the Catalan cuisine is excellent and the service warm and efficient. While going à la carte can push it up into the expensive category, they also do good-value set menus.

€€ Pont Vell, C/Pont Vell 28, Besalú, T972 591 027. Set in a medieval house overlooking the old bridge this restaurant makes for a memorable evening. Dishes served are based on recipes which date back to the Middle Ages.

€€ Quatre Estacions, Passeig de la Farga s/n, Banyoles, T972 573 300. Uses the freshest local produce for its excellent, Catalan cuisine. They've got a great range of local liqueurs as well.

€€ Taberna de l'Abat, Plaça Santa Llúcia 6, T972 219 704. Exposed stone walls give this rustic spot plenty of atmosphere. Delicious Catalan dishes are served on the terrace in summer.

€ Boira, Plaça de la Independència 10, T972 203 096. This bar has a perfect location on the river edge. There's a good-value lunch menu and tapas or you could head upstairs for the fancier restaurant.

€ Café Arts, Rambla Llibertat 25. One of dozens of popular cafés on Girona's lovely, arcaded rambla. A great place to muse over a coffee on the terrace.

€ Café Context, C/Pou Rodó 21, T972 486 390, www.cafecontext.com. A delightful bookshop and café serving tapas, drinks and light meals.

€ La Crêperie Bretonne, C/Cort Reial 14, T972 218 120. A good choice for veggies, this friendly, French-owned crêperie is easy to spot thanks to the old caravan at the entrance. Budding artists can draw their impression of Girona on the paper table-cloths with the crayons provided.

Figueres and around *p123*
The most acclaimed restaurants in the region are the hotel restaurants in the **Duran** and the **Empordà** (see Where to stay) in Figueres.

€€ El Bon Retorn, Av de Barcelona 36, T972 504 623. Another of Figueres' good hotel-restaurants serving excellent modern Catalan cuisine.

€€ España, C/Jonquera 26, T972 500 869. An old-fashioned restaurant serving good local dishes.

€ El Café del Barri Vell, Plaça de las Patates, T972 505 776. A simple, laid-back and cheap, vegetarian café on a pretty little square just behind the Dalí museum, which puts on poetry readings and concerts out on the terrace in summer.

Olot and La Garrotxa *p125*
Many *fondas* (guesthouses) and hotels in the area around Olot have good, traditional restaurants offering tasty local dishes.

€€€ Les Cols, Ctra de la Canya s/n, Olot, T972 269 209. Spectacular restaurant and stunning rooms in glassy cubes in the garden.

€€ La Deu Ctra de la Deu, T972 261 004, www.ladeu.es. One of the best options for trying local 'volcanic cuisine', which features locally sourced produce.

€ El Mig, Plaça del Mig 1, Olot, T972 270 298. Relaxed café-bar with cheap snacks and coin-operated Internet terminals.

🌙 Bars and clubs

Vic and the Parc Natural de Montseny *p116*
Vic's nightlife isn't exactly pumping, but there are a few good bars around the Carrer Sant Miquel de Sants.

Girona *p119, map p120*
Lola Café, C/Força 7, T629 794 360. Cocktail bar in the heart of the old city, popular with students.

Room 118, Gran Vía Jaume I No 20, T972 417 409. A fancy bar in the sleek **Hotel Vitòria**, with amazing city-wide views.

Olot and La Garrotxa *p125*

There are dozens of bars concentrated on and around the Plaça Carme.

Bar Carme, right on the square, with a small terrace.

Bar Cocodrilo, C/Sant Roc 5, T972 263 124. Also on the square with marble tables and a long list of cocktails.

❀ Festivals

Terrassa *p114*

Mar International Jazz Festival, with the city's main festival (dedicated to **San Pere**) held on the following Sun when you'll see plenty of traditional Catalan traditions from *gegants* to human castles (Terrassa has got a couple of champion *castellar* teams).

Vic and the Parc Natural de Montseny *p116*

Mid-Sep Music Festival, www.festival gualba.com, is always a good event with bands playing on the square and in venues across the town.

Girona *p119, map p120*

Mid-May Temps de Flors (Festival of Flowers).

Sep Jazz Festival and a pretty low-key **Cinema Festival**.

Oct-Nov Festa de Sant Narcís, the city's biggest festival, when devils, dragons and giants parade though the streets.

Nov and Dec Fira d'Artesans, a traditional craft fair where you can do your Christmas shopping.

Ripoll *p127*

Jul and Aug Music Festival, low-key, when weekend concerts are held in the monastery and the church of Sant Pere next door.

⛰ What to do

Vic and the Parc Natural de Montseny *p116*

The countryside around Vic is great for riding, walking and hot-air ballooning – there are dozens of companies offering trips in hot-air balloons. The **tourist office** has a full list of tour operators and dozens of useful leaflets, or you could contact:

Baló Tour, C/Bisbe Morgades 49, Vic, T934 144 774, www.balotour.com. One of the biggest companies offering balloon rides across the Vic plain.

Club Nautic Vic-Sau, C/Granollers 3a, T630 877 011 www.vicsau.com. Sailing lessons, canoes, kayaks and more on the Pantà de Sau.

Olot and La Garrotxa *p125*

There is plenty of walking and horse riding in this region. Olot tourist office has a list of local tour operators, or you could contact:

Aventura Natura, C/Major 37, Santa Pau, T626 599 706. A range of tours, including walks around the medieval village and the volcanic peaks of the area. Also offer Segway tours.

⊖ Transport

Terrassa *p114*

Frequent (at least 4 an hour) **trains** from Sants station in **Barcelona**, or **metro** from Plaça Catalunya. Return tickets on the train or metro cost less than €5. If you are travelling by **car**, take the E9 from Barcelona.

Montserrat *p115*

There are several ways of getting to Montserrat from Barcelona. A daily **bus** (**Autocares Julià**, T932 615 858, www.autocaresjulia.es) departs 0915 from outside Sants Station, returns 1700 in winter, 1800 in summer, €4.70 one way. The **FGC train** (R5), departs from Plaça d'Espanya, get off at Monistrol de Montserrat to connect with the **cable car**, Aeri de Montserrat, which makes a hair-raising ascent in 5 mins

(€10 return), or stop at Monistrol de Montserrat to take the *cremallera* (rack-and-pinion railway) up the mountain in 15 mins (€9.50 return). A range of all-inclusive tickets, which include the FGC train, plus the *cremallera* and the funiculars on top of the mountain (€27) and, optionally, museum entrance and lunch (€43), are available: see www.cremallerade montserrat.cat for details.

There are several **walking paths,** including the Montserrat Pilgrimage Path (also known as the Camí de les Canals i de l'Aigua) from Barcelona: see www.montserrat visita.com for more details.

Vic and the Parc Natural de Montseny *p116*
Vic is less than 1 hr away from **Barcelona** by train (trains leave half-hourly from Plaça Catalunya and Sants). **Sagalés**, T902 130 014, run a regular service; **TEISA**, T973 268 500, www.teisa-bus.com, run twice-daily services to **Lleida** and another to **Girona**.

There are infrequent local buses from **Vic** to **Viladrau**, **Sant Hilari Sacalm** and **Rupit** and infrequent buses to other local villages but the region is best explored with your own transport. Trains stop regularly at **Hostalric** (on the Barcelona–Girona line) and **Aigufreda** on the Barcelona– Puigcerdà line.

Girona *p119, map p120*
Air Girona's airport is used mainly for charter flights and low-cost flight operators, including **Ryanair** and **Thomson Airways**. For information, see www.aena.es.

Bus There are regular local buses from Girona and Figueres to **Banyoles** (very frequent in summer) and **Besalú** with **TEISA**, T972 570 053, which also runs less regular services to these villages from Barcelona. Services arrive at Girona from Estació del Nord, Barcelona. **Olot** and **Besalú** are linked

with Girona by regular direct buses from Barcelona with **Garrotxa Exprés**, T902 177 178, and **TEISA** (T972 201 796). **SARFA**, T902 302 025, run services from the beach resorts of the Costa Brava.

Train Services leave regularly from Sants and Pg de Gràcia in **Barcelona** for Girona.

Figueres and around *p123*
The bus and train stations are next to each other a 10-min walk from the city centre. The Dali Museum is signposted.

Bus There are regular SARFA, T902 302 025, buses to **Roses**, **Cadaqués**, **Sant Feliu de Guíxols** and other coastal towns. Barcelona Bus/Sagalés, T902 130 014, run daily services from **Barcelona** to **Figueres** via **Girona**, and **TEISA**, T972 201 796, run services to **Besalú** and **Olot**.

Train There are frequent (at least hourly) trains to **Figueres** via **Girona** from Estació-Sants and Passeig de Gràcia in **Barcelona**. These continue on to **Llança** and **Port Bou**.

The area around Figueres is comparatively little-visited and very difficult without your own transport. You can get a **taxi** from Figueres out to the surrounding villages or wait for the single **bus** on Thu to **Sant Llorenç de la Muga** and **Albanyá** with SARFA, T972 301 293. There are daily services between **La Jonquera** and **Maçanet de Cabrenys** with David i Manel, T972 672 853.

Olot and La Garrotxa *p125*
There are regular bus services to **Olot** from **Girona**, and twice-daily services from Barcelona via **Banyoles** and **Besalú**. There's also one bus a day from **Lloret de Mar** and one from **Ripoll**. There are bus connections from **Olot** to **Santa Pau**, which run daily in summer but only twice-weekly in winter (Mon and Wed).

Ripoll *p127*
TEISA, T972 702 095, has bus services between **Olot**, **Girona**, **Camprodon**, and **Sant Joan de les Abadesses**. Ripoll is on the main train line from Barcelona-Sants to Puigcerdà and the French border via Vic.

Northeast of Ripoll to the French Border *p127*
Buses between Barcelona, Olot, Girona, **Camprodon** and **Sant Joan de les Abadesses**. Buses between Camprodon and Setcases, but you'll need your own transport to reach some of the more remote villages.

Catalan Pyrenees

The Catalan Pyrenees cover a vast swathe of the region. The highest and most dramatic peaks are in the northwest corner of Catalunya, near Puigcerdà and La Seu d'Urgell. This is where you'll find the best ski resorts as well as the spectacular National Park of Aigüestortes and the Romanesque churches in the remote Vall de Boí. If you are approaching from the south, the massive Cadí range is not, strictly speaking, part of the Pyrenees proper, but still offers some demanding climbing and hiking in the Cadí-Moixeró Natural Park. One of the most popular sports in the region is white-water rafting along the powerful Noguera Palleresa river, and you can head also over the border into Andorra for some shopping and magnificent scenery.

Vall de Núria → *For listings, see pages 147-152.*

A tiny rack-and-pinion railway makes the spectacular, vertiginous journey to the Vall de Núria, set more than 2000 m up in the Pyrenees. A low-key ski resort in winter, and hikers' favourite in summer, it's also famous for a miraculous statue of the Madonna in the ugly sanctuary which dominates the valley. Núria is second only to Montserrat as a girl's name in Catalunya. The Vall de Núria can get surprisingly crowded in summer and winter but most people just come for the train ride and a picnic by the lake – so even a 20-minute walk will take you away from the hordes.

La Cremallera
Heading directly north of Ripoll on the N-152 which meanders along the Freser Valley, you'll reach **Ribes de Freser**, a low-key town with a spa (Balneari de Ribes), sheep-trials every September, and a weekly market where you can pick up some of the local farmhouse pâté, *pa de fetge*. This is the departure point for **La Cremallera**, a rack-and-pinion train line, which makes a spectacular and magical journey through the mountains. It makes one stop, at the attractive town of **Queralbs**, a huddle of stone and slate houses with an elegant Romanesque church, which hasn't quite been overwhelmed by the new developments springing up like toadstools on its outskirts. The train continues onwards and upwards across viaducts, through tunnels, past dramatic cliffs, forests and waterfalls, finally disgorging its passengers up at the Vall de Núria, 1,000 m above Ribes de Fraser and more than 2000 m above sea level. The lugubrious sanctuary of **La Mare de Deu de Núria** overlooking the valley was built in the late 19th century, and looks more like a prison than a place of worship. Like Montserrat, the valley has long attracted pilgrims, who still come to venerate the 12th-century carved wooden statue of

the Madonna, which is almost as famous as Montserrat's La Moreneta. The Madonna is the patron saint of shepherds, but she's also credited with helping women with fertility problems: there's a hole in part of the Choir and anyone hoping to conceive should put their head in it while the bell tolls.

There is a ski station, especially popular with families (11 ski runs, including two black and three red runs), a lake where you can hire boats, horse-riding facilities, and plenty of easy to moderate walking trails; www.valldenuria.com has all the details.

Berga and Parc Natural de Cadí-Moixeró → *For listings, see pages 147-152.*

Berga, on a rocky slope 50 km west of Ripoll, is the capital and main transport hub of the Berguedà *comarca* (county). The old quarter has an old-fashioned faded charm, but the town is best known as a base for the nearby Parc Natural de Cadí-Moixero which offers spectacular hiking and rock-climbing, including the celebrated peak of Pedraforça. If you've got your own transport or plenty of patience with bus schedules, there are some delightful stone villages scattered around the edges of the park which make more attractive bases for exploring.

Berga
Berga doesn't have any particular sights or monuments, and serves mainly as a base for visits to the nearby natural park of Cadí-Moixero. The old town, shabby but still picturesque, is a pleasant place for a stroll. During Corpus Christi, in May or early June, the town explodes with one of Catalunya's most exhilarating festivals, the three-day **Festa de la Patum**, with *gegants* (dragons spitting fire) dancing in the streets to the sounds of strange hornpipes, plenty of carousing by red-capped Catalans, and, for a grand finale, a wild dance by masked men covered in rushes.

Some 14 km west of Berga is the **Rasos De Peguera** ski resort, the closest to Barcelona and a favourite for day-trippers. Small and low key, it's good for families and beginners. For information, see www.rasos.net.

Parc Natural de Cadí-Moixeró
Beyond Berga, the foothills of the Pyrenees loom with startling abruptness, pale and forbiddingly craggy. These dramatic peaks are part of the Sierra Cadí, one of the most spectacular sights in Catalunya, and part of the Parc Natural de Cadí-Moixeró. The sheer Pedraforca ('stone pitchfork') peak is a serious challenge for experienced mountain climbers, who descend in droves during the summer months.

Bagà and around The park information office is in Bagà, a few kilometres further up the C-1411, a tranquil town with another pretty medieval core. From here, a small paved road heads up through a valley of Alpine lushness and beauty, ringing with the soft sounds of cow bells, climbing higher into forested peaks and finally emerging at the heady Coll de l'Escriga. Just beyond it is the attractive hamlet of Gisclareny, a good base for trekking.

Back a mile or two before Bagà is the dreary roadside straggle of **Guardiola de Berguedà**, which hides the elegant Romanesque **Monestir de Sant Llorenç** – get keys from the Ajuntament (Town Hall), mornings only – and is the starting point for the single daily bus which heads west to the more remote, prettier villages of **Saldes** and **Gósol**.

Saldes sits right at the foot of Pedraforca and is the usual point of departure for the most difficult routes; lofty Gósol, a dense stone warren of ancient streets, once inspired Picasso who spent the summer of 1906 painting and walking here and is the starting point for a number of easier, if less dramatic, trails up the back of Pedraforca.

La Pobla de Lillet East of Guardiola de Bergueda, a small road follows the thin trickle of the Llobregat to La Pobla de Lillet, with two sturdy stone bridges straddling the river, and an appealing old quarter to wander around. There's also a delightful garden, the **Jardí de la Font** (Spring Garden) designed by Gaudí on the bank of the river, and a couple of fine Romanesque churches on the outskirts – the **Monestir de Santa Maria**, and the **Santuari de Falgàs**. There are ancient churches tucked into almost every fold of these mountains; one of the loveliest is at **Sant Jaume de Frontanyà**, south of La Pobla de Lillet (get the keys from the tourist office), and there are several within a couple of miles of Berga itself, including **Església de Sant Quirze de Pedret**, a pre-Romanesque church with Moorish sides, and the humble little **Església de Sant Pere de Madrona**, clamped in a little hollow just below the shrine of Queralt.

Castellar de n'Hug and ski resorts Heading north of Pobla de Lillet, the road winds up towards Castellar de n'Hug, an ancient stone sprawl hugging the mountain which has a special place in every Catalan's heart, thanks to the Fonts de Llobregat, a spring which has famously never dried up – it's the source of the great river which meets the sea just south of Barcelona, but here it's a lazy trickle tumbling over stones and overhung with trees. The town makes a good, if touristy, base for walking and isn't too far from the adjoining ski resorts of **La Molina** and **Masella**. La Molina has 53 pistes, with plenty for skiers of all abilities including intermediate and advanced skiers. For information and to book accommodation call T972 892 031 www.lamolina.com. Masella has 37 pistes including six black and 15 red runs. For information and to book accommodation, T972 144 000, www.masella.com. The **tourist office** ① *Castellar de n'Hug's Ajuntament, T938 257 097*, has lists of accommodation.

Toses To the southeast of the ski resorts on the N-152 to Ripoll, Toses stands precariously balanced high on a lofty peak and boasts the enchanting frescoed Romanesque Església de Sant Cristófol. The original frescoes have been taken to MNAC in Barcelona but copies of the surviving fragments in situ hint at their former splendour.

Cerdanyà Valley → *For listings, see pages 147-152.*

North of Bagà, the mountains are pierced with extraordinary tunnels – including the Tunel de Cadí, Spain's longest – which lead into the lush valley of the Cerdanya, shaped like 'the handprint of God' according to local tradition. The capital of the region is Puigcerdà, jauntily set on a promontory overlooking the valley and surrounded by snow-capped peaks. Most of its monuments were wiped out by bombing during the Civil War, but it's still got a few pretty squares which are the centre of the town's buzzy nightlife. The best times to visit depend on whether you are interested in walking, best in late spring and early autumn, or skiing, you can count on snow in January and February.

Puigcerdà

Puigcerdà was once the capital of the kingdom of Cerdanya which spread across the Pyrenees before being divided between France and Spain in the 17th century. Bombing wiped out most of its ancient monuments during the Civil War, including the Gothic church of Santa Maria on the main square, although its formidable belltower survived, along with the 13th-century church of Sant Domènech on the city's eastern flank. Inside, barely discernible in the gloom, there's a macabre series of murals depicting the saint's head being split in two with a sabre.

A cheerful, appealing town, Puigcerdà has plenty of bars and restaurants, and bustling squares full of outdoor cafés. In summer, you can join in with some typical Catalan sardana dancing on Wednesday afternoons, although check with the tourist office as it takes place on different squares. There are easy strolls down to a lake where you can hire a boat and laze about among the swans and weeping willows, and the town has also got an enormous ice rink (a hangover from the Olympics) and is the capital of Spanish ice hockey.

Llívia

When the former kingdom of Cerdanya was being divided up between the French and Spanish, the French claimed the 33 villages between the Ariège and Roussillon. But after the deal was done, the Spanish triumphantly claimed Llivia by pointing out that it was a town and not a village. As a result, Llívia is now a curious Spanish colony tucked a couple of miles inside the French border. It's a tiny, attractive town, with a twisting medieval hub guarded by a **fortified church** ① C/dels Forns, Tue-Sat 1000-1300, 1500-1800 (until 2000 in summer), and a medieval pharmacy, now part of the **Museu Municipal** ① C/dels Forns 10, T972 896 313, Apr-Jun Tue-Sun 1000-1800, Jul-Aug daily 1000-1900, Sep Tue-Sun 1000-1900, Oct-Mar Tue-Sun 1000-1630, €1. The Esteva pharmacy dates back to the 15th-century, and only stopped doling out potions and unguents in 1918 – there's a collection of jars and bizarre apothecary's instruments and some delightful hand-painted herb boxes. The rest of the museum's holdings are a bit musty – Bronze Age relics and old maps – and the entrance ticket also allows admission into the 15th-century Torre Bernat de So next to the church. It's a good place for a stroll and a long, lazy lunch on one of the squares. You can find a **tourist information office** ① C/Forn 11, www.llivia.org, T972 896 011, in the town hall.

Bellver de Cerdanya

South of Puigcerdà lie a string of relaxed, country towns: Bellver de Cerdanya, heaped on a hill overlooking the river, is one of the largest, with a handsome porticoed square and pretty, flower-decked balconies strung along the old stone houses. The **Romanesque Església de Santa Eugènia de Nerellà** just south of the town is pierced with a peculiar leaning belltower, and has an ancient polychrome statue of the Madonna. The village is also one of the access points for the Parc Natural de Cadí-Moixeró (see page 138).

Strung along the main road to the west, **Martinet** is less obviously alluring, but has a good reputation for its country cooking and lies just beneath the small ski resort of **Llés**, which also has a lake, the Estany de la Pera, for messing about in boats and kayaks.

La Seu d'Urgell and Castellciutat

At the western end of the valley is La Seu d'Urgell, on the banks of the River Segre, a relaxed market town which was named for its imposing seu (cathedral). After mouldering away for years as a remote backwater, La Seu d'Urgell got a new lease of life when the Olympic canoeing events were held here in 1992 and it now has excellent watersports facilities. It's also the main point of access on the Spanish side of the border for Andorra (see page 153).

Fortunately, the new development has left the medieval centre almost untouched, and the cobbled streets linking a chain of little squares are a relaxing place to amble. The **cathedral** ① *T973 353 242, www.museudiocesaurgell.org, Jun-Sep Mon-Sat 1000-1330 and 1600-1930, Sun 1000-1300, Oct-May Mon-Fri 1200-1330, Sat-Sun 1100-1330, €3, concessions €1*, was first established in the eighth century, but completely rebuilt in 1184. There's an elegant cloister with finely sculpted capitals, and the **Museu Diocesana** holds a good collection of ecclesiastical treasures, including an illuminated copy of the *Beato de Liébana*.

La Seu d'Urgell has one odd little curiosity: the **Cloister of Vallira**, in the park of the same name on the edge of town, was designed by Luis Racionera and, instead of the usual saints and beasts, the capitals depict 20th-century icons, from Marilyn Monroe to Picasso.

Castellciutat, up on a rock overlooking the town, is the site of the ancient settlement which was wiped out by the Moors during the eighth century; there are some scenic trails leading along the valley and up to the ruined castle which is all that remains. La Seu d'Urgell's tourist office has a range of leaflets describing walks in some of the surrounding villages, including a particularly beautiful walk to a waterfall near the tiny hamlet of Estana.

Noguera Palleresa Valley and Parc Nacional d'Aigüestortes

→ *For listings, see pages 147-152.*

Heading west of La Seu d'Urgell, the mountains are studded with steep valleys, ancient stone villages of slate-roofed houses and powerful rivers: the most powerful of them all is the Noguera Palleresa, which has become a paradise for rafting and adventure sports. The stunning park of Aigüestortes spreads across this northeastern corner of Catalunya, one of only 14 national parks in Spain, and certainly one of the most enchanting and beautiful regions in the whole country.

Tremp and Talarn

The southernmost large town on the Noguera Palleresa Valley, Tremp is squeezed between two massive hydroelectrical plants which harness the energy of Catalunya's most powerful river. Talarn, tucked behind chunky walls on a hilltop just north of Tremp, makes a much more attractive stopover.

La Pobla de Segur and around

La Pobla de Segur was the final destination for the rafters from the Pyrenees who nudged their loads of felled treetrunks down river to the factories in an epic journey which is re-enacted annually from Sort (see below). A couple of Modernista mansions, including the Casa Mauri (now the Ajuntament, or town hall), are left over from the years of prosperity, but the town is now really a tourist and transport hub for buses into the Pyrenees.

There are some interesting, isolated villages with their own forgotten Romanesque churches nearby; **Ribert** is beautifully set in wooded countryside by the Riu Verde, and **Claverol** is topped by the ruins of an ancient castle. Heading northeast towards Sort, the road passes through a spectacular gorge, the **Congost de Collegats**, pummelled by the Noguera Pallaresa in its rush from the mountains and the inspiration, some say, for Gaudí's La Pedrera. **Gerri de la Sal**, peacefully sitting by the side of the river was, as its name indicates, an important salt-manufacturing village. Salt has been gathered here since Roman times, but a flood wiped out almost all the salt flats in 1982; a small eco-museum describes the process and the history of salt-production. The town is dominated by the 12th-century **Benedictine Monestir de Santa Maria**, with a striking, if shabby, wall of bells looming above the entrance.

Sort
The biggest centre for rafting and adventure sports is Sort, where the pretty old town is rapidly being swallowed up by hasty development. The word *sort* means 'luck' in Catalan, and Sort in fact boasts one of the highest percentages of lottery winners in Spain. The streets are now lined with tour-operators and outdoor kit shops, offering an incredible array of activities in the surrounding canyons and valleys. Every year in late June or early July, there's a spectacular festival of **Raiers** (Rafters) who scud down the river on simple rafts made of lashed together branches just as the old timber pilots used to do.

Llavorsí and Port-Aíné
Llavorsí is also full of adventure tour operators offering rafting trips on the Noguera Pallaresa (it's the starting point for many of the trips), and is easily the prettiest town along this stretch. Northeast of Sort is the ski resort of Port-Aíné, a smallish ski station which has a good range of pistes suitable for intermediate and advanced skiiers. For ski information and to book accommodation, T973 621 100, www.skipallars.cat.

Espot and Parc Nacional d'Aigüestortes i Estany de Maurici
Further up the valley, there's another ski resort at Super Espot above the small village of Espot which is the western gateway to the preternaturally beautiful Parc Nacional d'Aigüestortes i Estany de Maurici. This is Catalunya's only national park, a spellbinding landscape of green meadows flecked with scores of crystal-clear lakes and surrounded by jagged, forested peaks. There are hikes for walkers of all fitness levels, and it's also an excellent destination for serious climbers; the **park information office** ① *Casa del Parc, C/Sant Maurici 5, Espot, T973 624 036*, has maps and information on the refuges scattered through the park. These are usually staffed with fulltime wardens during the summer, and it is worth calling in advance to ensure a place. Jeep taxis will drop you off at the park boundaries (or you can avoid the road and walk along the GR11), where you can make the short stroll to the Estany de Maurici, a still, clear lake of hallucinatory beauty, looked over by the strange stone eruptions of Els Encantats (The Enchanted Ones). Legend has it that two hunters and their dog sneaked off one Sunday morning instead of attending mass; they were lured deeper into the mountains by an elusive stag when a bolt of lightning shot down from the heavens and turned them into stone. For experienced walkers, there's a spectacular trek (about 10 hours from Espot to Boí) right through the park from east to west. The park information offices have details. See below for information on Boí, on the western edge of the park.

Vall d'Aran → *For listings, see pages 147-152.*

The lush Vall d'Aran was originally part of the French kingdomAquitaine, although it joined the kingdom of Catalunya and Aragón in 1389. It was often entirely cut off from the rest of the world during the winter until the massive Vielha tunnel was hammered through the Maladeta peak by Republican POWs in the 1940s. This is the only Atlantic valley in the eastern Pyrenees, drained by the River Garonne which meets the sea near Bordeaux; cooler, wetter and altogether neater than the surrounding valleys, it has preserved a distinctly French character audible in the local language, Aranès, a mixture of Gascon French, Catalan and even the odd Basque word thrown in for good measure. The valley's capital, Vielha, is a buzzy mountain town stuffed full of smart boutiques catering to the constant flow of French day-trippers. There are tourist information offices in most of the Aranese villages.

Vielha

The capital of the Vall d'Aran is Vielha, which is prettier when you get off the drab main drag and wander about the narrow streets behind it. Here you'll find the distinctive Aranese stone houses, with their stepped gables, slate roofs, and carved wooden balconies. Vielha is becoming increasingly smart, thanks to the droves of French visitors who have triggered a spate of fashionable shops, galleries and restaurants, and it doesn't hurt that the Spanish royal family traditionally choose this region for their skiing holidays.

In the heart of old Vielha is the 12th-century **Església de Sant Miquèu**, with an octagonal belltower overlooking a little square. The church holds a very beautiful 12th-century sculpture of Christ de Mijaran which is one of the finest examples of Romanesque sculpture in this region. Across the river is the **Museu de la Vall d'Aran** ① *C/Major 10, T973 641 815, Mon-Sat 1000-1300 and 1700-2000, Sun 1000-1300, €2, concessions €1,* in a 17th-century mansion, with a description of the butterflies unique to the valley, and exhibits relating to the history and folklore of the region.

Baqueira-Beret and the Port de la Bonanaigua

At the eastern end of the Vall d' Aran is the ultra-chic ski resort of Baqueira-Beret (www.baqueira.es), where the Spanish royal family like to belt down the pristine slopes. Their patronage has sparked a spate of chi-chi development throughout the Vall d'Aran, much of it in harmony with the ancient grey-slated villages (Baqueira-Beret itself being the exception, with some eye-poppingly dreadful modern architecture). Beyond Baqueira-Beret is the dizzying pass of the Port de la Bonanaigua, which at more than 2,000 m is one of the most spectacular in the Pyrenees. Shaggy mountain horses daydream in the middle of the road and, with admirable equanimity, refuse to budge for even the biggest lorries. The Port de la Bonanaigua chair lift also runs in summer (usually July to mid-September) and there are some excellent hikes across the top of the mountains.

Salardú and Artíes

Salardú and nearby Artíes make good bases for hiking in the valley, and are delightful crooked old towns of grey stone overlooked by a pair of Romanesque churches. In Salardú, the 13th-century Església de Sant Andreu is set in its own gardens, and has an imposing carved portal; inside, the remnants of its ancient frescoes have been restored revealing a glowing Pantocrater (Christ in Majesty).

Artíes, the most attractive village in the valley, has the Església de Santa Maria, fortified by the Templar knights, and the small Església de Sant Joan, which now holds a small local museum.

Vall de Boí → *For listings, see pages 147-152.*

South of Vielha, the Noguera Ribagorçana River forms a natural boundary between Aragón and Catalunya. Tucked just east of the river is one of Catalunya's greatest treasures, the Vall de Boí, scattered with ancient villages crammed with so many masterpieces of Romanesque art that the whole valley was designated a World Heritage Site in 2000. The finest frescoes have been taken to MNAC in Barcelona, see page 53, in order to safeguard them from rapacious collectors who were snapping them up at an alarming rate at the turn of the last century. They have been replaced by copies, which give a glimmering sense of their original splendour. Thoughtless development and heavy tourism has taken its toll on many of the villages, but the surrounding scenery is spellbinding and the churches themselves can be magical if you get there before the crowds. Most of the villages have several tour operators offering trekking, horse riding and mountain biking in the surrounding hills. The main tourist office for the Boí Valley is in Barruera, one of the first villages along the valley. Stop in at the **Centre d'Interpretació** (**visitor centre**) ① *T973 696 715, www.centreromanic.com*, in Erill la Vall to buy a combination ticket (€9) which allows you to visit all the Romanesque churches.

Coll and Barruera

From El Pont de Suert, a single road winds up through the Vall de Boí, with smaller roads splintering off to the villages; the first of these turnings leads up to **Coll**, often overlooked in the charge towards the biggest prizes at Taüll, but very prettily tucked into a hillside. Its Romanesque **Església de Santa Maria de l'Assumpció** is rarely open, but it is very occasionally possible to arrange guided visits with the valley's main tourist office in **Barruera**, the large town spread along the main road further north. The tourist office is right on the main road and provides plenty of helpful maps, leaflets and accommodation guides. Barruera's Romanesque **Església de Sant Feliu** ① *mid-Sep to mid-Jun 1000-1400, 1600-1900, mid-Jun to mid-Sep 1000-1400, 1600-2000 €2, concessions €1.50*, has a peaceful setting away from the constant whizz of traffic down by the river.

Durro and Erill La Vall

A turning to the right leads to **Durro**, smaller and more peaceful, with the imposing **Església de La Nativitat de la Mare de Déu**, and a humble Romanesque monastery hidden in the mountains beyond. North of Barruera, and just before the turning for Boí, is **Erill La Vall**, a quieter base than Boí or Taüll, with a handful of good restaurants and hotels. The spick-and-span 12th-century **Església de Santa Eulàlia** ① *Tue-Sat 1000-1400 and 1600-1900, Sun 1200-1400 and 1600-1900, €2, concessions €1.50*, has been thoroughly – perhaps too thoroughly – renovated, but still boasts a soaring six-storey belltower, and the town is hoping to build a visitors' centre which will give tourists a glimpse into the Romanesque tradition.

Boí

The tiny medieval centre of Boí is corseted by a grim ring of car parks and modern developments, but it's the closest base for western access to the **Parc Nacional d'Aigüestortes i Estany de Maurici**, see page 141. There's a **park information office** ① *Casa del Parc Nacional d'Aigüestortes i Estany de Sant Maurici, C/de les Graieres 2, Boí, T973 696 189*. The town is surrounded by good walking trails to the other villages of the valley. It's about 3.5 km to the park boundaries, unless you take a jeep taxi (book at the information office), and another 3.5 km to the waterfalls of Aigüestortes ('twisted waters').

Boí's ancient **Església de Sant Joan**, dating back to around 1100, has been extensively renovated and contains a copy of the startling murals which are now in MNAC and are some of the earliest examples of Catalan Romanesque art; there's a vicious depiction of the Stoning of St Stephen, and a lurid Heaven and Hell, in which monsters taunt a soul burning in Hell. The road through the Vall de Boí peters out at the spa complex in **Caldes de Boí**, which has been famous for its waters since Roman times, and is beautifully set in dense forest.

Taüll and Boí-Taüll ski resort

The road twists upwards through Boí towards the very pretty village of Taüll, which contains the most spectacular church in the valley, the beautiful **Església de Sant Climent de Taüll** ① *summer daily 1030-1400 and 1600-2000, winter Mon-Sat 1030-1400 and 1600-1900, Sun 1030-1400 €2, concessions €2*, with its distinctive soaring belltower. The image of the Pantocrater (Christ in Majesty) is one of the most important elements of Romanesque art, and the Christ which looms from the apse of Sant Climent, fixing the congregation with his limpid terrible gaze, is startling in its intensity. The views from the top of the slim belltower (included in entrance ticket but queues can take forever in summer) are breathtaking.

Taüll is a likeable little town, despite the rash of modern chalets which have sprung up in the wake of the nearby ski resort of **Boí-Taüll**, and another good base for walking in the surrounding hills. At the heart of the oldest part of the town, a stone maze of hunched cottages, is another medieval church, the **Església de Santa María** ① *1000-2000, free*, gently but determinedly subsiding and taking its belltower with it. For ski information and accommodation, T902 406 640, www.boitaullresort.com. The ski resort of Boí-Taüll is relatively new, but unfortunately some thoughtless modern development has already grown up around it. The resort itself has a respectable number of slopes – more than 50, including nine black and 24 red runs – and a wide range of accommodation in all price categories.

Lleida and around → *Phone code: 973. Population: 113,686.*

Cheerful, if rather nondescript, the provincial town of Lleida sits on a bump in the middle of a fertile plain close to the Aragonese border, a strategic location which led to the establishment of a Roman settlement and, later, the capital of a small Moorish kingdom. Nowadays the substantial student population gives Lleida a buzz, particularly around the lively Plaça de Sant Joan, but there are virtually no reminders of its illustrious past. It's the transport hub for bus services to the Pyrenees, with several services a day heading up the Noguera Pallaresa valley. With so few monuments or obvious attractions, few visitors bother spending much time in this region, but there are some tiny villages close to Lleida which make excellent bases for some serious walking and are well off the beaten track.

Arriving in Lleida

Getting there There are regular train and bus services from Barcelona to Lleida with connections for the Pyrenees, as well as connections to Madrid and other major cities in Spain. Lleida is on the high-speed train line between Barcelona and Madrid. Barcelona to Lleida by AVE is 57 minutes; from Lleida to Madrid is around two hours. You'll need your own transport to get to the more remote villages. For general bus information, T973 268 500 (morning only). ➤➤ *For further details, see Transport, page 152.*

Tourist information The main tourist office ① *Av Madrid 36, T973 270 997, www.turismedelleida.com.*

Places in Lleida

Lleida was once dominated by the 13th-century fortress of La Zuda, but it was virtually demolished by the Napoleonic armies in 1812, and then given a final battering during the Civil War. The remnants, called the **Castell del Rei**, merit a visit, and shelter Lleida's only remaining 'sight', the old cathedral, la **Seu Vella** ① *T972 230 653, www.turoseuvella.cat, Tue-Sat 1000-1330 and 1600-1930, 1730 in winter, Sun 0930-1330, €5, free Tue,* which can be reached by a rickety lift (€0.50) from Plaça de Sant Joan, or you can make the 20-minute slog up from the centre of town. Begun in 1203, the lofty cathedral is an elegant example of the Transitional style from Romanesque to Gothic, with a sturdy octagonal tower and traces of Mozarabic decoration. The Gothic cloister is particularly charming, with arcades of different sizes and shapes, harmoniously knitted together with delicate stone tracery.

The old cathedral was turned into a military barracks in the 18th century, when a new cathedral, back in town on the Carrer Major, was constructed. It's a dull and uninspiring building, illuminated by narrow stained-glass windows. Around the corner on nearby Carrer Cavallers, there's a collection of art by local artists.

On the other side of the cathedral, the elegant 16th-century Hospital de Santa Maria houses the little-visited **Museo Arqueològic** ① *T972 271 500, Tue-Fri 1200-1400 and 1800-2100, Sat 1100-1400 and 1900-2100, Sun 1100-1400, free,* with a rather tired collection of Roman odds and ends. It's worth a visit for the handsome patio, where you can drowse away an afternoon over a book.

The **Castell de Gardeny** ① *T973 271 942, www.domustemple.com; guided visits Sat 1000, 1200 and 1600, Sun 1000 and 1200,* an impressive castle on a windswept hill overlooking the city, was built by the Templars at the end of the 12th century. Now an interesting museum, it recounts the Templar occupation of the region in the 12th and 13th centuries. This is just one of a string of fortresses constructed by the Templars in what was then the front line of the struggle against the Muslim armies.

Around Lleida

Most of the towns heading towards the Segre Valley are entirely unexceptional, although **Balaguer** is worth a stop for the ruins of its medieval fortress, which was once the castle of the influential Counts of Urgell. There's another beautiful Gothic cloister in the Monestir de Santo Domingo, and the Gothic Església de Santa Maria is very appealing.

A wonderful train line, the Tren dels Laks, trundles between Lleida and La Pobla de Segur, taking in several charming towns and enjoying watery views.

North of Balaguer, a small road peels west off into the hills towards the 12th-century Monestir de Santa Maria de Bellpuig de les Avellanes, which was richly endowed by the Counts of Urgell who were buried here. Their sarcophogi were carried off the Metropolitan museum in New York where they are displayed in a cloister and muttered over by still-furious Catalans. There are wonderful views across the valley and down to the winsome castle-topped village of Àger. The original fortress was established by the Romans, then rebuilt by the Moors and finally converted into a church after the Moors were driven out of Catalanya.

Back on the main road north towards Tremp (C-147), a tiny road winds eastwards up to the old stone village of Llimiana, with another graceful Romanesque church and fine views of the surrounding almond groves, forests and the Sierra de Montsec. Below it is a lake, the Pantà de Terradets, where families come to windsurf and picnic at weekends.

Catalan Pyrenees listings

For Where to stay and Restaurant price codes and other relevant information, see pages 11-20.

🛏 Where to stay

Vall de Núria *p137*
€€ **Hotel Vall de Nuria**, T972 732 030, www.valldenuria.com. The sanctuary only looks like a prison from the outside, and inside you'll find light, attractive rooms and a good restaurant.
€ **Els Caçadors**, C/Balandrau 24, Ribes de Freser, T972 727 006. This small hotel, close to the Cremallera train station, has a good restaurant dishing up tasty local specialities.
€ **Pic de l'Àliga Youth Hostel**, Estació de Montaña Vall de Nuria, T972732048, which enjoys a spectacular setting right at the top of the ski-lift.

Camping
Up in the Vall de Núria, you can camp in a small area behind the sanctuary.
Camping Vall de Ribes, Ctra Pardines Km 0.5, T972 728 820. Wonderful, rural campsite with pitches arranged on terraces on the hillside. Few facilities, but fabulous views and lovely staff.

Berga and the Parc Natural de Cadí-Moixeró *p138*
€€ **Hotel Les Fonts**, Ctra Castellar Km 8, Castellar de n'Hug, T938 257 089, www.hotellesfonts.cat. The largest and best equipped although the decor is high-kitsch with plenty of flounces.
€ **Estel**, Ctra Sant Fruitós, Berga, T938 213 463, www.hotelestel.com. Modern and accommodating on the edge of town.
€ **Hostal Alt Llobregat**, C/Portell s/n, Castellar de n'Hug, T938 257 074, www.altllobregat.com. A simple but reasonably priced *pensión* with a café-bar.
€ **Hostal La Muntanya**, Plaça Major 4, Castellar de n'Hug, T938 257 065, www.hostallamuntanya.cat. A delightful, cheerful guesthouse with a popular restaurant.
€ **Hotel La Pineda**, C/Raval 50, Bagà, T938 244 515, www.hotelpineda.com. This is the best place to stay in Bagà; a down-to-earth hotel just off the main shopping street.
€ **Santuari de Falgars**, Poblet de Lillet, T937 441 095, www.falgars.com. A popular *pensión* with wonderful views.

Camping

Càmping Bastareny, Bagà, T938 244 420; **Càmping Cadí** at Gósol, T973 370 134 and 2 campsites in Saldes: **Càmping Repòs de Pedraforca**, T938 258 044 and **Càmping Mirador del Pedraforca**, T938 258 062.

Cerdanyà Valley *p139*

Puigcerdà has the best range of accommodation in the Cerdanyà Valley.

€€€€ Torre del Remei, Camí Reial s/n, Bolvir de Cerdanyà, 5 km from Puigcerdà, T972 140 182, www.torredelremei.com. One of the most luxurious hotels in Catalunya. It's spectacularly set in a Modernista palace surrounded by gardens, and rooms are individually decorated with a stylish mixture of traditional and new fabrics and furniture. The restaurant has a superb reputation.

€€€ El Castell, Ctra N-620, Km 229, Castellciutat, T973 350 000, www.hotel-castell-cintat.com. Tucked next to the ruins of the old castle, **El Castell** is a discreetly elegant modern building with all the luxury trimmings, including a fabulous restaurant.

€€ Del Prado, Ctra de Llivía s/n, Puigcerdà, T972 880 400, www.hoteldelprado.cat. A well-equipped, chalet-style hotel close to the ice-skating rink with a pool and a very good restaurant.

€€ Fonda Biayana, C/Sant Roc 11, Bellver de Cerdanya, T973 510 475. Delightfully rickety with a popular local bar and mid-range restaurant downstairs.

€€ Hostal Rita Belvedere, C/Carmelites 6-8, Puigcerdà, T972 880 356. An old-fashioned *hostal* with some old and some modernized rooms, many with good views.

€€ Hotel La Glorieta, C/Afores s/n, T972351045, www.hotehostallaglorieta.com. A modern hotel just outside town on the way to Castellciutat, with all mod cons including a pool and a good restaurant.

€€ Parador Nacional de la Seu d'Urgell, C/ Sant Domènec 6, La Seu d'Urgell, T973 352 000, www.parador.es. A mix of ancient and modern, this parador is built around a glassed-over Renaissance cloister.

€ Hostal Rusó, C/Frederic Bernades 15, Llivia, T972 146 264, www.hostalruso.es. The best budget option, set around a little courtyard in the town centre and has a decent old-fashioned and cheap restaurant.

Noguera Palleresa Valley and Parc Nacional d'Aigüestortes *p141*

The main access towns for Aigüestortes Park are Espot and Boí.

€€ Hotel Solé, Av Estació 44, La Pobla de Segur, T973 680 452. Conveniently central and perfectly comfortable aparthotel.

€€ Roya, C/Sant Maurici s/n, Espot, T973 624 040, www.hotelroya.net. Simple with an excellent restaurant and close to the park information office and the jeep taxi stand.

€ Pensió del Rey, Llavorsí, T973 622 011. A good budget option.

€ Pensió La Palmira, C/Marineta s/n, Espot, T973 624 072, www.pensiopalmira.com. Also has a cheap restaurant with a good *menú del día* for under €10.

Vall d'Aran *p143*

In Salardú and Artíes there are plenty of places to stay, from super chi chi ski hotels to humble guesthouses.

€€€ Melia Royal Tanau, Ctra de Beret s/n, in Baqueira-Beret, T973 644 446, www.solmelia.com. One of the smartest options, with a fantastic location next to the ski lifts to deliver you straight to the slopes, a heated pool, Turkish baths, gym and a jacuzzi for some post-skiing pampering.

€€€ Parador de Artíes, Ctra a Baqueira-Beret s/n, Arties, T973 640 801, www.parador.es. Luxurious, chalet-style parador with all kinds of extras including an outdoor pool.

€€ Besiberri, C/Deth Fòrt 4, Artíes, T973 640 829, www.hotelbesiberri.com. A delightful, family-run chalet-style hotel right by a stream with flower-filled balconies and delicious breakfasts.

€€ Hotel Aran, Av Castiero 5, Vielha, T972 640 050, www.hotelaran.net. Offers pretty wooden rooms, as well as a jacuzzi and sauna to soak tired limbs. Family run. Prices leap in Aug.

€€ Mont Romies, Plaça Major s/n, Salardú, T973 642 016. This traditional stone hotel is in a perfect location in the heart of the village.

€€ Parador de Vielha, Vielha, T973 640 100, www.parador.es. A modern and slightly soulless place but with great views of the valley.

€ Casa Vicenta, C/ Reiau 7, Vielha, T973 640 819, www.pensioncasavicenta.com. A sweet little *pensión* with simple, but very cheap rooms; those without bathrooms are cheaper.

Vall de Boí *p144*

€€€ Balneari Caldes de Boí, Boí, T973 696 219. A grand spa hotel with all the trimmings in a magnificent location. Closed in winter.

€€ Casa Peiró, La Plaça 7, Coll, T973 297 002, www.hotelcasapeiro.com. A typical 19th-century stone mountain house with a wooden gallery and rustically furnished rooms. The mid-range priced restaurant is particularly good.

€€ Farre d'Avall, C/Major 8, Barruera, T973 694 029. Very comfortable, and has a well-reputed, mid-range restaurant, but traffic noise can be a problem.

€€ Hostal La Plaça, Plaça Església, Erill la Vall, T973 696 026, www.hostal-laplaza.com. Attractive option which overlooks the main square and has another very good restaurant.

€€ Pensió La Coma, C/ Unica s/n, Taüll, T973 696 147. An old favourite with a cosy restaurant much loved by locals.

€ Pensió Pascual, Pont de Boí s/n, T973 696 014. A friendly little place on the outskirts of the village by the bridge. A good budget choice.

Lleida and around *p145*

€€€€ Finca Prats Hotel Golf and Spa, Ctra N240 Km 102.5, T902 445 666, www.finca prats.com. Ultra-luxurious spa hotel and golf course; one of the best hotels in Catalunya.

€€ Catalonia Transit, Plaza Berenguer s/n, Lleida, T973 230 008, www.hoteles-catalonia.es. Set in a turn-of-the-20th-century building above the train station, the rooms of this historic hotel are surprisingly crisp, modern and very comfortable.

€ Goya, C/ Alcalde Costa 9, Lleida, T973 266 788, www.goyahotel.es. Central budget hotel, with modern en suite rooms.

€ Urgell, C/Urgell 25, Balaguer, T973 445 348. Old-fashioned but impeccably kept.

❿ Restaurants

Berga and the Parc Natural de Cadí-Moixeró *p138*

€€ Balcó de Catalunya, Santuari de Queralt, Berga, T938 213 828. Head up here for a simple lunch enjoying spectacular views; set in the sanctuary of Queralt on a crag overlooking the mountains.

€€ Sala, Paseo de la Paz 27, Berga, T938 211 185, www.restaurantsala.com. The best-known local restaurant run by a welcoming father-and-daughter team, the **Sala** produces excellent regional cuisine with some inspired contemporary touches.

Cerdanyà Valley *p139*

Much of what's on offer in Puigcerdà is geared towards tourists. The cafés set around the two adjoining squares of Santa Maria and Herois at the centre of Puigcerdà are particulary tourist orientated and, consequently, the food here is usually overpriced and very ordinary. Those listed below are exceptions.

€€€ Torre del Remei (see Where to stay, above), Puigcerdà. An award-winning restaurant, for a special treat.

€€ Andria, Passeig Joan Brudeu 24, La Seu d'Urgell, T973 350 300, www.hotel andria.com. This celebrated old restaurant with Modernista decor in the heart of the old town is one of the best in the town. It serves delicious, local dishes. There are a few rooms (**€€**) upstairs.

€€ Can Ventura, Plaça Major 1, Llivia, T972 896 178, www.canventura.com. This delightful restaurant overlooks a lovely square and serves tasty local dishes out on the terrace in summer.

€€ Carlit, Av Catalunya 68, Llivia, T972 896 326. A welcoming restaurant serving unusual Basque specialities.

€€ El Galet, Plaça Santa María 8, Puigcerdà, T972 882 266. A friendly, old-fashioned spot on one of the city's main squares – perfect terrace in summer – offering good Catalan food at good prices.

€ Cal Cofa, C/Frederic Bernades 1, Llivia, T972 896 500. Serves succulent, cheap, grilled meats to a lively, local crowd.

€ Fonda Pluvinet, C/El Segre 13, Martinet, T973 515 075. An appealing stone building in the centre of the village, serving delicious, inexpensive Catalan food.

€ Restaurant Madrigal, C/Alfons I, Puigcerdà. A low-key bar which has freshly made tapas and basic meals at a good price.

Vall d'Aran p143

There are great places to eat in the Vall d'Aran; mostly for people with deep pockets.

€€€ Casa Irene, C/Mayor 3, Artíes, T973 644 364. One of the finest restaurants in the whole region, run by the charismatic Irene España, and well worth a splurge.

€€ Era Mola, C/ Marrec 4, Vielha, T973 642 419. A romantic and centrally located restaurant, which offers delicious Aranese specialities, featuring wild mushrooms and very good crêpes.

€€ Urtau, Plaça Artau s/n, Artíes, T973 640 926. Plain but cosy, with wooden beams, whitewashed walls, and a fireplace. Excellent,

local dishes, a good wine list and some of the best desserts in the Pyrenees. Next door, they also run a noisy, buzzy bar, where you can find Basque-style tapas (*pintxos*) – slices of bread piled high with all kinds of toppings – which are tasty, filling and very cheap.

€ Nicolas, C/Castèth 10, Vielha, T973 641 820. You'll find more delicious, local specialities and a fantastic array of *pintxos* (Basque-style tapas).

Vall de Boí p144

€€ El Caliu, C/Feixanes 11, Taüll, T973 696 212, www.elcaliutaull.com. Serving elegantly prepared dishes and an array of wonderful home-made desserts. One of the best restaurants in these parts.

€€ La Cabana, Ctra de Taüll s/n, mid-way between Boí and Taüll, T973 696 213, www.lacabanaboi.com. Serves tasty grilled local meat and Catalan mountain dishes.

Lleida and around p145

There is lots of choice in Lledia from good budget places catering to students to swish award-winning establishments for a posh night out.

€€ Xaler Suis, C/Rovira Roure 9, T973 235 567. Good local dishes such as roast kid, lobster raviole and tasty stews, and there's a fabulous chocolate fondue for dessert.

€ El Portón, C/Sant Martí 53. Stylish tapas bar with a huge range of tasty snacks.

€ Muixi, Plaça Sant Jaume 4, Balaguer, T973 445 497. Don't miss this award-winning confectioner's shop which makes delicious local cakes and other goodies.

✪ Festivals

Cerdanyà Valley p139

Aug Festival de l'Estany by Puigcerdà's lake on the last weekend in Aug, which culminates in a spectacular fireworks show.

⛰ What to do

Noguera Palleresa Valley and Parc Nacional d'Aigüestortes *p141*
Tour operators based along the Noguera Pallaresa river include:
Rafting Llavorsí, Llavorsí, T973 622 158, www.raftingllavorsi.com. Rafting, kayaking and hydro-speed trips are offered.
Yeti Emotions, Llavorsí, T973 622 201, www.yetiemotions.com. For rafting, canyoning, hydrospeed, mountain-biking and rock-climbing.

Vall d'Aran *p143*
Vielha tourist office has maps with good suggestions for walking trails close to the town. The town is also stuffed full of tour operators who can organize everything from horse riding and mountain biking to kayaking or heli-skiing.
Escuela de Equitació, Ctra Francia, T973 642 244, www.aranequitacion.es. For horse riding.
Horizontes, Catra Francia 22, T973 642 967, www.horizontesaventura.com.
Deportur, Cami Paisàs s/n, further up the Vall d'Aran in Les, T972 647 045, www.depotur.com.

☺ Transport

Vall de Núria *p137*
There are regular trains from Barcelona-Sants via Plaça Catalunya to **Ripoll** and **Ribes de Freser**, where you join **La Cremallera**, T972 732 044, up to the Vall de Núria. The rack-and-pinion train runs regularly (usually between 0900 and 1800, although hours are extended in season) daily except in Nov when it is closed (€22.30, children €13.35 for a return ticket from Núria to Ribes).

Berga and the Parc Natural de Cadí-Moixeró *p138*
This region is very difficult to explore without your own car, as buses are infrequent. There are 3 buses a day Mon-Fri, 2 a day Sat and Sun from **Barcelona** to **Berga** with ALSA, T902 422 242; 1 bus a day (except on Sun) to **Castellar de N'Hug** via **La Pobla de Lillet**.

Cerdanya Valley *p139*
Regular bus services link **La Seu d'Urgell** with **Andorra la Vella** and other towns in Andorra. There are regular trains from **Barcelona-Sants** via Plaça Catalunya to **Puigcerdà** via **Vic** and **Ripoll**. Regular local bus services link **Puigcerdà** with **La Seu d'Urgell** via **Bellver de Cerdanya** with ALSA (T902 422 242) who also run direct services to **La Seu d'Urgell** from the Estació del Nord in **Barcelona**.

Noguera Palleresa Valley and Parc Nacional d'Aigüestortes *p141*
This region is hard to explore fully without your own transport, although all the larger towns are connected by bus.

Bus The bus service is run by ALSA, T902 422 242, who run twice-daily buses from **La Seu d'Urgell** for **Sort** and **Llavorsí**, plus a regular bus service to **Llívia**. There are daily buses from **Barcelona** and **Lleida** for **Espot**, but you'll have to ask the bus driver to let you off at the turn-off for the village and walk the last 7 km, or call a **jeep taxi**, T973 696 314, www.taxisvalldeboi.com. There are direct buses from **Barcelona** to **La Pobla de Segur** and **Lleida**, but you'll need your own transport to get to the more remote villages.

Train There are regular trains from **Sants** to **Lleida**, where several buses depart for the Pyrenees, stopping at **Tremp**, **La Pobla de Segur**, **Sort** and **Port de Suert**.

Vall d'Aran *p143*
There are 2 buses from **Barcelona** to **Vielha** which travel via **Port de Suert** from the Estació del Nord with ALSA (T902 422 242).

Vall de Boí p144

There's only one bus up the Vall de Boí from **El Pont de Suert** (usually runs Jun-Sep only). El Pont de Suert has twice-daily connections to **Lleida** and **Vielha** with **ALSA** (T902 422 242) which are timed to connect with the Vall de Boí service.

Lleida and around p145

Bus There are direct buses from **Barcelona** to **La Pobla de Segur** and **Lleida**.

Train There are regular services from **Barcelona-Sants** to **Lleida**, where several buses depart for the Pyrenees, stopping at **Tremp**, **La Pobla de Segur**, **Sort** and **El Port de Suert**. The high-speed AVE runs about 8 times a day to Madrid (2 hrs 10 mins) See www.renfe.com for AVE and regional timetables and ticket information.

Andorra

Andorra gets a bad press, and it's sometimes hard to find reasons to defend it, particularly during the high season and at weekends, when a stream of traffic pours in to the principality to stack up on cheap goods at the ranks of hideous hypermarkets. In the unrelenting drive to plonk a resort on every mountainside, few regions have been left untouched. To find an unspoiled corner takes serious effort; you'll have to tramp your way to tranquillity whenever you come, but it's easiest during the early summer and autumn.

Background

The Principality of Andorra has been squabbled over by the Counts of Foix and the Archbishops of Seu d'Urgell for centuries; a treaty signed in 1278 allowed the Andorrans some autonomy but the community was obliged to pay tribute to the rulers on either side of their borders in alternate years. The remoteness of the region meant that in practice it was difficult for anyone to intervene in local affairs, and the Andorrans zealously protected their rights and privileges, even managing to maintain neutrality during the Civil War and the Second World War. Smuggling was big business during the wars, and was the basis for the legitimate tax-free business which grew up in the 1940s and 1950s. Money also began to roll in from the increasingly popular sport of downhill skiiing, opening up new transport connections and allowing an alarming rate of development. Andorra was getting richer and richer and no longer needed the help or patronage of its neighbours. Finally, in 1993, the locals voted overwhelmingly for independence and a democratic constitution to replace their ancient feudal obligations.

Andorra la Vella and around → *Phone code: outside Andorra 00 376.*
Population: 22,200. Altitude: 1029 m.

The capital of Andorra, Andorra La Vella, enjoys a spectacular setting but is an ugly modern city lined with hideous, shoddy architecture and neon-lit shopping malls. The city's raison d'être is shopping, and there's virtually nothing else to do. Head for the hills and escape to some of the surrounding hiking trails where you can put all crowds and neon behind you.

The old quarter (Barri Antic) is worth a visit for the **Casa de la Vall** ① *Carrer de la Vall, T829129, Mon-Sat 1000-1400 and 1500-1800, Sun 1000-1400 (closed Sun between Nov and May), admission by guided tour only, reserve in advance, free*, which was the seat of the Counsell de la Tera, the representatives of Andorra's seven valleys who ruled the country until 1993, and is now the seat of the national parliament.

Slope facts

Check out the comprehensive website www.skiandorra.ad for weather reports, links, and information on all the resorts.

There are two enormous ski resorts in Andorra, which each encompass several villages: **Grandvalira**, www.grand valira.com) is the largest, with 205 km of pistes (118 in total). It includes villages and towns such as Soldeu and Pas de la Casa. **Vallnord** has more than 70 pistes, and includes the villages of Arcalís, Arinsal and Pal.

Heading northeast of Andorra la Vella, there's some gentle walking around the **Estany d'Engolasters**, overlooked by the Romanesque Església de Sant Miquel with a statuesque belltower. It's a suitably picture-book setting for a handful of old legends including one which states that all the stars of the sky will be so entranced by the beauty of the lake that they will fall to the bottom and stay there until the end of time.

Northeast to Pas de la Casa

The road wiggles along to the French border at **Pas de la Casa**, a hideous high-rise conglomeration of duty-free shops with another big ski-resort, but passes some prettier stopping points along the way. **Canillo** has not managed to survive unscarred, but the old quarter with its balconied houses is quietly attractive with its fine old Romanesque church and characteristic lofty Andorran belltower. On the outskirts of the town is one of the best Romanesque churches in Andorra, Sant Joan de Caselles, with a glittering Gothic retablo and a richly decorated wooden ceiling. **Soldeu**, a popular ski town, is surprisingly small and unassuming, and the villages have some fantastic walking in the surrounding forests during the summer.

Northwest to Ordino

Northwest of Andorra La Vella, the other main route through the principality heads up the Ordino valley. **Ordino** is another good base for hiking, with some handsome old stone buildings still holding their own among the ring of modern apartments. It's also got a pair of small museums on the Carrer Major: one is devoted to a history of Andorra's postal service and the other is the **Areny-Plandolit House Museum** ① *T836908, visits on request*, which carefully recreates the life of a 19th-century Andorran merchant's family with exhibits and original furnishings.

There's also a **Nature Interpretation Centre** ① *on the outskirts of Ordino in La Cortinada, call T849849 for opening hours*, which aims to show the effect mankind has on nature (you'll never forget your litter again). It's very child-friendly with plenty of touchy-feely exhibits and clever multi-media exhibits. Almost opposite is a big, modern sports' centre which has everything you can think of from a pool, gym, and squash courts to a Turkish bath and jacuzzi.

There's a **tourist information office** ① *Traviessa d'Ordino 7, T878173, www.ordino.ad*.

Villages north from Ordino

The string of villages which unfurls along the river further north includes **La Cortinada** and **Llorts**, which are sleepier but less over-developed. There are two more ski resorts at **Arsinal** and **Pal** to the west of Ordino; Arsinal is bigger and more dynamic, but Pal, huddled around another Romanesque church, is smaller and prettier thanks to local planning laws which have banned ugly ferro-concrete developments. Up near the border with France, **El Serrat** sits near the Tristaina lakes and is surrounded by waterfalls; beyond it is the ski resort of **Arcalís**, which is a big favourite with British snow boarders and probably Andorra's most attractive resort.

Andorra listings

For Where to stay and Restaurant price codes and other relevant information, see pages 11-20.

🛏 Where to stay

Andorra la Vella *p153*
Only serious shopaholics will want to use Andorra la Vella as a base, but if you get caught overnight, there are dozens of places to stay.
€€€ Husa Cèntric, Av Meritxell 87, T877500, www.husa.es. Modern, very well-equipped hotel with spa, restaurant and a roaring fire in the lounge.
€€ Hotel de l'Isard, Av Meritxell 36, T876800, www.hotelisard.com. A charming stone-built hotel with bright modern rooms.
€€ Hotel Plaza, C/Maria Pla 19-21, T879444. With gym, jacuzzi, sauna and beauty centre. One of the plushest.
€ Hotel Cisco de Sans, C/Anna Maria Janer 4, T863188. A simple spot in the historic quarter, family-run and friendly.

Northeast to Pas de la Casa *p154*
€€ Hotel Roc Sant Miquel, Ctra General s/n, Soldeu, T851079, www.hotel-roc.com. Has a good little restaurant and there's a great bar area where the local ski-instructors play in a band. Warm and friendly.
€€ Petit Hotel, C/Sant Jordi 18. Comfortable little hotel in the centre, with friendly staff and tasty breakfasts.

€€ Sport, Ctra General s/n, Soldeu, T870500, www.sporthotels.ad. The best-equipped hotel in Soldeu and the closest to the ski-lifts. Views of the slopes, a pool, sauna and gym.

Northwest to Ordino *p154*
€€ Hotel Santa Barbara, Ordino, T837100, www.hotelstabarbara.com. Has spacious, immaculate rooms, some of which look out over the main square. There's a good restaurant (**€€**) too.

🍴 Restaurants

Andorra la Vella *p153*
€€ Bodega Poblet, Carrer de l'Alzinaret 6, T376 862 722. Chic and sophisticated, serving some of the best and most creative tapas in town.
€€ Borda Estevet, Ctra de la Comella 2, T864026. A good choice, this traditional, Pyrenean restaurant specializes in delicious grilled local meat and fish – famous all over Andorra.
€€-€ Don Denis, C/Isabel Sandy 3, T820692, off the main shopping drag. An old favourite with locals which does a good-value set lunch at €15, but also serves some of the finest and freshest seafood in the area. Highly recommended.

Northeast to Pas de la Casa *p154*
€€ Cort del Popaire, Plaça de Poble,
Soldeu, T851211. One of the town's best
restaurants, set in a old stone barn offering
friendly service and roaring fires in winter.
€ Molí del Peano, Crtra General, Canillo,
T851258, offers local specialities like rabbit
and home-made desserts. Friendly, cheap
and cosy.

Northwest to Ordino *p154*
€€-€ Topic, Ctra General s/n, Ordino,
T736102, www.topicordino.com. An
enormously popular restaurant and bar,
which offers good regional specialities, as
well as fondues and a huge range of
international beers spread over 4 levels.

▲ What to do

Andorra la Vella *p153*
Almost all the Barcelona travel agencies offer
skiing packages, which include transport,
lift-passes and accommodation. The website
www.skiandorra.ad offers great deals and
packages too.

☻ Transport

Andorra la Vella *p153*
Bus There are regular buses to Andorra
La Vella with **ALSA** (www.alsa.com) from
Estació del Nord bus station, Barcelona, and
buses with **Julià** (www.autocaresjulia.es)
from Estació de Sants, Barcelona. **Novatel**
(www.andorrabybus.com) offer a minibus
service from Barcelona airport if you can't
wait to get on the slopes. Within Andorra,
there are local bus services to **Pas de la
Casa** with La **Hispano Andorrana**
(www.andorrabybus.com).

Train You can also take the train from
Barcelona-Sants to **Puigcerdà** and get a bus
from there (services are run by **ALSA**).

Contents

Footnotes

Index

Titles available in the Footprint *Focus* range

Latin America	UK RRP	US RRP
Bahia & Salvador	£7.99	$11.95
Brazilian Amazon	£7.99	$11.95
Brazilian Pantanal	£6.99	$9.95
Buenos Aires & Pampas	£7.99	$11.95
Cartagena & Caribbean Coast	£7.99	$11.95
Costa Rica	£8.99	$12.95
Cuzco, La Paz & Lake Titicaca	£8.99	$12.95
El Salvador	£5.99	$8.95
Guadalajara & Pacific Coast	£6.99	$9.95
Guatemala	£8.99	$12.95
Guyana, Guyane & Suriname	£5.99	$8.95
Havana	£6.99	$9.95
Honduras	£7.99	$11.95
Nicaragua	£7.99	$11.95
Northeast Argentina & Uruguay	£8.99	$12.95
Paraguay	£5.99	$8.95
Quito & Galápagos Islands	£7.99	$11.95
Recife & Northeast Brazil	£7.99	$11.95
Rio de Janeiro	£8.99	$12.95
São Paulo	£5.99	$8.95
Uruguay	£6.99	$9.95
Venezuela	£8.99	$12.95
Yucatán Peninsula	£6.99	$9.95

Asia	UK RRP	US RRP
Angkor Wat	£5.99	$8.95
Bali & Lombok	£8.99	$12.95
Chennai & Tamil Nadu	£8.99	$12.95
Chiang Mai & Northern Thailand	£7.99	$11.95
Goa	£6.99	$9.95
Gulf of Thailand	£8.99	$12.95
Hanoi & Northern Vietnam	£8.99	$12.95
Ho Chi Minh City & Mekong Delta	£7.99	$11.95
Java	£7.99	$11.95
Kerala	£7.99	$11.95
Kolkata & West Bengal	£5.99	$8.95
Mumbai & Gujarat	£8.99	$12.95

Africa & Middle East	UK RRP	US RRP
Beirut	£6.99	$9.95
Cairo & Nile Delta	£8.99	$12.95
Damascus	£5.99	$8.95
Durban & KwaZulu Natal	£8.99	$12.95
Fès & Northern Morocco	£8.99	$12.95
Jerusalem	£8.99	$12.95
Johannesburg & Kruger National Park	£7.99	$11.95
Kenya's Beaches	£8.99	$12.95
Kilimanjaro & Northern Tanzania	£8.99	$12.95
Luxor to Aswan	£8.99	$12.95
Nairobi & Rift Valley	£7.99	$11.95
Red Sea & Sinai	£7.99	$11.95
Zanzibar & Pemba	£7.99	$11.95

Europe	UK RRP	US RRP
Bilbao & Basque Region	£6.99	$9.95
Brittany West Coast	£7.99	$11.95
Cádiz & Costa de la Luz	£6.99	$9.95
Granada & Sierra Nevada	£6.99	$9.95
Languedoc: Carcassonne to Montpellier	£7.99	$11.95
Málaga	£5.99	$8.95
Marseille & Western Provence	£7.99	$11.95
Orkney & Shetland Islands	£5.99	$8.95
Santander & Picos de Europa	£7.99	$11.95
Sardinia: Alghero & the North	£7.99	$11.95
Sardinia: Cagliari & the South	£7.99	$11.95
Seville	£5.99	$8.95
Sicily: Palermo & the Northwest	£7.99	$11.95
Sicily: Catania & the Southeast	£7.99	$11.95
Siena & Southern Tuscany	£7.99	$11.95
Sorrento, Capri & Amalfi Coast	£6.99	$9.95
Skye & Outer Hebrides	£6.99	$9.95
Verona & Lake Garda	£7.99	$11.95

North America	UK RRP	US RRP
Vancouver & Rockies	£8.99	$12.95

Australasia	UK RRP	US RRP
Brisbane & Queensland	£8.99	$12.95
Perth	£7.99	$11.95

For the latest books, e-books and a wealth of travel information, visit us at:
www.footprinttravelguides.com.

 footprint travelguides.com

 Join us on facebook for the latest travel news, product releases, offers and amazing competitions:
www.facebook.com/footprintbooks.